But What Can I Do?

Also by Alastair Campbell

NON-FICTION

The Blair Years

The Alastair Campbell Diaries Volume One: Prelude to Power

The Alastair Campbell Diaries Volume Two: Power & the People

The Alastair Campbell Diaries Volume Three: Power & Responsibility

The Alastair Campbell Diaries Volume Four: The Burden of Power: Countdown to Iraq

Alastair Campbell Diaries Volume Five: Outside, Inside, 2003–2005

Alastair Campbell Diaries Volume Six: From Blair to Brown, 2005–2007

Alastair Campbell Diaries Volume Seven: From Crash to Defeat, 2007–2010

Alastair Campbell Diaries Volume Eight: Rise and Fall of the Olympic Spirit, 2010–2015

The Irish Diaries

The Happy Depressive: In Pursuit of Personal and Political Happiness

Living Better: How I Learned to Survive Depression

Winners

FICTION

All in the Mind

Maya

My Name Is . . .

Saturday Bloody Saturday (with Paul Fletcher)

But What Can I Do?

Why Politics Has Gone So Wrong, and How You Can Help Fix It

ALASTAIR CAMPBELL

HUTCHINSON
HEINEMANN

9 10

Hutchinson Heinemann
20 Vauxhall Bridge Road
London SW1V 2SA

Hutchinson Heinemann is part of the Penguin Random House group of companies
whose addresses can be found at global.penguinrandomhouse.com.

First published by Hutchinson Heinemann in 2023

www.penguin.co.uk

A CIP catalogue record for this book is available from the British Library.

ISBN 9781529153330 (hardback)
ISBN 9781529153347 (trade paperback)

Typeset in 12.5/15.25pt Dante MT Std by Jouve (UK), Milton Keynes
Printed and bound in Great Britain by Clays Ltd, Elcograf S.p.A.

The authorised representative in the EEA is Penguin Random House Ireland,
Morrison Chambers, 32 Nassau Street, Dublin D02 YH68

www.greenpenguin.co.uk

Contents

But What Can I Do?

Preface

I am dedicating this book to the people who write to me . . . day after day, in they come: people's views, experiences, anxieties and, above all, their questions. They come by letter, by email, to my website, or in reaction to *The Rest Is Politics* podcast I do with former Tory Cabinet minister Rory Stewart, or the newspaper I write for, *The New European*. They come in their droves too, amid the bot abuse and troll insults, on social media. And if I had to boil down the essence of the questions to just one, it would be this: '*But what can I do?*'

Hence the title of the book; and hence the dedication to those who write to me in such numbers, for it is they who have inspired me to help them find the answer, so that they just do it, in whatever way they can. Because if we do not get new blood flowing into our politics, then I fear for the worst: a country already in decline could spiral further and further down.

Where I am optimistic is that amid the anger I see in all these comments and conversations, I also witness so much passion and potential that, unleashed, really could change things fast. Unfortunately, that potential all too often threatens to be overwhelmed by a deep sense of frustration and powerlessness: people feel powerless not just to fight for the changes they think we need, but powerless even to confront the barriers preventing them from trying. That feeling of powerlessness in turn swiftly becomes one of hopelessness, which all too often not only makes people give up the fight, but threatens their mental health too. As human beings, we are nothing without hope – hope that we can make a difference and so have a sense of purpose in our lives, hope that we can improve life for ourselves and for others we care about.

The questions I receive come from people of all ages, but many are from teenagers and students. It strikes me that if a young person is getting in touch with a man in his mid-sixties like me – not a politician but in the political arena, not a journalist but in the media world, with strong views I am always prepared to defend, with lots of experience of campaigns and trying to make change happen, and lots of experience of managing poor mental health and still going – it's because they haven't yet reached the hopeless stage, but they might be heading there. I try my best to come up with answers, but I confess there are times when I share that sense of hopelessness. After all, I'm living in a world facing the existential threat of the climate crisis; and in a Britain defined by austerity; then the lies and failings of Brexit; then the mayhem of Boris Johnson's morally corrupted and corrupting leadership; then the economic chaos and incompetence unleashed by Liz Truss on a scale never before seen so early in a premiership; and now with Rishi Sunak, the UK's fifth Tory prime minister in six not very good years. He is the second in a row who has lacked the mandate of a general election, and yet he has ushered in a second wave of tax rises and public spending austerity that nobody voted for. As for Labour, the party I have supported all my life, it is true that they are much stronger under Keir Starmer's leadership than they were under Jeremy Corbyn's. But Labour's sustained lead is as much due to a loathing of the Tories as it is to floating voters flocking enthusiastically to a compelling alternative.

More generally, I sometimes worry that the tide seems to be running against constitutional and democratic government – not just in the UK but across vast swathes of the globe. Despite its transparent failings, populism has taken a grip in countries both large – such as India, Brazil and the Philippines – and small, like Hungary; while across the Atlantic there are plenty of voters who believe that Donald Trump should get a second go at confirming his position as the worst and most divisive president in US history. Almost everywhere, evidence-based politics is under threat from a politics based on gut reaction and deep-seated prejudice, distorted values and culture wars.

As democratic values come under attack from within, it's no wonder how often and how easily and effectively dictatorships exploit democracies' weaknesses. How is it that Vladimir Putin can keep getting away with his crimes and misdemeanours, after more than two decades in power? Are we really as helpless as it seems in the face of the rise of repressive, domineering China? And while I can and I do find hope in the passion and enthusiasm of the young, why is it that surveys show that more and more young people – proportionately more than the old – are giving up on the very notion of democracy, and support the idea of 'strongman' leadership or military rule in its stead?

It's a chilling thought that when Trump was US president, and Johnson UK prime minister, Vladimir Putin president of Russia and Xi Jinping the hugely powerful general secretary of the Chinese Communist Party, it meant that of the five Permanent Members of the United Nations Security Council, only France, with Emmanuel Macron as president, had a leader who was non-populist, non-extreme or non-dictatorial. And we wonder why our major international institutions are failing to hold international support.

One of the most worrying recent trends has been highlighted by ex-Venezuelan politician and executive director of the World Bank, Moisés Naím, in his brilliant book, *The Revenge of Power.* He analyses political leaders who gain power through reasonably democratic elections and then set out to dismantle the checks on executive power through what he calls the 3Ps . . . populism, polarisation and post-truth. 'As they consolidate their power,' he writes, 'they cloak their autocratic plans behind walls of secrecy, bureaucratic obfuscation, pseudo-legal subterfuge, manipulation of public opinion, and the repression of critics and adversaries. Once the mask comes off, it's too late.' I am sure we can all recognise the likes of Putin, Trump, Modi in India, Orbán in Hungary, Erdoğan in Turkey, Duterte in the Philippines, Chávez and some of his successors in Venezuela, Bolsonaro in Brazil, Obrador in Mexico, Fujimori and Castillo in Peru (one from the right, one from the left, both currently in the same jail), among the '3P autocrats' Naím describes. For a UK citizen, the shaming thing is that Boris Johnson features so large among the rogues' gallery of lying, anti-democratic, rule-of-law-defying leaders analysed by the former Venezuelan minister.

'*But what can I do?*' It's the 'but' that signals the sense of powerlessness. So many people seem to be saying: 'I really care, I want to make a difference, I just don't know how to do it.' There is so much fear and anger about the state we are in. Yet whenever I look at my inbox or visit a school or college, or chat to fellow passengers on a train or plane, I also sense so much energy, so much commitment, so much passion for better causes and ideas.

'*But what can I do?*' Even how you ask the question gives a different sense of the challenge. When people ask me the question, some are saying, 'But what can *I* do?' with the emphasis on them looking for a role, but feeling they are small and powerless in the face of enormous challenge. Others ask something closer to 'What can I *DO*?', which carries with it a sense of yearning for ideas rather than merely agency.

In this book, I want to try to answer both forms of the question. Because, frankly, if too many of us decide that the only way to deal with the anxiety and anger that politics creates within us is to ignore it, and do nothing, we are part of the problem too. What's more, we leave the field clear for those we might blame for the problem in the first place. We cannot afford to stand on the sidelines. If we think things are wrong, and we want to change them, we have to get involved. And 'we' includes 'you'!

Introduction

I have worked in politics and media all my adult life. I have never felt greater despair about both.

Our country is in a mess because our politics is in a mess.

But it does not have to be like this. Politics can do so much good. Political leaders can do so much good.

I worked alongside Tony Blair, and saw him achieve real progress, not least helping to bring peace to Northern Ireland. I saw Gordon Brown deliver record investment in schools and hospitals, and lead the world in managing the horrendous fallout of the global financial crisis of 2008.

It's not just Labour leaders that I can respect. For years as a journalist I covered Margaret Thatcher, and though I disagreed with a lot that she did, I never once doubted that she was driven by a real vision, by her own deep values and convictions, a phenomenal work ethic, and genuine commitment to public service ahead of personal gain.

Then there was John Major, who, sick of scandals within his own party that were damaging the reputation of politics as a whole, brought in and legislated for the principles and standards he believed should govern public life: Honesty, Openness, Objectivity, Selflessness, Integrity, Accountability and Leadership.

These principles have been comprehensively trashed in recent years, especially, though not exclusively, under Boris Johnson. We must find the leaders who can bring those standards back, and so help to take our country forward.

With those words, in what the producers portentously called an 'Address to the Nation', complete with the Union flag behind my left shoulder, I launched last autumn's Channel 4 TV series, *Make Me Prime Minister*. No, not make *me* prime minister, though I have often wondered whether I should have stood for Parliament and become a politician in my own right, instead of being the guy helping the ones out front (I shall explain later why I haven't). Rather, the series focused on people often described by politicians and journalists as 'ordinary'. Several, as my co-presenter, Tory peer Sayeeda Warsi, and I soon discovered, turned out to be anything but.

Hundreds of applicants were auditioned, a shortlist of twelve was selected, and by the final, after they had been tested on a range of policy issues as well as crisis management, media management, campaigning and head-to-head debating, there were just three still standing. Then there was one – the winner, Natalie Balmain.

As I stood in the wings watching those final three – all strong, passionate women, the youngest twenty-five, Natalie the oldest at thirty-six – I felt proud to have played a part in finding them, giving them a platform, and hopefully launching them on a political journey that will give real purpose to their lives, and bring hope and improvements to our country and beyond.

Don't let anyone tell you that people don't care about politics. They do. I see, feel and hear it everywhere I go. But there is widespread loathing and disgust at much of what politics has become, and a widespread sense of powerlessness that anything can be done to change it, that all too easily lead to a sense of despairing apathy. That suits the chancers and the charlatans. It also suits them that there are so many barriers preventing so-called 'ordinary people' getting into politics in the first place. Can anyone seriously look at the House of Commons, let alone the House of Lords, or the broadcast studios and newspapers from where the story of our national politics is told, and say: 'That's modern Britain right there!'? It's why the barriers need to be taken down.

As Natalie set out her plans for a new tax system that could finally tackle multinational tax avoidance, so that public and community services could be properly funded; as Holly Morgan explained what was needed to end institutional racism; as Kelly Given argued for a housing revolution that would end homelessness and redesign the housing market and house-building rules to benefit the young and the poor, a cameraman muttered to me: 'Why do we have Priti Patel, Liz Truss and Nadine Dorries in the Cabinet when we could have women like this?' (This was recorded shortly before Liz Truss went on to even higher things, before catastrophically crashing first the UK economy, then her own career and a forty-nine-day premiership.)

It's a good question, and one that reminded me of something LBC broadcaster Nick Ferrari told Sayeeda and me, after he interviewed our semi-final candidates (one of the many challenges we put them through). 'They had better ideas, and explained them better, than any of the ministers and shadow ministers I've had in here recently.'

There are few things wrong with Britain that we don't have the people to fix. The passion is there. The ideas are there. It's just that too few of the brightest and the best, the passionate and the committed, are even thinking about going into politics. They can't see the point, or they can't get into the system. And that's the problem. Purpose and system won't change by themselves. People have to get engaged; they have to get involved.

The populist leaders who have been dominating politics at home and abroad are a symptom of rotten politics and media cultures, as well as a cause. People with values, passion and real commitment to others are the cure. We must all do what we can to find such people, inspire them, build them up and get them into the political arena so they can deliver the massive kick up the backside, dare I say revolution, that is needed. They are the future. My generation – of people and of politics – we are the past. What we should now be doing, as Sayeeda and I did with the candidates in the TV show, is to help, support, aid, assist, so we can pass the baton on. At the time of writing, two of those three finalists, despite the reservations about politics they expressed, have indicated they hope to become candidates in parliamentary elections, Natalie for Labour, Kelly for the SNP, while Holly is already getting engaged in the continuing struggle to defeat racism. All three admitted, too, that during the making of the series, they developed a better appreciation of how hard political life and decision-making is, which makes it all the more encouraging that they have chosen to stick with politics and go further, despite the challenges, setbacks and pressures they experienced.

If I have one simple goal for this book, it is this: to help people who want to make a difference to do so. That means, first of all, getting them to believe that they can and should. But it also means getting them to understand what politics involves – or, rather, *should* involve. There is the simple definition of the word politics – the activities of governments, politicians and political parties. That is the part that people all too often turn away from. But then, there is the broader definition, based on the original Greek word, *politiká*, which involves all the activities and relationships associated with making decisions in groups, such as the distribution of money or status, and which ultimately takes you to more or less everything that matters in our lives. Politics, by its broadest definition, is the place where we have to campaign and be active if we really want to effect the change needed to make people's lives better.

Getting people engaged in this way means persuading them to resist cynicism, despite their so-called betters and elders – and maybe some of their friends too – providing so many reasons to be cynical. There's a popular assumption that politicians are all the same – they're not – or that they're in it for themselves – not all of them are – or simply that they achieve nothing for the people who elect them – some achieve a lot. I am very critical of a number of politicians, but have direct experience of a sufficient number of others to know that there are plenty of good ones among the bad.

It's also important to get people to realise that it's precisely because the political process does feel so remote and irrelevant to so many that it so badly requires the input, energy and activism of new people. Protest is good. People power is great. Ultimately, though, we need individuals with intelligence, energy and ideas to enter elected politics. Because if we don't achieve this, we're condemning ourselves to drawing our leaders from an ever-narrowing gene pool, with more than its fair share of the fanatics, incompetents and mavericks who further alienate normal people from politics. As I will argue, there is always going to be an enormous role for good old-fashioned campaigning, and I would never dissuade anyone from fighting outside Parliament for a cause they believe in. However, if I am pleading with people at least to think about going into politics, it is because of the fundamental truth that if you want to change opinion you can do so as a campaigner, but if you really want to change the course of a country, and certainly if you want to change the laws of the land, you have to get into government.

Oh, go on, I will admit it, I have an altogether more ambitious hope . . . that there is someone now in their teens, twenties or early thirties, who is so inspired by something they read in here that they decide to embark upon a life in politics, someone who one day becomes an outstanding prime minister, is in office on the day I die, and posts a selfie with a dog-eared copy of *But What Can I Do?* and says: 'This was the book that convinced me I could change the world.' Allow me my idle fantasies: they might help you fulfil yours . . .

My call to action, though, is to people of all ages, to anyone who is worried about the state of the country and/or the world, to people who are developing political awareness and understanding, and trying to find their place in the political arena. It is also aimed at people on the cusp of political engagement and activity, but perhaps needing that extra push to move from thinking to doing, from complaint to commitment. I hope, too, that there are parents and teachers who read this book, and who are inspired to encourage their children and students to take an active interest in politics.

Politics is the area I know best, and which currently worries me most, but I hope there are thoughts and ideas in here that will help anyone who has it within them – as we all do – to do something special. Science, medicine, invention and innovation, enterprise, architecture and planning, music, writing, culture and art, the law, charities . . . there are lots of ways to change the world. It is up to us to change it, and every one of us can play a part.

I want to raise your hopes as we go through the book. I also want to show you – without going all lifestyle guru on you – how important it is to look after your physical and mental health, whichever path of action you decide to take. But, first, we need properly to analyse and understand the extent of the crisis we currently face. That is what Part 1 is all about: where it all went wrong. It is important to understand why and how we got into the mess we are in, and identify some of the deeper forces at play, because unless we really understand them, we cannot defeat them. And defeat them we must – as soon as possible, and hopefully in my lifetime.

Part 1, I confess, is pretty depressing, scary even. Populism and polarisation are with us, threatening democracy around the world, and fascism is a real threat. Inequality within and between nations is growing. The climate crisis is an existential one. But stick with me. By the end of the book, with any luck, you'll be in a mood to understand that, as the song went and can go again, 'Things can only get better.' I will share some thoughts on how to make this happen.

That D:Ream song provided the soundtrack to New Labour's first election win in 1997. Despite the inconvenience of having been expelled from the party a few years ago, I remain Labour to the core. But that doesn't mean I'm speaking only to those who share my political views. I genuinely hope to offer ideas and insights that help people of all political persuasions, including those who are unsure what they believe in as yet. The book is for supporters of democracy everywhere who feel their political way of life is under threat. It is for those who believe in international cooperation rather than narrow national self-interest; it's for Tories who perhaps want to see their party return to being a serious national party rather than a populist Brexit tribute band; it's for Scottish Nationalists who want not merely to campaign for independence, as is their right, but who also want their leaders to answer rather than will away the really tough questions at the heart of their project; it's for climate campaigners who want not only to save the planet – don't we all? Well no, actually, there are some very powerful right-wing forces who couldn't give much of a damn – but also, as some have done in other parts of Europe, to advance to a role in government. And though I doubt I will ever see Brexit as anything other than a catastrophic act of national self-harm, if there are Brexit true-believers who see in here ideas that can help them fix some of the issues they know in their hearts need fixing, then that's fine by me.

I hope, too, that current politicians read the book, and reflect that they, and their parties, are a big part of the problem. They need to change, or be changed. They need to open up to new people and ideas, new structures, new ways of being funded, new ways of doing politics, or risk becoming irrelevant. That is the challenge to them, and they need to confront it head on.

Ultimately, though, I am most interested in the millions of individuals who are not currently fully active or engaged, but who have a feeling they might want to get involved in changing things for the better. I hope people who have never thought a political party or a political campaign might be for them are persuaded otherwise. At the very least, I hope they will take on one big issue – something they really care about, and where they really want to make a difference – and that they will find things here that will help them do so with power and conviction.

PART ONE

Why Did It All Go Wrong?

Our Polarised World

If there is one thing that makes me optimistic that we can get things back on track fairly quickly, it is the fact that they went off track as swiftly as they did. Of course, it is entirely possible for things to get even worse, and in my bleaker moments, I imagine a near future in which fascism sweeps the world, societies collapse, the nation-state breaks down as companies and corporations become more powerful than any constraint upon them, the climate crisis continues unchecked, and we all self-destruct and go to hell in a handcart. But there is another way to think about where we are: if change for the worse can be historically speedy, so can change for the better, and that is what we have to try to bring about. And given that change for the worse seems to have stemmed from a period when things appeared to be going well for the liberal democracies in which most of us wish to live, perhaps this moment, when so many feel anxious and/or angry about the direction we are taking, is one from which the pivot to something better can come. Because, for all the talk of populism and polarisation – to which I will be adding plenty in the pages to come – there remain millions of people in Britain, and billions abroad, who are desperate to reject and defeat them, and want something better from their politics and their political leaders. They, or I should say WE, have to take back control of the political debate, and of politics.

Our world certainly felt very different in the early nineties. The Berlin Wall had fallen in 1989; the Cold War was coming to an end, and with it the threat of nuclear annihilation receded; and for a while, as economies on both sides of the Atlantic picked up, the term 'global community' seemed as though it actually meant something. It was an optimistic and forward-looking era in other ways, too. Personal computers and mobile phones started to become an integral part of people's lives. The worldwide web was beginning to develop. The first artificial heart was created. DNA profiling was enlisted in the fight against crime. Universities expanded and educational opportunities were enhanced.

Yet it is also possible to see in that period early signs of some of the harmful trends that led us to where we are now. The rise of the cult of the individual over the power of community. The growth of the belief that if the wealthy have more money, it will somehow trickle its way down to the poor. These messages, most clearly enunciated in the 1980s by Ronald Reagan in the US and Margaret Thatcher in the UK, may at the time have seemed rooted in aspiration and enterprise, but time would show they could all too easily become corrupted by greed and selfishness.

Historians, economists and political geeks will argue for ever about the pluses and minuses of the ideologies adopted by some of the major world leaders of the last quarter of the twentieth century. Take 'Reaganomics' – the free-market doctrine espoused by US president Ronald Reagan that focused on cutting taxes and regulation, and on tight money supply. Its supporters argue that it saw off an era of stagnant growth and high inflation ('stagflation') and ushered in one of growth and enterprise. Its critics point out that it led to a tripling of the national debt during Reagan's two terms in the White House, widened the socio-economic gap between the haves and have-nots, and caused social mobility to stall as real wages fell and the number of people living in poverty rose (Liz Truss and her chancellor, Kwasi Kwarteng, were to dabble – briefly and disastrously – with an extreme form of Reaganomics in the summer of 2022). In the UK, Margaret Thatcher's economic approach has similarly been praised for helping the country get back on its feet after the turmoil of the 1970s, and criticised for opening up social division. Other policies pursued by her to build what she believed would be a one-way road towards change for the better have similarly turned out to have adverse consequences. The sale of council houses – a significant vote-winner at the time – might now be seen as a prelude to the current housing crisis, something which many young people cite as the reason they feel pessimistic about the future, and angry about politics. The Thatcher privatisation revolution, viewed by many Tories as part of her great radical reforming legacy, may, in its promotion of a share-owning democracy, have seemed a noble political goal at the time. But, several decades later, the fact is that it is the big money of private equity that now owns the shares and calls the shots, while many consumers are left with poor performance and rising prices. It's been calculated, for example, that 20 per cent of consumers' annual water bills go simply to reward shareholders and to service the debt that the utilities' owners have landed on their purchases.

I would argue that the Labour governments led by Tony Blair and then Gordon Brown did a lot to reverse some of the downside of Reaganism's UK twin, Thatcherism, not least in our record-funding of schools and hospitals, and a concerted effort to get the young and long-term unemployed into work. But I concede that our critics on the left would argue that we accepted too much of the Thatcher economic agenda. For its part, the current Conservative government has moved to undo significant parts of the New Labour government record, whether that is abolishing Sure Start and Education Maintenance Allowances, or ending the Building Schools for the Future programme, which even former education secretary Michael Gove now recognises was a mistake. In Mr Gove's new area of responsibility as Secretary of State for Levelling Up – very Johnsonian to create a job title from a slogan – there was the scrapping of Regional Development Agencies, which had actually been delivering the kind of levelling up the current government claims to believe in, and similarly the scrapping of the New Deal for Communities.

There are long-term causes, then, for the position we find ourselves in now. But if we're looking for a single trigger moment, a tipping point that ushered in the current era of instability over stability, division over unity, it was surely the global financial crisis of 2008. The cocktail of causes included the taking of excessive risks by the financial institutions we trusted to look after our money; the greed and unscrupulousness of predatory lenders in the sub-prime mortgage market, who targeted people on low incomes; inadequate supervision and regulation by governments; and the bursting of a housing bubble in the States. The cocktail of consequences included the collapse in value of securities and derivatives, enormous damage to financial institutions, the bankruptcy of Lehman Brothers bank, and a full-scale global banking crisis.

Governments, anxious at the prospect of a complete collapse of the global financial system, had to step in with enormous bailouts of the financial institutions who many blamed for the crisis in the first place. Unsurprisingly, this led to a widespread feeling among people whose lives and living standards were damaged by what had happened that 'they' – the greedy bankers – were getting away with it, while 'we' – the people hit hardest despite doing nothing wrong – were paying the price, and were likely to be doing so for many years to come. And though governments had little choice but to act as they did, they became very much part of the 'them' in the equation, and many were toppled as a consequence, not least Labour under Gordon Brown.

It is hard to overstate the economic and political consequences of the GFC. The recession which followed was greater than any since the Great Depression of 1929–1939. The World Bank reckoned the economy of the world was set back a decade, not merely in terms of growth, but also in the fields of investment and innovation, and efforts to narrow inequalities within and between nations. Unemployment soared. Millions were plunged into poverty. As businesses failed and homes were repossessed, suicide rates rose. A young generation became the first unable to say with confidence that they would be better off than their parents. The European debt crisis followed, with several Eurozone member states unable to repay or refinance their government debt or to bail out their banks without the help of other EU countries, the European Central Bank and the International Monetary Fund. This too was easily and eagerly exploited by populists of right and left. Not surprisingly, trust in political and financial institutions, already in decline, fell sharply. When in 2010 the new British prime minister David Cameron announced that we were 'all in this together', it sounded like a hollow joke. Not surprisingly, societies became further polarised.

Polarisation thrives on uncertainty and fear – uncertainty about our future prosperity and position in society, fear of what others might do to us, deny us, or take away from us. We retreat into our group of like-minded people. Once we're there it takes an awful lot to draw us away from it. We become certain that 'we' are doing the right thing; we don't necessarily trust 'them' to follow suit. Humans have always been prone to confirmation bias – defined by the *Encyclopaedia Britannica* as 'the tendency to process information by looking for, or interpreting, information that is consistent with one's existing beliefs'. In tandem with this, contradictory evidence is avoided or ignored and, as a result, people's existing beliefs are strengthened. In a polarised society, confirmation bias becomes further entrenched – indeed Michael Hogg, Professor of Social Psychology at Claremont Graduate University in Los Angeles, coined the term 'uncertainty identity theory' to describe how we identify much more strongly with our 'own' group and the beliefs it holds at times when the future seems unsure. Once a society or an issue is polarised, people on either side of an argument not only find it hard to find common ground, they stop trying, and then begin to question not merely each other's views and arguments, but their motives too.

A polarised society, then, is a toxic one where reasonable debate is driven out, compromise is shunned, and people take extreme positions. People come to believe that there is an enemy – 'they' – who have more than 'us', and who have it because they have exploited 'us'. 'We' have tried to do the right thing – work hard, pay tax, play by the rules, live by traditional norms and values. 'They' – the government with power, business with money, the elites with access and status – have let us down.

So strong is the pull that, on occasion, the 'them' assumes mythical proportions. Who, for example, are the 'woke' brigade that right-wing politicians and certain parts of the media claim are behind so many of our current woes? 'Woke' has become the catch-all term of abuse and derision to capture anything on the culture war front that can be used to suggest 'they' want to do something bad to 'us', or take something good away from 'us'. There was me thinking woke meant that you had a social conscience and cared about others, when, in the hands of the right-wing media, and right-wing politicians like Suella Braverman and Nadhim Zahawi, it turns out it is people like me wanting to destroy anyone and anything that doesn't fit with my narrow, liberal intelligentsia worldview. If only I was as powerful as they seem to make out, I would use this amazing force for something else, I'm sure.

Here, of course, the right wing is playing on the basic human tendency to want to cling on to the past and project it as much better than it was when they feel that the world they are living in – its ideas and values – is changing too fast. It's why, for example, they find it so hard to accept there may have been anything wrong with the way the British Empire was run. To suggest otherwise is to be dismissed as woke – or even to be viewed as a traitor.

The 'woke' brigade, as viewed through the lens of polarisation, comprise an astonishingly diverse range of individuals and groups. Judges who question government decisions on the basis of their lawfulness or unlawfulness – woke. 'Lefty lawyers' who defend people accused of a crime, or help asylum seekers with their claims – woke. Journalists who stray from the favoured narrative of the government and its media cheerleaders – woke. Charities and NGOs – woke. LGBTQ+ campaigners – woke. Former royals who hold hands or talk about their feelings – woke. Civil servants who submit challenging analyses to ministers – woke. Priests and bishops who speak up about poverty – woke. Footballers who stand up to, or kneel down against, racism – woke. It's a bit like horoscopes: when you use the vast, vague definition offered by the right, you can find something in anyone that can be tarred as a little bit woke. Hilariously, the right often seek to defend their anti-woke diatribes as being rooted in a love of free speech. Yet 'woke', and its ally 'snowflake', are used in practice to try to shut down any criticism or questioning of the populist, polarising, post-truth approach. In other words they are aimed at shutting down the free speech of others! 'Politically correct' used to perform a similar purpose, but 'woke' as an insult has spread its net far wider. Be proud to be woke, I say, and stand up for what it really means, namely – the Merriam-Webster dictionary definition – 'to be aware of and actively attentive to important facts and issues, especially issues of racial and social justice'. You can see why the racists, shock jocks and right-wing cheerleaders on both sides of the Atlantic find it difficult, and seek to corrupt not just the word, but the causes that brought it into being. 'Us' is good. 'Them' is 'woke'.

We see a similar conjuring up of a 'them' in the dismissal and derision of 'experts' by the populist right. I have to say that I'd rather have an expert fly my plane or operate on my tumour than an unqualified amateur. But apparently – whether for the Tory right in Britain or the MAGA crowd in the States – individual 'common sense' beats the collective wisdom of the experts. Donald Trump regularly denigrates expert opinion, suggesting that he alone possesses true wisdom. For his part, when Cabinet minister Michael Gove notoriously said during the EU referendum that 'the people of this country have had enough of experts' he was aware precisely what he was doing. He knew that most expert opinion, whether on the economy and trade, on security, on diplomacy, on the future of peace in Northern Ireland, would be pointing to the many negatives inherent in the UK leaving the European Union. By attacking that expert opinion, he was encouraging people to dismiss those who had studied the issues that were on the ballot paper, and could offer informed advice, and listen instead to like-minded friends with little knowledge. He was seeking to create a dividing line between 'we the people', who are good and true, always well motivated, and 'them', the shadowy establishment figures ('the elite', as they so often get termed) who resent 'our' common-sense approach to life. In so doing, he was encouraging the elevation of feeling over fact, emotion over evidence.

We saw at times during the pandemic and afterwards that experts proved fantastically useful whipping boys. You could blame them for everything, even though all they were doing was advising – they didn't have the power to legislate. The *Daily Telegraph*, which for much of Boris Johnson's premiership operated more like a fanzine for its former columnist than a serious broadsheet newspaper, preferred to attack experts for the lockdown that their hero alone had the power to implement. Interesting, too, how right-wing journalists and politicians can somehow blame experts at the Treasury and the Bank of England both for seeking to undermine government economic policy and for implementing it. It doesn't matter that Tory economic policy under Johnson, Truss and Sunak has pinballed between wildly different positions. Their inconsistency is irrelevant once you've discovered that whatever happens, you can just blame 'them', the experts. That's the constant that their detractors hold on to.

The great paradox in all this is that those who claim to represent 'us', so often turn out in reality to be 'them'. It is truly remarkable that Trump, the inherited wealth real-estate billionaire; Johnson, the Eton- and Oxbridge-educated, *Telegraph* journalist son of a Eurocrat; Rishi Sunak, the wealthiest chancellor and prime minister we have ever had; Jacob Rees-Mogg, the multi-millionaire hedge fund son of a *Times* editor; and Nigel Farage, the privately-educated City-trader-turned-professional-Brussels-basher, have all been able to ally themselves to the cause of 'us', when they are so clearly members of the self-interested 'elite' class they claim to fight. It is testament to their success as populists and polarisers. Listen to a Donald Trump speech and hear him seek to polarise in virtually every statement. He is fighting for the 'us' against the 'them', who, at any given moment, may be 'the elite', Democrats, pre-Trump Republicans who dared to criticise him, Mexicans, migrants, Muslims, the FBI, Congress, Washington, the United Nations, China – even London mayor Sadiq Khan, when it suits him. An attack on any of the above will bring his supporters running. In a deeply polarised environment such as the one we currently inhabit, Trump's claim that 'I could stand in the middle of Fifth Avenue and shoot somebody and I wouldn't lose voters' is not as far-fetched as it should be.

People don't just polarise on such specific issues as the economy or immigration. They also tend to polarise around broader world views. If, for example, you're an ideologically extreme Brexiteer or a US right-wing libertarian who believes there should be no gun controls, you'll probably be very sceptical about climate change. There may be no intellectual link between Brexit and gun control on the one side and global warming on the other. But there is a wider set of values and gut instincts involved that seemingly bring these disparate issues together. Libertarians don't want to be told what to think. Hence the scepticism about 'experts'. They prefer to listen to their gut and their friends on social media than to people trying to explain complicated issues in complicated language, with nuance and shades of grey. Right-wingers more generally, particularly wealthy ones, seem to fear any suggestion of a restraint on their ability to access resources or raw materials. They also view securing a market-led economy free from virtually all government oversight as some kind of religious mission. Once formed, these broad outlooks are very difficult to break. You view everything through the lens of your 'tribe', and you don't want to be seen to step out of line with it, even if the facts show you're wrong. Yale law and psychology professor Dan Kahan found that participants in his study who believed climate change is real were further persuaded by the testimony of a Harvard expert. Those who were climate change sceptics simply dismissed the expert's credentials.

Of course, even in a polarised society, there are plenty of people who do not adopt extreme stances – people with whom we might not agree but whose genuinely held beliefs we never-theless respect. In the US, there are many Republicans who do not support Trump. In the UK, as we have seen in recent opinion polls, there are numerous Conservative voters who do not align themselves with the likes of Johnson, Truss and Sunak. Yet you only need to glance at the policies now frequently espoused by both political parties, and compare them with those of a gener-ation or so ago, to see how far the polarising forces now at work have pushed those parties towards the extremes.

In this context, and in case people think that I believe every-one on the right is 'them', and can never be anything but, let me reference Ronald Reagan, US president from 1981 to 1989, more favourably perhaps than I have above, not least to show just how far Republican Party politics have moved under the polarising influence of Trump. Reagan was something of a hate figure for the left, inside and outside America. Yet if you want to see great, moving oratory, go online and find 'Reagan's last speech as president'. There are several highlights in the speech, but for me the finest is when he quotes a letter he received shortly before leaving office, from a man who wrote: 'You can go to live in France but you cannot become a Frenchman. You can go to live in Germany or Turkey or Japan but you cannot become a German or a Turk or a Japanese. But anyone from any corner of the earth can come to live in America, and become an American.'

The whole speech, with his explanation of the symbolism of the Statue of Liberty welcoming outsiders to a place of freedom and opportunity, his focus on how each wave of new arrivals from other lands and regions has renewed and enriched the country, his bold assertion that newcomers from overseas end up feeling more American than those born there, reads like a love letter to immigrants and immigration. 'We lead the world because, unique among nations, we draw our strength from every country and every corner of the world . . . If we ever closed the door to new Americans, our leadership in the world would soon be lost.'

Read it through from start to finish, and there is barely a word you could imagine falling from Trump's lips, or indeed the lips of other Republicans hoping to be their presidential candidate next time around. The Republican dial has shifted way to the right, and it is polarisation that has propelled it there. Compare and contrast Reagan's soaring, inclusive oratory with Trump's snarling, sneering rantings; or his rambling defence of his attack on four Congresswomen of colour, three of them born and raised in the US, who he had suggested should go back to where they came from. The othering trope of racists and fascists down the years.

Whatever the outcome of his policies, in Reagan's tone, rhetoric and manner, he clearly showed that he wanted an inclusive society. Trump, flourishing in a polarised US, sucks in support for an exclusionary one.

Brexit was won on similar polarising messaging to that used by Trump. Indeed, the success of the Brexit campaign in 2016 fuelled Trump's belief ahead of his victorious presidential bid that he was right to seek to divide, to create chaos, to dominate the airwaves with lies and insults, to dismiss the opinion of 'experts', to polarise. He had witnessed, and been impressed by, the use of such tactics by Boris Johnson and Nigel Farage – the former a latecomer to Brexit and Trump, the latter a true believer in both – to win their campaign to get the UK out of Europe. 'They' (Brussels) take your money. We will take it back and give it to the NHS. 'They' (the Turks) are coming. We will stop them. 'They' (the economists/business/status quo) say Brexit will make you worse off. Don't believe them. Only we will tell you the truth. Because 'we' are with 'you', against 'them'.

Within days of victory, the Brexit camp had retreated from some of the central promises its leading campaigners had made. As the Brexit negotiations unfolded, commitments that the UK would stay in the single market and the customs union were dropped. Once Boris Johnson became prime minister, the promise that a border down the Irish Sea would be laid over his dead body was broken. Johnson breathed on, to tell more lies and break more promises. Yet, all the while, Brexit true-believers insisted both that the very different Brexit now emerging was exactly what people had voted for, and that it was going well. Anyone who suggested otherwise, or sought to raise the actual crimes committed by the winning campaign, or the many lies it told, was at best a 'bitter Remoaner', at worst a traitor. It was all straight out of the polarisation playbook: extreme tribalism, the replacement of facts with 'alternative facts', and the demonisation of whoever was deemed to be 'them'.

In fairness, I have to concede that I, too, am very tribal about Brexit. I'm acutely aware of my reluctance to see any benefits that it might have delivered (though I do, honestly, struggle to find any!). Equally, I am conscious that when I get into an argument about Brexit today, several years on from the referendum, the exchanges can all too quickly become emotional, rather than intellectual. That, as I have already intimated, is a consequence of polarisation. I have to force myself, and often fail, to see the argument the other person is putting forward on its own merits. But it is hard. I have experienced too often the frustration of presenting people with firm evidence, facts, data, only to discover it is not enough. Time and time again, your interlocutor doesn't want to listen, because they don't trust you, because you are not in their tribe. You, the messenger, are questioned, and your message does not get past first base.

Sometimes, this dialogue of the deaf is a product of wilful deception. We saw plenty of this from the Brexit campaign leaders during the referendum, and have seen plenty more since, as they have sought to pretend that what we are getting is what we were promised, and that the Brexit benefits are clear for all to see. But on my side of the argument, it is not just because we are disputing the legitimacy of facts. The problem sometimes is that we are unable even to understand or appreciate what the other side cares about, or what makes them anxious.

On a train journey back from the annual conference of the Confederation of British Industry in Birmingham last year, I found myself sitting opposite a retired engineer who asked me, in a perfectly friendly way, if I would ever stop 'banging on about Brexit'. I said, in all probability, no, I wouldn't, because I felt it had done so much damage to the country, and I worried that the *Brexomertá* of the political classes would make things worse, because the only way you ever solve a problem is to admit to its existence in the first place. I then went on to ask him if he felt that the country had become better off financially as a result of Brexit.

'No,' he said. 'Not yet anyway.'

'Do you think the NHS has got the extra money we were promised?'

'No.'

'Do you think the other benefits that were promised have materialised?'

'No.'

'Do you think our reputation in the world has been weakened or strengthened?'

'Well, I am guessing you think it has been weakened. Maybe it has.'

'So what was it about?'

'For me, it was about sovereignty. Laws being made here, nowhere else.'

'Which laws do you have in mind?'

'Well, none specifically. But it's the principle of the thing.'

'Even if it makes us poorer, weaker, less influential in the world?'

'Yep.'

'Fair enough,' I said. 'At least that's an honest view.'

It's something that David Cameron experienced in the lead-up to the 2016 referendum. He was sure that if he focused on the hard economic facts, he would win the day. That approach, he believed, was what had helped him oust Gordon Brown to become prime minister, first leading a coalition government in 2010, and then a majority Conservative government when he defeated Ed Miliband's Labour five years later. A similar hard-headed approach to hard economic fact, he believed, had also been key to winning the battle against independence in the referendum in Scotland in

2014. But he had not reckoned with how quickly the landscape was changing.

A few years before it became perhaps the single most divisive and polarising political issue of my lifetime, Brexit barely figured in the public debate at all. Even the most Eurosceptic of the Eurosceptics talked of being 'in Europe, not run by Europe'. They weren't saying 'out' of Europe at all. David Cameron was sufficiently confident in his position as a leader who wanted to keep the UK in the EU to dismiss UKIP, who at that time were very much leading the charge against Europe, as 'fruitcakes and loonies'. What he didn't appreciate was how powerful, persuasive and ruthless the fruitcakes and loonies were becoming, not least within his own party. Nor, in his confidence in his own abilities and his own arguments, had he fully appreciated how, in a polarised landscape, Brexit would come to symbolise a whole range of attitudes and issues that had nothing to do with the hard facts of Britain's relationship with the EU. To those promoting Brexit, the EU, and all who wished to stay part of it, simply became 'them' – the people responsible for all our ills – while 'we' were its victims.

The Leave side seemed to see from very early on that people had very different reasons for voting for Brexit. Some thought it would reduce immigration, some thought it would make Britain richer, some thought it would save the NHS, some wanted all UK laws to be made in the UK alone. It didn't matter to Leave why someone voted Leave, they just needed the numbers. So they told people what they wanted to hear. Having discovered, for example, that for some people animal rights is a defining issue, they targeted a campaign at those people by assuring them a vote to leave was a vote for stronger protections for animals. As with much else in the campaign, a lot of what they said was tendentious at best, outright untrue at worst. It mattered not, so long as they achieved their objective.

'Leave means Leave' became one of their mantras, when in truth Leave meant whatever proved to be useful in the argument at the time. Leave were less prescriptive about what Leave actually meant than Remain were about what Remain meant.

Here, it is perhaps worth mentioning how other seeming plus points from the recent past – the increasing prevalence of computers, smart phones and social media – brought their negative aspects with them. Come 2016, the technological revolution was being harnessed in ways the Remain camp was too slow to understand, and too worried about Tory party division to fight against properly. Data laws were broken. Funding laws were broken. A blind eye was turned to Russian interference, still denied to this day despite a welter of evidence, not least in the Intelligence and Security Committee report whose publication Johnson delayed for so long it was treated like ancient history by the time it finally saw the light of day. Cameron instructed the Remain camp that he did not want to see 'blue on blue' attacks, thereby allowing Johnson and co to peddle their lies and fantasies untroubled by effective rebuttal from Conservatives on the other side. It was like a match between Gentlemen and Players, with Cameron leading the Gentlemen. One side relied on fact; the other on anything it took to win, true or false, right or wrong – the more emotional and polarising the argument the better.

Cameron cannot say he wasn't warned. Chancellor George Osborne was strongly against holding the referendum. Former French president François Hollande recounted to me how both he and then German chancellor Angela Merkel had told Cameron that in holding a referendum on anything, let alone such a contentious and complex subject, a government risked being punished for other, seemingly unrelated, issues. Cameron, wearing what Hollande called 'an arrogant mask of serenity', assured them he knew what he was doing, and he would be fine. Cameron also mistakenly believed that his Etonian charm would enable him to persuade the Europeans to grant enormous concessions that he would be able to sell back home as evidence both of our strength and standing within the EU, and of the need for us to stay in it. On that, too, Merkel and Hollande warned him he was overstating the possibilities, that they would agree to nothing that went against the core principles of EU membership. Cameron should have learned the lesson of someone who worked for years alongside Merkel, who said: 'Her great strength is that she is uncharmable. She deals in fact.'

The referendum itself, far from settling the debate, if anything widened and entrenched the polarisation. Leave and Remain became the badges of two groups who prior to 2016 may have had much in common, but now appeared to have totally opposing perspectives and beliefs. Long before Trump had introduced us to the concept of 'alternative facts' as a strategy, the Leave side seemed to base their entire approach upon them. They had won, and that was all that mattered. The 'facts' on which they had won, and the promises they had made, were largely forgotten, rewritten or elided into a political drama of passion and personality.

From a polarising perspective, the messaging had been faultless. 'Take back control' fed the sense that we had lost it in the first place (John Major and Tony Blair have both pointed out that they cannot recall a single thing that they wanted to do as prime minister which 'Europe' prevented them from doing). It also implied that in so doing, we were going to give ourselves a better future. We would put the country to rights. We would resurrect national pride. And all with the big NHS lie thrown in: a big red bus travelling the country with the message that all we had to do to get an extra £350 million a week for the NHS was get out of the EU. Much of the fuel for the campaign came from fearfulness, not just about the non-existent threat of Turks 'swamping' the country, but about immigration more generally. Then there was the 'threat' of 'Brussels', unelected bureaucrats, experts and elites (this from the most elitist leadership team ever assembled). The very word 'Europe' itself became a byword for the enemy. The language of war was often employed, with the 'them' of France and Germany hellbent on taking ever more from 'us', the plucky Brits.

Projecting themselves as the underdog was essential to the Brexit campaign. 'They' were Goliath, an all-powerful establishment hoodwinking the public for their own interests. 'We' were David. Labelling the hard economic analysis of the Remain side as 'Project Fear' was a brilliant piece of strategic rebuttal, as it allowed the Leave side to evade engaging with the realities of the situation. Instead, they could focus on querying the motives of the messenger, further strengthening the message that it was somehow all about 'them' keeping the status quo for themselves. Cameron and his right-hand man Osborne – and I admit that until the late stages of the campaign I thought they were right – were sure that ultimately fact and detail would beat fantasy and emotion. We were all proven catastrophically wrong. The Brexit outcome changed the terms of political debate, and they have yet to change back again. Had the Leave campaign spelled out openly the length and complexity of the exit process, the costs en route, the loss of rights and access, the damage to trade and diplomacy, the risks to stability in Northern Ireland, and all the other things they denied would ever happen, they know they would not have won. They had to win on one basis, govern on another, and hope that the people, opposing politicians and the media would move on in time. It's fair to say that their hopes have been largely fulfilled, with both main parties reluctant properly to address the elephant in the room: the damage Brexit is already doing, and what needs to be done to fix it, given it has taken at least a 4 per cent chunk out of the economy.

In more normal times, people who fail to deliver on their promises generally receive their come-uppance. In polarised times, they appear to have the space and capacity to double-down on their failure, explain things away with a new promise or a fresh outburst of wishful thinking, or blame the ever-present, ever-useful 'them'. In the case of Brexit, any suggestion of an economic downside was waved away as Project Fear. Prices would fall, not rise. The pound would strengthen, not weaken. Trade would grow, not shrink. When those benefits failed to materialise, we were told that a 10 per cent devaluation of sterling the day after the vote was 'to be expected', but that the sunlit uplands would soon hove into view. Another government department was created, and later shelved, to pretend there was substance to their slogans, with Jacob Rees-Mogg appointed minister for Brexit Opportunities.

We were assured that a quickly agreed trade deal with the United States would be one of the major wins of Brexit. Four Brexit prime ministers later, we are still waiting. When Liz Truss, ahead of her first meeting with US President Joe Biden, admitted it would be a long time coming, it led to more insouciant shoulder-shrugging from the Brexit ideologues. 'Ah well, it was never about trade deals . . .' Wasn't it? At the time of the referendum, the notion that we would even think about leaving the customs union and the single market was denied outright; the very suggestion was all part of the same 'Project Fear'. When these once unthinkable moves happened, we were suddenly asked to believe that this was always part of the plan. And when Brexit was exposed as not being a done deal at all, but barely half-baked, and going badly, it all became the fault of the Europeans, who, according to David Frost, the man who negotiated the deal on Boris Johnson's behalf, had exploited our weakness.

Ironically, when it comes to Northern Ireland it is the EU that takes the peace process more seriously than Northern Ireland's actual sovereign government. How do you reconcile all that with the claims made at the outset that 'we hold all the cards' and 'they need us more than we need them'? Or that Johnson and

Frost boasted of the 'brilliant' deal they had struck, which they later condemned when its manifest weaknesses became exposed?

Another popular strategy – in an era of 'alternative facts' – is to deny any link between cause and effect. A labour market shortage created by EU citizens choosing or being forced to head home was 'nothing to do with Brexit'. Supply chain disruptions were 'nothing to do with Brexit'. The continuing depreciation of sterling was 'nothing to do with Brexit'. One of my stand-out moments in the first of the two Tory leadership elections in 2022 came when Liz Truss and Rishi Sunak were asked in a televised debate whether they believed the enormous queues at the port of Dover – it was taking many hours for holidaymakers to get through, and far longer for lorries – had anything to do with the decision to leave the EU. Both went into an immediate race to see who could be fastest to the draw in denying any such link. This gaslighting was especially stunning because in their answers to the previous question, which was about how they would differentiate themselves from the lying of the Johnson era, both had said that we would always get the truth from them. The deal seems to be: I promise you'll always get the truth from me, until I am faced with an inconvenient truth about the real world and the mess we have helped to make of it.

I've dwelt on Brexit in some detail here, not just because I despair at the damage it is doing, and the reluctance of politicians to address it, but because it demonstrates so many of the poisonous characteristics of populism and polarisation. The same pattern has been seen in the US or Italy, Hungary or Poland. The precise causes and triggers vary from country to country, and may well have not just economic and social components but cultural and religious ones, too (the polarisation to be found in contemporary Israeli politics has very different roots from those that set off divisions in, say, Bolsonaro-era Brazil). The playbook, though, is generally the same: the division of society into 'us' and 'them'; a contempt for facts and reasoned argument alongside organised deceit and lying, and far too much acceptance of both; and an equal contempt for the values and institutions that are fundamental to a functioning democracy and the holding of the powerful to account. Israel is instructive, also, in revealing the sheer pace with which a move to the extremes can take place. Its current government, under Benjamin Netanyahu, who has been prime minister on and off for a total of fifteen years since 1996, is by some stretch the most right-wing in its history. It has been driven there by people and policy ideas once on the outer fringes of Israeli debate, now dominant in its government. A hard-right finance minister claiming greater authority over Jewish settlements and civilian affairs in the occupied West Bank; a minister in charge of policing who has a history of anti-Arab activism; ultra-Orthodox ministers demanding more autonomy and funding for religious schools; insisting, too, on greater political control of the appointment of judges and the rulings of the Supreme Court. The notion of Israel as a liberal democracy feels fragile indeed, and the notion of the 'two-state solution' as the way to fix the Israel–Palestine conflict, which for so long felt difficult but at least possible, feels currently like a pipe dream.

To make matters worse, polarisation by its very nature tends to turn more extreme unless its causes are tackled at the root. Division begets further division. 'Them' and 'us' become ever more mutually antagonistic. Take the following grim statistics from the US. According to the researchers Gabriel Almond and Sidney Verba, in 1960s America 5 per cent of Republicans and 4 per cent of Democrats said they would be unhappy if their son or daughter married someone from the other party. By 2008 the figures were 27 per cent for Democrats and 20 per cent for Republicans, and by 2020, 38 per cent of Republicans and 38 per cent of Democrats declared they would be upset or very upset by one of their children marrying someone from the other political tribe. The direction of travel here is pretty worrying.

Polarisation, though, is only one of the ingredients of the toxic cocktail that is polluting the current political scene. Its force would not be so effective without the political force that takes advantage of it: populism.

2.

The Rise of the Populists

The classic definition of populism is a form of politics aimed at 'ordinary people' who feel their concerns are not addressed by 'the elite'. 'The elite' is an easy target, because it is such a vague term that it can be interpreted as comprising anything and anyone who seems to lie outside the direct experience of 'ordinary people'. 'Ordinary people' is a nice, vague phrase, too. Most people consider themselves to be 'ordinary', yet, of course, no two people are the same. The double-vague combination lends itself well to exploitation by politicians who seek to persuade anyone with a grievance that it is the fault of someone else, who has something they don't, be that power, wealth or opportunity. Then the next step is to persuade them that they should switch their political allegiance from Politician A, who tells them that the problem is difficult and complex, to Politician B, who assures them it can be solved by turning against this mythical 'elite', represented by that MP, that civil servant, that institution, that banker, that business, that judge, that academic, that diplomat, that anything or anyone who does not share your own worldview.

I feel the following definition, however – offered to me by an Australian who called himself 'sleuthfortruth' and was responding on Twitter to an interview I had done there – gets closer to the heart of things, for it recognises populism's negative effect as well as its negative motive: 'Populism', he said, 'is the art of agitating disaffected voters to vote *against their best interests* by amplifying problems and not really offering anything in return.'

'Voting for a populist party,' he added, 'is like diving head-first into an empty swimming pool because you're angry that there's no water in it.' Arguably, it's even worse than that. You not only hurt yourself because the pool is empty, you also allow yourself to be persuaded by the anti-elite elitists who told you to jump in the first place that it was someone else's fault that there was no water there. As I made clear in the previous chapter, my view of Brexit is that it was an act of national self-harm secured by populist politicians falsely promising to improve people's lives when in fact they were about to make them, in many ways, worse; and that those self-same populists then doubled down on their failure, inventing new bogeymen and new issues to blame for all ills, such as climate activists, 'lefty lawyers' and 'wokery'. The end result is that we now see the same people who fought for Brexit seeking to leave that particular disaster and its consequences behind them, and move on to bigger ones. Consider leading Brexit campaigner Nigel Farage. It is as if he wakes up each morning and says: 'Right, I have helped do irreparable damage to my own country; now let's see if we can do the same to the rest of the world by stopping all this Net Zero nonsense.'

How do populist leaders come about, and prosper? There's little doubt in my mind that they are both driver and product of a polarised society. They thrive on division, claiming to be on the side of 'the pure people', honest and hard-working, in their struggle against 'the corrupt elite'. They thrive on the uncertainty and instability that have provoked that polarisation. In 'normal' times we are prepared to compromise, to accept nuance and a degree of complexity in our lives. In uncertain times, we seem to want simple solutions and strong leaders who we think can deliver them. We saw this play out in parts of Europe in the 1930s, with catastrophic consequences, and we are seeing it again in different regions of the world now. Sadly, the lessons of the Second World War and the Holocaust are all too distant for those people on the lookout for a saviour leader who will tell them what they want to hear about the obstacles to their own happiness and prosperity, and identify the enemies they are encouraged to blame.

The reason that populists tend to like referendums is that they play brilliantly to their binary view of the world, where it's 'us' or 'them', 'yes' or 'no'. I find myself revisiting a speech by Margaret Thatcher, from 1975, when she was arguing against the use of referendums except in very special circumstances, such as on issues over which voters were fundamentally divided but on which the major parties agreed. She maintained that without the protections and definition afforded by a constitution, referendums sacrifice parliamentary sovereignty to political expediency. In a system such as Britain's, this would threaten minorities by trading liberal democracy for majoritarianism. 'Perhaps the late Lord Attlee was right,' she observed, 'when he said that the referendum was a device of dictators and demagogues.' Attlee, the UK's post-war Labour prime minister, was right. Thatcher was right.

It should come as no surprise, then, that Vladimir Putin likes to cement rigged constitutional change with the device of the referendum, as in September 2022, when he orchestrated referendums in the Ukrainian regions of Luhansk, Donetsk, Kherson and Zaporizhzhia on joining Russia. It was a blatant attempt to make it appear he had 'the will of the people' behind him in his invasion of Ukraine and attempted annexation of these regions. Nor should it come as a surprise that when a referendum was held in Egypt in 2019 to decide on changes to the constitution, a huge effort was made to boost turnout. Voting took place over three days; there were offers of free rides to the polls, even free food, and in some places reportedly threats of fines for not voting. Turnout was ultimately just 44 per cent, but victory for change was secured with almost 90 per cent support. President Sisi immediately saluted the Egyptian people for backing his changes, though fewer than half had actively done so. So what, his supporters can argue. The changes – to extend the length of a presidential term from four to six years; remove the limit on two terms; restore the right of the president to appoint the vice-president; increase presidential power over the judiciary and the military – were passed 'by the people'.

Meanwhile in the UK, just three years earlier, Cameron felt he could contain the forces he was warned the referendum would unleash. He was wrong. Until Brexit, our two-party constitutional monarchy had been spectacularly good at keeping extremes and revolutionaries away from the levers of power. With the 2016 referendum, something just snapped.

Key to the appeal and success of the polarising populist is that they present themselves as an anti-politics politician. Joe Biden may have reached the very top in part *because* of his many decades of experience, but plenty of election-winning politicians, not least Trump, have used their lack of experience in politics as an asset. This can be exploited as another form of them versus us. The career politicians, the so-called professional politicians, are 'them'. The 'us' politicians are those who share the widespread public contempt for politics. Johnson rose as an anti-politics politician. Farage too. Berlusconi in Italy. Bolsonaro in Brazil. Imran Khan in Pakistan. The appeal is that they're 'different' . . . 'not afraid to say what the people are thinking' . . . 'breath of fresh air' . . . 'he makes me laugh'. They also often benefit from the common human assumption that someone who has enjoyed success in one field is bound to prove equally adept in another, wholly unrelated one. Trump became a household name by projecting himself, often against the evidence, as a supremely successful business-man. Many people therefore believed his claim that he could run the country just as effectively as he said he ran his businesses. Berlusconi did likewise in Italy. It is the same phenomenon, when allied with the populist disregard for expertise, that means a C-list celebrity is as likely to appear on television, simply because of their celebrity status, talking about important issues on which they know little, as is an actual expert.

Ultimately, the populist's model message, which the mega-elitists use to persuade angry people they're on their side, is really quite straightforward. 'You are angry. You are right to be angry. I get your anger. Because they (elites/vague enemies undefined) are not giving you what you want and need and deserve. They keep everything for themselves. Because they are not on your side. I am on your side. Because only I understand you, and only I have the strength to deliver for you on your priorities.'

The them/us scenario isn't just created on a national scale, either. It includes the wider world. British populists, for example, gleefully celebrate the removal of the rights of EU citizens to live, work and travel here freely (and without regard for the fact that in doing so they have taken away reciprocal rights from their own citizens). 'We' are the citizens of an exploited and beleaguered country. 'They' are the foreigners who are taking our jobs, crossing our borders or, according to home secretary Suella Braverman, invading our country. In much the same vein, the Tories under Johnson scrapped the Department for International Development and reneged on a pledge to spend 0.7 per cent of GDP on overseas aid and development – a policy for which broad consensus had been built over time – strongly hinting all the while that 'they' were nefariously siphoning off the money that belongs to 'us'. In the US, meanwhile, Trump won an election by promising to build a wall across the country's southern frontier.

It might matter fractionally less if populists actually delivered on the main promises made, and/or delivered real, tangible, enduring improvements to the lives of the people who elected them. But they so rarely do. It's hard to resist the conclusion that the sole purpose of many populists' pursuit of power . . . is power itself. Power to amass more power, wealth and influence for themselves, their friends and supporters. Power also to undermine the institutions which are there to act as a check on their power, and the electoral systems that might otherwise ultimately see them ejected from office.

Despite the economic and social chaos viewed as the legacy of Hugo Chávez's rule of Venezuela, you will still find defenders who argue that, especially in his early years in power, he lifted many out of poverty. More recently, the violence provoked on the streets by President Pedro Castillo's arrest in Peru came partly from working-class people who felt he had made a difference for the better in their lives and living standards. I find it hard, however, to think of a populist leader who has delivered sustained progress for the people who put them in power, and/or who resisted the pressures and temptations to fall into corruption and the abuse of power. What about Berlusconi in Italy? Or Erdoğan in Turkey? Or, for that matter, recently departed Australian prime minister Scott Morrison, whose simultaneous lack of achievement and debasement of Australian politics was recently brilliantly skewered in the book *Bulldozed* by journalist – and former operative in Morrison's own party – Niki Savva?

To a Brit like me, perhaps the most damning line among many is her description of Morrison as 'Boris Johnson without the hair or the humour'. But how similar to Trump does Morrison appear under the microscope of friends and enemies interviewed by Savva . . . 'petty, vindictive, messianic, megalomaniacal, plain mad, missing that part of the brain that controls empathy'. The sense is not merely of a leader incapable of leading in a coherent way – his unconstitutional seizing of several ministries to be headed by himself was bizarre in the extreme – but who thus corrupts and debases politics more generally, as did Trump and Johnson. The losers are the people, whose needs and interests seem barely to figure in the machinations going on around him.

The reason populists seek to consolidate their power and undermine the institutions which are there to act as a check on their power is that, once the public is alert to the reality, they are less likely to support the politicians who have created it. So, the politicians do what they can to make it harder for the public to eject them from power, up to and including, in Trump's case, a refusal to accept the outcome of an election he had clearly lost.

It's perhaps to conceal this naked ambition and desire for self-promotion that what a populist says is so often precisely the opposite of what they mean. Johnson was a past-master when it came to obfuscation and lying, seeking to conceal his true intentions behind an air of false friendliness and bonhomie. Others have emulated his gaslighting approach. Consider the following examples, which have emerged at various points from the Conservatives under our three recent prime ministers. Let's start with some Johnson favourites.

'I am a huge admirer of the BBC' (which is why we bully and intimidate it, pack it with our friends, donors and supporters, and play along with the defund campaign of the hard right).

'Our friends and partners in the EU' (whom we insult at every turn, and blame for problems of our own making).

'Levelling up' (it sounds good, even if the policies move in the opposite direction).

'Global Britain' (did anyone say Little England?).

Here are a couple of the best Trussisms:

'Let me level with you . . .' (words often followed by a lie or the explanation for a broken promise, though the breach is never admitted).

'I've been very clear' (the opening to a sentence that invariably sought to explain how two opposing views expressed by the same person within a short distance of each other are actually the same).

Now a couple of Sunak specialities:

'I love the NHS, it is the jewel in the British crown' (I'm sorry it's on its knees thanks to austerity and general undermining, so if we have to open it to the American market to get a trade deal, so be it, and I'm sorry we can't pay nurses a decent wage, but I did clap for them during the pandemic, so you should just trust me when I say that there is no right-wing hidden agenda at work here).

'This government will have integrity, accountability and pro-fessionalism at every level' (but if it helps me to become prime minister by securing the backing of a former home secretary, sacked recently for a lack of all three, with a promise she can walk straight back into Cabinet, so be it. Needs must).

And finally, here is a selection of bogus or contradictory argu-ments I have heard from all three PMs:

'We are absolutely committed to helping the poorest people in the world' (so we will slash overseas aid and get rid of the Depart-ment for International Development).

'Peaceful protest has a vital role to play in our democracy' (which is why we are legislating to make it harder to do).

'Everyone should have the right to vote' (so even though there has been only one recent case of voter fraud using fake identity, we will force everyone to show ID when they vote, because that will suppress turnout among the young and the poor, who are more likely to vote against us).

Once a polarising populist leader has a strong cohort of people – often referred to as 'the base' – willing to believe anything they say, and support anything they do – the ability of that leader to withstand criticism over their mistakes and failures, lies and broken promises, or their rejection of hard evidence exposing all of the above, grows. That it took a riot at the Capitol Building in Washington, and lockdown-law-breaking parties in Downing Street in London, to make it clear to all but their most sect-like followers that Trump and Johnson respectively were unworthy of the offices they held, underlines the potential fragility of our institutions when bad people, who do not play by any rules but their own, are in charge of the rules which are supposed to govern all. Even now, you can find plenty of people who claim Trump is victim rather than villain, or who defend Johnson's lies and law-breaking on the grounds that 'all politicians lie' (not true), and 'everyone played fast and loose with the rules in lockdown' (also not true).

The impact of rule-breaking is not restricted to the country where it takes place. It does real damage to the wider world. When leaders of supposedly enlightened countries such as the US and the UK follow the autocracies down the road of cheating and lying, why should we be surprised that their counterparts in China, Russia and their satellites continue to believe they can behave with impunity? The post-war world has, with some terrible exceptions, been held in check by a set of internationally agreed rules, many of them born amid the global reckoning which followed the Second World War. Once those rules are treated with contempt or indifference by those nations who formerly championed them, then everything descends into a dangerous free-for-all. We have seen considerable solidarity among the democracies for Ukraine in the face of Putin's invasion. However, there are plenty more atrocities happening around the world to which both global politics and media tends to turn a blind, or at least indifferent, eye.

As former UK foreign secretary and current head of the humanitarian International Rescue Committee David Miliband has pointed out, when Saudi Arabia bombs a bus carrying Yemeni schoolchildren, or President Bashar al-Assad targets health facilities in Syria, and indeed President Putin drives up food and fuel prices to create division and even famine well beyond Russia or Ukraine, they are doing so because they have ever less reason to fear being held to international account. 'Impunity is on the march,' Miliband argues. And impunity has a devastating human cost. Each year between 2016 and 2020 an average of 32,000 civilians were killed in conflict – more than double the rate of the previous five-year period and nearly ten times that of 2005 to 2009. Around the world, more than 100 million people were forced to flee their homes, primarily as a result of conflict. Attacks on health facilities have also increased. Since the UN Security Council passed a resolution condemning attacks on hospitals in May 2016, there have been over 4,000 such attacks worldwide. Even during the pandemic lockdown of 2020, more health workers and patients were killed than in the previous year. Meanwhile, ethnic cleansing and killings of aid workers have accelerated as well.

From the poisonous, non-beneficial aspects of populism, it's only a short step to what the eminent American historian Timothy Snyder describes as sado-populism, in which leaders win support for actions and policies that will actually damage many of those who vote for them. Trump and Putin, Professor Snyder argues, are often described as 'populists'. A populist, however, 'is someone who has a policy offering a promise to the people' to make their lives better. 'I don't see that in Trump and Putin,' Snyder goes on. 'I see policies that if implemented would hurt the people . . . it is sadism, the deliberate administration of pain.'

This, of course, begs the question: how can you govern by hurting the people who put you in office? The answer is that you do so by fuelling their fear, rage, resentment, hate. But you also make 'your people' feel better about themselves by assuring them that they are better than others. Donald Trump may correctly have identified that many among the white working classes felt that globalisation was passing them by, that their jobs and industries were being outsourced to China, and that they were being screwed over by the elites. But as a sado-populist, he was less interested in helping them than in exploiting these genuine grievances, while simultaneously telling them that they were superior to the 'them' – whether Blacks, Hispanics or Muslims – whom he identified as the source and cause of their problems. Closer to home in the UK, people have, at various times, been encouraged to blame Poles and Romanians, gypsies, Brussels, bureaucrats, 'wokies', welfare scroungers and asylum seekers seeking to 'invade across the Channel' (even though we had 'taken back control' of our borders) – and, at the same time, to feel superior to them.

The Tories' Rwanda policy, under which the government said asylum seekers would be sent to the African nation for processing, asylum and resettlement, is a classic example of sado-populism. The public want to see a practical solution to a genuine problem. This policy is not designed to provide that. It's an exploitative move to appeal to those on the right who are so central to ensuring that the Tory-party-turned-Brexit-party stays popular with its base. Base being the operative word. In this context, what was remarkable during the leadership campaign that followed Boris Johnson's fall was that all eleven candidates backed the Rwanda plan, or said they did. In so doing they were taking policy attitudes and ideas once confined to the extremist fringes of far-right parties like the National Front, the British National Party or Britain First, dragging them into the mainstream of government policy, and making them a prerequisite for anyone wishing to rise to power or prominence in the Conservative Party.

Moisés Naím, author of the term '3P autocrats' as a label

for those new leaders who use (sado-)populism, polarisation and post-truth (to which I'll come shortly), went on to describe how this tripartite approach has resulted in the development of pseudo-democracies with pseudo-elections, pseudo-law and a pseudo-press. The three Ps themselves have been with us in some shape or form for ever, but have rarely been deployed by the same people at the same time and never, until recent times, with the technological tools that would-be autocrats can now harness to their benefit. Russia offers perhaps the most obvious example here. We should not, however, be at all complacent about how quickly the UK was moving towards such a pseudo-democracy under Johnson, nor imagine it is impossible that another rogue populist leader could take us down the same dangerous route very quickly.

Populism in its current form is less an ideology than a tool-box for gaining and wielding power that can be coupled with virtually any worldview. Hence we have populists of the left and of the right, as in France, where despite being re-elected for a second term as president, rare in modern times, Emmanuel Macron quickly found his powers curbed by the parliamentary electoral success of populist right-wingers led by Marine Le Pen, and populist left-wingers led by Jean-Luc Mélenchon. Both pre-sented themselves as the voice of the people against a corrupt elite. In post-financial crisis Greece we witnessed the phenom-enon of a country faced with both a left-wing populist movement in the form of SYRIZA, and a right-wing one in the shape of Golden Dawn. The two were very different from one another in terms of policy. But they shared a disdain for liberal democracy, an eagerness to exploit polarisation, and, at best, a relaxed atti-tude to the use of authoritarian techniques. Those on the far left rightly decry right-wing populists. They are, however, often blind to similar populist tactics being used by the left, simply because they happen to share some of their values. While Hugo Chávez, who was president of Venezuela for most of the period between 1999 and 2013, brought in reforms to help the poorest in society, he also dealt severely with critics and opponents, clamped down on the press, and manipulated the constitution to stay in power. And, late last year in Peru, President Castillo, a left-wing populist, was arrested after staging what amounted to a self-coup, as he tried to dissolve Congress illegally in a bid to stay in power. At the time of writing, he is one of two inmates in a police prison specially adapted to house the other one, Alberto Fujimori, a right-wing populist former president, in power from 1990–2000, now serving a twenty-five-year sentence for human rights abuses and corruption.

So populism takes many forms. Indian prime minister Narendra Modi's populism is rooted in a view of vegetarian Hindus as the pure people of India, and beef-eating Muslims and foreigners as the threat. In Brazil, Jair Bolsonaro's populism cast the people as honest and hard-working souls whose aspirations had been thwarted by a left-of-centre, globalised and globalising political-managerial class residing in Brazil's big cities. In each case, the specifics are irrelevant. What matters is the basic pitch. 'You the people are good. They the elite are bad, and do you harm. Only I can protect you from them.'

To the polarising populist, compromise or agreement between opponents is to be avoided. I reckon that part of the success of the podcast I do with ex-Tory Cabinet minister Rory Stewart, *The Rest Is Politics*, is down to the fact that while we come from different backgrounds and have different political views, we try to 'disagree agreeably'. This approach seems to strike a chord with a lot of people. But it is anathema to the polarising populist, who needs divisiveness, who feeds off anger and hate, who wants disagreements to be disagreeable. Remember Trump's insulting nicknames for all his opponents? Yes, it revealed his character. But it was also all part of his strategy. Are you with me or against me?

If you're against me, you're against the people, and I'm going to do all I can to make sure they hate you as much as you hate me. Oh, and by the way, I love that you hate me.

'A talented populist at the helm of a determined campaign of polarisation,' Moisés Naím wrote in an article I commissioned for *The New European*, 'can quickly put democratic institutions under considerable pressure. Sometimes the institutions hold. Sometimes they do not.' This is the dangerous moment in which we find ourselves, unsure about the strength of democratic institutions to withstand the anti-democratic intent of people in power who have used the three Ps to get there, and use them even more once they do.

I know I ought to be comforted by an interesting piece of research last January by Cambridge University's Centre for the Future of Democracy, which showed that the Covid-19 pandemic saw a disproportionate fall in the popularity of populist leaders compared with such non-populists as Angela Merkel in Germany, Emmanuel Macron in France or Justin Trudeau in Canada. Not surprisingly, perhaps, when it came to a life-and-death crisis, people wanted to listen to scientific experts and politicians focused on fact ahead of leaders banning masks (Bolsonaro), suggesting a swig of bleach was the cure we were waiting for (Trump), or urging us to believe we could send the virus packing in twelve weeks if we sang the national anthem twice while washing our hands (Johnson). In June 2020, according to this study, approval of government handling of the crisis was 11 percentage points lower on average in countries with populist leaders than in those with more centrist governance. By the end of 2020, this gap had widened to 16 points.

While I find this trend encouraging, though, I also think it's fragile. Yes, it's true that – for example – Bolsonaro, Trump and Johnson have gone – for now, at least. But their supporters have not, as the attack on the Capitol in Washington on 6 January

2021 or the attempted insurrection in Brasilia on 8 January 2023 showed. Populism remains an insidious threat. And in an era when so many people have turned away from politics in disappointment or disgust, things can all too easily be turned on their head by a highly motivated minority.

3.

The Third P:
Post-Truth and the Uses of Lying

By its very nature, populism involves holding up a distorting mirror to society and telling people, 'Ignore the evidence to the contrary, this is how things really are.' And it is here that the third P, post-truth, comes into play. This is not just lying. It is a strategy designed to distort the factual base of debate so that we lose sight of the distinction between truth and lies. It has long been part of the armoury of totalitarian regimes. The last couple of decades or so, however, have seen it spill over into the liberal democratic arena. It is this third P, former New Zealand prime minister Helen Clark believes, that has provided the fuel for the rise of polarisation and populism. 'It is putting some of the oldest and most respected democracies under pressure,' she told me. 'It has had a profound impact on the US, the UK, Italy, France, where the parties of the broad centre right and centre left are barely able to fend off the far right. Then to see a party described as neo-Nazi doing well in Sweden, these are really concerning trends. They can only be countered by the broad centre coming together against populism, and *for* fact and reason and truth in political debate. Without that, it will be hard to get back on an even track.'

Given its totalitarian roots it should come as no surprise that a contemporary master of post-truth is Vladimir Putin. As Peter Pomerantsev explains in his seminal book, *Nothing Is True and Everything Is Possible*, the Russian leader has built his career on post-truth foundations, and lying – flamboyantly and shamelessly – has remained an essential tool in his armoury.

'There are no Russian tanks involved.'
'We have pictures.'
'They are fake.'
'No, they're not. Look. Here they are crossing the border.'
'The CIA has a history of faking things.'

'You killed people on our streets.'
'No, we didn't.'
'We have proof.'
'It is a provocation by your security services.'
'We have evidence of your spies and assassins, and what they did.'
'They were visiting your lovely cathedral.'

Back in 2003, during the US-led invasion of Iraq, Iraqi information minister Muhammad Saeed al-Sahhaf became known as 'Comical Ali' on account of his incessant claims of military success, which the reporters he was briefing knew from their own eyes to be nonsense. At the time, his approach was laughed at around the world, and became the subject of satire. And yet, by the mid-2010s, it seemed to have become the communications modus operandi of several major countries, democracies among them.

Putin is confident that, provided he persists with his lies and dismisses out of hand any inconvenient evidence to the contrary, he will ultimately leave his questioners and opponents with nowhere to go. They end up either confused, repelled, frustrated, in jail, or dead. The invasion of Ukraine was not an invasion, remember, but a special military operation, and laws were brought in to protect that lie. Telling the truth about what was happening became a crime. And since lying is strategy in the hands of men such as Putin, they don't need to make an effort to conceal it. They even smile as they lie, so that they can let you know that they know you know they're lying – and they don't care. In their worldview, truth is just another element of the battlefield, with manipulation and distortion weapons in hybrid warfare, to be used so that 'truth' is shaped according to what Russian interests are deemed to be at the time. From denied tanks in Ukraine to denied massacres in Syria; from denied interference in electoral campaigns in the EU and the US to denied assassinations home and abroad and denied downing of planes carrying civilians, it's all grist to Putin's post-truth mill. It invites the disbelief of most in the West, but the belief and/or amusement of many in the Russian audience, as well as the Putin-bankrolled useful idiots dotted around hard-right and hard-left parties and causes around the world. Bot-army influence campaigns help spread the lies further, while simultaneously trashing the reputations of opponents and truth-tellers. These Internet soldiers are every bit as important to Putin's aggressions as the real soldiers in uniform. They are huge teams of people paid by the state to take part in trolling and disinformation campaigns all over the world aimed at promoting the Russian worldview and undermining its opponents. Key to this is the so-called Internet Research Agency, a Saint Petersburg-based company run by Yevgeny Prigozhin, a Putin ally who now leads the Wagner mercenary fighting force in Ukraine.

Putin's Russia was perhaps quicker than the West to grasp that social media enables lying to be deployed as a strategic tool, undermining opponents home and abroad through the constant dissemination of misinformation. But some of the same techniques are present in advanced democracies too. The ubiquity of this form of communication, the fact that it is now where news almost always breaks first, gives it a speed and an agency that helps the populist, who doesn't care too much about detail or facts. Get the message out, don't worry about accuracy, just get people paying attention and onside.

When it comes to the use of post-truth strategies in Western democracies, perhaps the first big mover was the media magnate Silvio Berlusconi, Italy's colourful former prime minister. One of his favoured tactics was the regular vilification of judges as 'men in togas', to justify judicial reforms that would help undermine investigations into the many business scandals in which he was involved. Though Berlusconi was voted out of power, more than once, his 3P style of politics lived on in others, not just on the far right, but also incarnated in what Moisés Naím has called 'a true anomaly . . . a centrist populist movement, the Five-Star Movement'. And when the popular and broadly respected government of Mario Draghi fell in the summer of 2022, Berlusconi was yet again at the centre of the action as populists and nationalists moved in for the kill. His Forza Italia party became part of the coalition government headed by post-fascist leader Giorgia Meloni.

What Berlusconi started in the West, Trump seized on and developed. That lying for him was not just a personality trait, but a post-truth strategy, was revealed the moment his adviser Kellyanne Conway introduced the concept of 'alternative facts' the day after Trump was sworn in, when he falsely claimed there had been more people in Washington to celebrate his inauguration than there had been for Barack Obama's. The *Washington Post* fact checker – oh that we had papers in the UK who had done the same systematically with the Tories in recent years – calculated that in his four years as president, Trump made false or misleading claims on 30,573 occasions. The day before he became president, campaigning across the country on 2 November 2017, they recorded 503 such statements. The normalisation of his strategy was revealed by the steady rise in his lying stats. There was an average of six misleading claims per day in his first year, sixteen per day in his second, twenty-two in the third, and thirty-nine in the fourth. The *Post* has a five-million-word database to support its claims, and it is a compelling, disturbing read. The US continues to battle with the post-truth toxin even though Trump was voted out of office, and it is evidence of the damage he has done to the fabric of US politics and democracy that he remains the potent force he is, not least via those parts of the media which have themselves embraced post-truthery.

'But perhaps the most unexpected victim of the 3P wave,' says Moises Naím, 'has been Britain, which has yet to recover from the carnival of populism, polarisation and post-truth that gave rise to Brexit.' 'Since then,' he goes on, 'not one but both of its major parties have fallen prey to populist leaders. And while the left-wing populism of Jeremy Corbyn atop the Labour party proved ineffectual and short-lived, a serial fantasist installed himself solidly in 10 Downing Street. By sidestepping key guardrails against abuse, such as the longstanding norm that a minister who lies to Parliament must resign, Boris Johnson put Britain's democracy under a level of stress it has not known before, with new laws restricting the ability to protest showing that even the Mother of Parliaments is not immune to autocratic tendencies.'

That Johnson is, like many of his fellow populists, a liar by nature is unquestionable. Dominic Cummings, who strategised for him during the Brexit referendum, and then became his senior adviser in Downing Street, until their fallout became terminal, said of him that he lied so often, so effortlessly and so shamelessly, that he no longer knew when he was telling the truth or lying. Given Cummings is a friend turned foe, who latterly dedicated himself to Johnson's destruction, and given the lies at the heart of the Brexit campaign, he is perhaps not the most reliable analyst of his former boss. The fact remains, though, that lying has always featured in the Johnson story. He was fired for lying, early on in his career, by *The Times* (it is further evidence of the decline in our standards that years later the same paper backed him to be prime minister). Lying then became his journalistic norm when he worked as a correspondent for the *Daily Telegraph* in Brussels, where he specialised in inventing stories about 'EU plans' to make British life less fun and more difficult, for example by banning flavoured crisps and bent bananas, or insisting that there should be one-size-fits-all condoms based on the dimensions of the average Italian penis, rather than the much larger – in Johnson's puerile imagination – British version.

But for Johnson, as for Putin and Trump, lying was a deliberate strategy as well as an unpleasant character trait. In typically populist style he employed it to present a mirror image of reality, where he – with all his privilege and celebrity – was on the side of 'us', the people, against 'them', the 'establishment' (whatever that was). Lying as strategy was also revealed on the occasions when Johnson shook his head and muttered the words 'I never said that', in response to journalists and politicians reading his own words back to him. Or when a man in a hospital said Johnson was only there for a photocall, and he replied, 'there are no press here', as he looked directly at a pack of media people who were recording the entire exchange. It is the Putin playbook. Though the truth may be staring you in the face, deny it and set out your alternative reality instead. The Johnson version. Leave people confused or amused and all will be well.

Each lie emboldened him. The more he got away with the small ones, the more confident he felt about moving up to big ones. The less he was challenged by an all too supine media and Parliament, the less he thought it mattered. It's how the normalisation of the abnormal works. It was not normal to win an election on a false promise – the oven-ready Brexit deal – and then for there to be no consequences once the election votes had been counted and it was clear that what Boris Johnson had assured us would happen did not, in fact, materialise, and that the deal was oven-ready in exactly the same way as a turkey is oven-ready when it is waddling around the farm.

Johnson's casual attitude to the truth also served his highly opportunistic approach to day-to-day politics. Leaders such as Berlusconi, Putin and Trump have pushed a broadly unified agenda and simple messages with a projection of their own power and authority. Johnson pushed the simple message of Brexit, but his broader agenda was as dilatory and short-breathed as his attention span, seemingly inspired by what might prove popular at that particular moment, or (just as often) to get him out of whatever trouble he found himself in. It was interesting how regularly a visit to Kyiv or a call with President Zelensky in Ukraine coincided with a new and damaging development in the investigations into his personal conduct. Even with Brexit, it's questionable how ideologically committed he ever was to the cause. In campaigning for Leave in 2016, Johnson was not seeking to deliver Brexit for the country, nor acting out of political or ideological conviction, given he was not sure which side to back until the last moment. (This is something we know not merely because he famously wrote two different *Daily Telegraph* columns, one for Leave, one for Remain, but also from reports of conversations he had with friends and colleagues at the time, most of whom believed he would back Remain.) He was making a personal political calculation about the best way to position himself as the darling of the Tory Party. If he had lost, he would have been the hero of the right wing. Instead, his victory brought forward David Cameron's departure from office and Johnson's next step towards the pinnacle of power. Win-win for him. Lose-lose for the country. Hey ho.

Where Johnson differed most from other post-truth populists was in the image of himself he tried to present. Trump, Putin, Erdoğan, Modi and their ilk like to appear powerful and in control. Johnson sought to project not so much power and authority (which might not have gone down well with a notoriously cynical electorate in challenging times) but a kind of bumbling amiability that could serve as a smokescreen for the lying, the incompetence and the moral corruption he allowed into the system. Even so, there were moments when the mask slipped, and he resorted to vicious personal attacks that could have come straight out of Trump's playbook. One such occasion was when he accused the Labour leader Keir Starmer of having dedicated time in his days as director of Public Prosecutions to prosecuting journalists, while failing to prosecute paedophile Jimmy Savile. As the facts emerged – Starmer had nothing to do with the mistakes made in the Savile case – even Johnson's long-standing head of policy resigned in disgust. MPs called on him to apologise. One or two Cabinet ministers distanced themselves. But Johnson is not an apologiser, unless for tactical reasons, or on behalf of others in order to shift the blame onto them. And, of course – on at least one level – his doubling down on his big lie proved effective, as he knew it would be. A few days later, the Labour leader was surrounded by an angry mob shouting abuse about Starmer's supposed protection of Savile.

It's fortunate that Starmer remained level-headed: he called out what Johnson had done, though in a way that suggested to me that he was not letting Johnson into his head about it. He was going hard, not low or high. Joe Biden has adopted a similarly successful approach to Donald Trump. But the depressing fact remains that lying works with a certain element of the populist's base. And, unless they are careful, it can put the populist's opponents off their stride. I fear that Hillary Clinton, who had the misfortune to be the first victim of Trump's uniquely unpleasant campaigning style, was distracted by it. He got inside her head, and perhaps no wonder.

Johnson's post-truth career exemplifies just about all the qualities demonstrated by modern demagogues, which have been described in an excellent book by two Austrians, economist Walter Ötsch and journalist Nina Horsczek: *Populismus für Anfänger* (Populism for Beginners; you'll need to be able to understand German to read this one). They portray leaders for whom the performance, the show, takes precedence over the delivery or the fulfilment of promises. This is a political approach in which the failure to deliver on policy only opens the door to more promises, to more blaming of the mythical, obstructing elite, whether that's judges, 'lefty lawyers' or civil servants. Here, problems exist to be exploited, not addressed. Very helpfully, Ötsch and Horsczek set out the following post-truth, populist strategic checklist:

Propaganda is more important than policy.

Simple untruths beat complex realities.

You must demand loyalty of others but not give it yourself.

Stirring up division is vital; build slavish media backing and sect-like support.

Develop a unique way of speaking, rich in imagery and the exploitation of emotions and symbols.

Rewrite national history.

Say unsayables.

Use baseless claims and insults.

Ignore conventions.

Weaken Cabinet, Parliament and bodies that threaten 'the will of the people' as you define it.

Never admit you're wrong, never accept your opponents are right, and always blame others if things go wrong.

Trump, Putin, Johnson to a tee. Go back and read the list again.

★

It was strange, given how many hundreds of thousands of words, and hundreds of hours, I had devoted to campaigning for Johnson's demise, how little joy I actually felt at the moment when he departed Downing Street. Partly it was because his resignation speech was clouded in the kind of lies, half-truths and gaslighting deceptions that have been his hallmark through decades as a media personality and then a political figure. He couldn't even bring himself to say the word 'resign', or apologise for the many misdeeds that had led his party to turn on him. He was only 'sorry' that he was leaving a job he had coveted for so long, with all the perks and privileges he had enjoyed, such as a country home and government planes to help ferry him to holidays and parties at public expense.

He will go down in history as the most dishonest, the most morally corrupt, the most disgraced, and, on a par with Truss, the most incompetent prime minister we have ever had. A man who has wrought incalculable damage on our Parliament; on the rule of law; on our media, including the BBC; on our diplomacy and our strength in the world; and on the peace process in Northern Ireland. That President Joe Biden could not even bring himself to name Johnson in his short statement on the resignation announcement underlined the damage done to our special relationship with the US. As for the alliances with our neighbours closer to home across the Channel – not least with a French president who tired of the lies and clowning long before his British counterpart's departure – they have been trashed as badly as the rooms in which the illicit pandemic parties were held, on such a scale that no workplace in the entire country was fined for as many lockdown breaches as Johnson's 10 Downing Street.

No doubt, there will be those who say that the fact that he did fall in the end – his final demise precipitated by his appointment of a serial sex pest to an important post in government – shows that a post-truth attitude to life contains the seeds of its own destruction. But he had survived far bigger scandals before, including several that in my view merited at least an investigation into the criminal offence of misconduct in public office. I think, for example, of the negligence that occurred during the Covid pandemic, during which huge sums of public money were awarded to Tory friends and donors for PPE supplies they were unable to provide, or of his relationship with, reliance on, and very strange meetings with, the Lebedevs (the father was a former KGB spy; his son a newspaper owner elevated to the House of Lords by – who else? – Johnson).

So far, I've focused on post-truth as a weapon in the hands of individuals. But it's more insidious than that. Entire political campaigns can rest on a post-truth version of reality and gain their force from it. Take the Brexit campaign again. Many of Leave's core claims were based on untruths, and yet far from hindering them, such untruths actually served to advance their cause. Remainers made doggedly factual arguments that bored many people or came across as finger-wagging. Brexiteers, untroubled by facts, could say whatever seemed to land best. Indeed, the more they were called out for their lies, the happier they seemed to be. When David Cameron denied that Turkey was about to join the EU, they turned a non-issue into a salient one, flooding voters concerned about immigration with social media ads calling on them to seize their last chance to repel the Turkish invasion. When the head of the Statistics Authority challenged Leave's claim that if the UK left the EU, more money would be secured for the NHS, they turned the observation into supposed further evidence for the way in which the 'establishment' (here, the Statistics Authority) was seeking to browbeat and mislead people. In both cases, they recognised the power of hot emotion over cold fact. And since most of the media in Britain preferred to report 'he said, she said' style, rather than, as per the *Washington Post*, holding the claims and the people making them properly to account via factual analysis, their claims were allowed to spread virtually unchecked. Indeed, the more the lies were talked about, the more the pro-Leave campaign exploited them in their communications. It was one of the most sophisticated, and at points illegal, campaigns in political history.

Nor is lying as strategy confined to political campaigns. Former US vice-president Al Gore refers to the work of the climate change deniers as 'the moral equivalent of a war crime'. From the early 1990s, the Global Climate Coalition (GCC) – which represented the oil, coal, auto, utilities, steel and rail industries – worked to make the public and policy-makers as confused as possible about the growing body of scientific evidence pointing to fossil fuels as a prime cause of man-made climate change. There will surely be an especially hot place in hell for those behind a strategy designed to persuade the world of the existence of a 'rising awareness of the scientific uncertainty' about the subject – an awareness actually created by those people and their paid hands. 'I think it is, in many ways, the most serious crime of the post-World War Two era, anywhere in the world,' said Gore. 'The consequences of what they've done are just almost unimaginable.' The Brexit lies have done enormous harm to one country. The climate lies have put the entire future of the planet at risk.

4.

The Slow Death of Democracy

In February 2022, former prime minister John Major made an important speech, entitled 'In Democracy We Trust?' – note the question mark – in which he said this: 'Democrats were so confident that their way of government was the way of the future that they stopped arguing for it. Their confidence was premature. In each of the last fifteen years, democracy has shrunk a little, as political and civil liberties have been diminished. In many countries, democracy has never taken root. Where it has, it risks being weakened by populism – often with added xenophobia, or muzzled by elected autocracy.' His analysis is supported by the assessment of Freedom House, the American non-profit which researches and advocates for democracy and human rights. It calculates that only 20 per cent of the global population live in countries that are fully free. Fifteen years ago, that figure stood closer to 40 per cent.

What is remarkable about John Major's speech is that he had Britain, the country that he had governed less than a quarter of a century earlier, in mind as he made it. In his view, Britain is not yet part of the unfree 80 per cent, but it is moving worryingly in that direction, largely thanks to Johnson and those who backed him. Unfortunately, the Tory party, along with the wider country, failed to heed the warnings of Major when, six years previously, during the Brexit referendum campaign, he and Tony Blair travelled to Northern Ireland together to warn of the dangers to the peace process if we left the EU. We would be wise to start listening to him about this broader democratic threat now.

Major's observation that Britain was an 'unexpected victim' of populism, polarisation and post-truth underlines the fact that, for all the faults we may have felt lay within our political systems, in the main our politics has generally been well regarded overseas – with Parliament viewed as a genuine crucible of debate where, whatever the passions, MPs were 'honourable' and strove to tell the truth. I have considerable experience of prime ministers, both as a journalist writing about them, and as an adviser working for them. Whether Tory or Labour, none were in my view liars. Johnson was, and is. Fact. Indisputable. It was this that set him apart from all previous prime ministers, Tory or Labour. Had I ever gone on TV and called Ted Heath or Margaret Thatcher a liar, or David Cameron or Theresa May, the presenter would quickly have shut me down, warned me against making such a statement without evidence, and the chances are a lawyer's letter might have followed. There is no such fear about Johnson. You can call him a liar in any forum you like, without any fear of comeback.

The fact remains, though, that while Johnson may have proved the most destructive of our recent leaders when it comes to upholding democratic values, the direction of travel both immediately before and after his time in office has been worrying – and of course that worrying direction of travel is not unique to the UK.

Recent events have shown that even democracies with written rules and constitutions can be undermined by determined populists. Trump regularly denigrated the countervailing systems carefully built into the US political framework by the founding fathers, to the point where he threatened to weaken them fatally. The UK, of course, has no formal written constitution. Instead, it relies on rules and precedents and the supposed good intentions of those who wield power, as well as on the strength and independence of the institutions that can act as brakes on the exercise of that power. In the words of John Major, it rests 'upon respect for the laws made in Parliament; upon an independent judiciary; upon acceptance of the conventions of public life; and on self-restraint by the powerful'. As Major goes on to point out: 'If any of that delicate balance goes astray – as it has – as it *is* – our democracy is undermined.' It's worth adding that this erosion of democracy is not solely down to parties on the right of the political spectrum, though they are the prime culprits. As I have argued elsewhere, one has only to look at recent events in some south American democracies (for example) to realise that hard-left populists have anti-democratic tendencies, too.

Major's reference to 'conventions' and 'self-restraint' invokes what might be termed the 'good chaps' theory of democracy: the assumption that people in public office will behave in a way that serves the public good, by respecting rules, tradition and precedent, and putting the interests of the country ahead of personal or political interests. He himself was responsible for bringing in the Nolan Principles on standards of conduct in public life after a series of scandals during his period in power in the mid-1990s. Some very bad chaps, lower down the political food chain, had brought politics into disrepute. Major was determined to restore some good chaps principles to public life. The problem with the Johnson administration was that the bad chaps were not lowly backbenchers or junior ministers; they were in charge.

While Johnson was in office, I took to reciting those seven principles on TV and radio any time I could, predicting that ultimately Johnson's inability to abide by any of them would one day be his downfall, which, I am glad to say, eventually they were. Let me remind you . . . Honesty. Openness. Objectivity. Selflessness. Integrity. Accountability. Leadership. He failed on all seven. Indeed, none of them would have registered on his radar. And before anyone shouts 'Pot. Kettle. Black,' and 'Iraq', as happens occasionally on social media when I tackle the phenomenon of Johnson the liar, I merely point you to the several official and parliamentary inquiries that took place, none of which concluded that I lied.

Johnson not only trashed the 'good chaps' approach to democracy, he exposed its fragility, even with Major's framework in place. And, indeed, he continued to do so after he left office, as he sought to stuff the House of Lords with his cronies in a resignation honours list which, given he was forced to resign in disgrace, many would argue he should not have been allowed to put forward in the first place. Yet both he and Liz Truss were given this privilege, precisely because prime ministers are assumed to be honourable, worthy human beings. Meanwhile, as he continued to take a salary as an MP in a constituency he rarely bothered to visit, and a former prime minister's allowance he will get for life, out of office he set off to the US to make a series of jokey speeches for a quarter of a million pounds a time, and pull in a few friends to help fund his extravagant lifestyle.

The UK Parliament, so long seen as one of the great democratic institutions of the world, struggled to deal with Johnson's elastic relationship with the truth, his subversion of norms and his breaking of rules. It has long been the generally accepted view that, for all the argy-bargy of our parliamentary politics, the reason that ultimately politicians are felt to be 'honourable' is that they are motivated not just by their own and their party's interests, but by the genuine national interest too. It explains why the Commons speaker, Lindsay Hoyle, slapped down and even expelled any MP who directly called Boris Johnson a liar, though there was not a single person in that chamber who didn't realise that is exactly what he is. According to convention, in the so-called Mother of Parliaments, all MPs are honourable, none is a liar. This idea was stress-tested to breaking point, and Parliament didn't know how to handle it.

Football fans will definitely know who I am talking about when I say the name Gary Neville. More and more non-football fans will too, because he has been developing a more clearly defined political profile. He has a great backstory, having gone from a working-class upbringing to a career as a top footballer, and then as a pundit, businessman and social media campaigner against rotten politics. I have talked to him often about political issues, and I hope one day he gets a seat as a Labour MP. But if he does, he will have to pick and choose his fights.

'I wouldn't do all that honourable and right honourable stuff,' he told me. 'No way. How can you call Johnson right honourable when you know he is a total bloody liar?'

'Ah, this might not work, Gary. You can't call another MP a liar.'

'Why not? He is a liar.'

'I know that, you know that, he knows that, the speaker knows that, the whole bloody country knows that. But it's the rules. Same as you can't handle the ball unless you're the goalkeeper.'

'It's ridiculous. It has to change.'

'Well, you'd have to get in and persuade everyone else to want to change it. But what would you rather spend your time on – that, or jobs and schools and hospitals and getting kids playing sport?'

'So, what can I say if I can't say he lied?'

'He inadvertently misled the House.'

'Jesus . . . I can't wait to tell Jamie Carragher . . . we should say Harry Maguire inadvertently handled the ball and Harry Kane inadvertently smashed the penalty into the net.'

It may seem absurd, but that is because, until Johnson, the 'all MPs are honourable, most ministers strive to tell the truth' approach – in other words, that people followed the rules and conventions of the institution – had more or less held, and had a broadly positive impact on the nature of debate. The public may love to think 'all politicians are liars', but, historically, I would argue, that's largely not been the case. It is true that politicians may at times have to conceal their real views in the interests of party unity, not least to fulfil the principle of collective responsibility on which our Cabinet system is founded. It's also the case that sometimes the full facts of a situation may have to be withheld, perhaps for reasons of national security or market sensitivity. However, out-and-out liars are the exception. I know from experience that most politicians in the UK *hate* lying, not least because they realise that, if exposed, it can be fatal to their careers as, eventually, proved to be the case with Johnson. They are also acutely aware that their honesty and the trust essential to a country's proper functioning go together. When governments announce restrictions to our freedoms during Covid, or raise taxes, or make changes to the way we can live our lives, it's vital that the public trusts their decisions and believes they are acting in good faith. Once that trust is broken, moral authority drains away. Johnson, as we have seen, experiences no moral qualms when he lies, and the effects of that lying will long outlast him. Should we ever become so used to lying in public life on this scale that we react to it with a shrug, we really are in trouble.

For populists such as Johnson, it's not just about ignoring the convention of behaving honourably. It's also about determinedly and systematically undermining the institutions that are there to counterbalance the power of government and hold it in check. As John Major said in his February 2022 speech: 'The prime minister and our present government not only challenge the law, but also seem to believe that they – and they *alone* – need not obey the rules, traditions, conventions – call them what you will – of public life. The charge that there is one law for the government, and one for everyone else, is politically deadly – and it *has* struck home. Our democracy requires that the truth and the law should be respected and obeyed – above all, by the government.' In this speech, Major was specifically referring to Partygate – the shorthand given to serial Covid lockdown law-breaking in Downing Street, in defiance of new emergency legislation made in that very building. But as he and I chatted when we were making a film for the People's Vote campaign, he cited other breaches of our democratic norms, most egregiously Johnson's prorogation of Parliament to avoid debate on Brexit, and his silence when a newspaper condemned judges upholding the law as 'enemies of the people'.

Major struck me as being genuinely, viscerally offended by what Johnson and his followers were prepared to do. They had seemingly forgotten what an earlier Conservative leader, Mrs Thatcher, had said back in 1975. 'The first duty of government is to uphold the law. If it tries to bob and weave and duck around that duty when it's inconvenient, if government does that, then so will the governed, and then nothing is safe – not home, not liberty, not life itself.' Wise words. Unheeded by the party that claims to worship her.

Trump's conduct after he lost the 2020 presidential election took this approach to its logical, extreme conclusion. Claiming, on the basis of no evidence whatsoever, that the election had been 'stolen', throwing doubt on the integrity of election officials, seeking even to conjure votes out of thin air, he then whipped up his supporters to stage an attempted coup. He continues to make his unsubstantiated claims, and to endorse his chosen followers as they seek key political roles. True, the coup attempt based on claims of a so-called election 'steal' failed last time. But there are elements of the Republican Party already preparing for a similar 'we win whatever the actual result' assault in the next presidential election. Since Trump's defeat, more state legislatures have been pressed to make the changes that would be needed to help him get away with it next time. More votes are being suppressed in advance. Greater attempts have been made to make it nigh-on impossible for President Biden to implement the promises on which he was elected. China and Russia look on, happy to feed to their peoples the narrative that Western-style democracy is not working, and that their not-so-benign dictatorships are.

It might be argued by some that the fact that Trump and Johnson were ultimately ousted could be seen as evidence that democratic institutions can stand up to extreme pressure. I'm less confident. I would argue that the fact that Johnson became prime minister, stayed in post as long as he did, and inflicted so much damage, underlined those institutions' weakness. I would similarly argue that Donald Trump's ability to rise to what is considered the most powerful elected office in the world despite – or worse, because of – his character flaws being laid out so openly over decades is evidence of a malaise at the heart of the US democratic process. That he continues to hold sway over large parts of the Republican Party, and that that party appears not to have been fundamentally damaged in the eyes of millions – either by his presidency, or even the attempted coup which was its culmination – suggests that in the US, as in the UK, ejecting a populist is not the same thing as defeating populism.

So far, I've focused on the ways in which individual populist leaders manipulate the levers of power. But they are not the only guilty ones. The fact is that leaders cannot subvert norms and conventions on their own. They need enablers, lots of them. Nor do institutions which are designed to act as checks and balances on power change of their own accord. Human beings, especially when those institutions are part of the state, and covered by law, have to change them. If a government in the developing world was bringing in new laws to curb the role of the judiciary, and the right to protest, to limit protection of whistle-blowers and journalists, to curb the power of the Electoral Commission to investigate wrongdoing by parties, to limit academic freedoms, to make it harder for younger and poorer people to vote, I know what Tory

MPs would call it. Yet they voted for all of those things in their own country, and both Liz Truss and Rishi Sunak continued to take them forward post-Johnson. The plain fact of the matter is that, month after month, week after week, we have witnessed a slow chipping away at the foundations of liberal democracy, as institutions and conventions that are there to hold the powerful to account, and prevent power being abused, have been slowly diminished. It has not stopped with Johnson's departure, and that chipping away has not taken place simply because Johnson and his ilk have said that it should. The Cabinet has to agree it. Legislation has to be written. MPs have to vote for it. I doubt many of those MPs, when they were seeking election, would have said to their constituents that these were the causes that got them out of bed in the morning, but once the government machine kicked in and demanded their support, they gave it, almost without exception. Enablers. Johnson, and those who have followed him, could not have survived as long as he did without them.

Such enablers are present at all levels of political and public life. Trump was enabled by senior members of the Republican Party, including those he had previously denigrated and belittled. Johnson was crowned by Cabinet colleagues and Tory MPs who knew they were electing a proven liar as prime minister, who knew he had secured victory by destroying one prime minister, David Cameron, before serving as what civil servants called 'the worst foreign secretary in history' to Cameron's successor Theresa May, and then destroying her, too. They continued to support him as he used the highest office in the land as the base for industrial-scale sloganising, gaslighting and unadulterated lying; and they forgave and defended him when his lies and his narcissism were repeatedly exposed in moral corruption, illegality, and gross incompetence across so many fronts.

Indeed, it is remarkable how many within the Tory party stood by him to the end, and beyond – among them the woman who succeeded him, Liz Truss. Right-wing apologist Jacob Rees-Mogg is always loudly defending the monarchy and the principles of parliamentary democracy. But he was remarkably comfortable with being a part of Johnson's gambit of lying to the Queen about the reasons for proroguing Parliament in 2019. And, as Johnson struggled to stay in office in the summer of 2022, Rees-Mogg was also happy to argue for a subversion of our democratic system. He claimed that since all the votes for Tory candidates at the previous general election had actually been cast for Johnson, MPs had no right to withdraw their support from him. Rees-Mogg had to be reminded we do not have a presidential system.

When Johnson was finally prised from office, his successor, Liz Truss, made a point of praising him to the skies in her victory acceptance speech. She, like her opponent Rishi Sunak, promoted the myth that, when it came to issues like Covid, or Ukraine, Johnson did better than other world leaders and 'got the big calls right'.

Equally shocking was the lengthy list of institutions that Johnson's attack dogs were prepared to savage to protect him. I honestly never thought I would see the day when UK government ministers went for judges; or when an entire Cabinet, including the attorney-general, defended the law-breaking of a prime minister. I never thought I would see the day when we had a government that seems to think its time and energies are better suited to attacking the BBC, the NHS and the Bank of England than attacking child poverty or homelessness. I never thought I would see the day when ministers were seemingly unable to appear in public without criticising the civil service, rather than seeking its support and cooperation in the delivery of policy which, in my experience, most civil servants are more than willing to provide. Doctors and nurses, teachers, police, local councils: they've all at times been whipping boys and girls for a government that has a very strange way of motivating those they pay to help them deliver for the people who elected them.

As to why Johnson's enablers acted as they did, various motivations seem to have been in play. Some supporters were merely venal: they were looking for rewards and promotion and understood his character sufficiently well to know that total support was the best way to get what they wanted. Some were weak, happy to take whatever seemed the easiest way in the face of something they knew to be wrong. Some had a sense of loyalty to party that overrode any personal ethical quibbles they might have had. Some had become so tribal that they could not recognise that 'we' might have become 'the enemy'.

The reasons why such people were ultimately prepared to force Johnson from power were scarcely more praiseworthy. It was not some sudden discovery of a moral compass that brought about their change of heart. It was their dawning realisation that Johnson, now widely despised across the country, was not a winner any more. He was a loser. If he stayed, he risked losing power for his party. Rishi Sunak may have helped bring about Johnson's demise. But he did so only when it was clear that Johnson's power was waning. Prior to that, he did more than most to prop him up.

Let's not forget either the other enablers who help to keep populists in power and spread their poison: their friends in the media. In the US, outlets such as Fox News, Breitbart and multiple shock jocks were quite happy to disseminate Trump's lies for him. It's only very recently that second thoughts seem to have set in – at least at Fox – no doubt because after the US midterms in 2022 he's no longer seen as quite the winner he once was. But for far too long, before Trump became Trumpty Dumpty on the front page of the *New York Post* – another sign of the Murdoch regime turning against him – Fox owners, hosts and editors shaped an agenda for Trump and against Biden, using truth-twisting tactics that bore more than a passing resemblance to those used by media operating under the control of totalitarian regimes past and present.

By contrast, in the UK, where news channels are subject to, and largely seek to conform to, regulations on impartiality and fairness, the enabling propagandists invariably work for the print media, and for think tanks with close links both to them and to the politicians in power. Indeed the reason why the government was happy to see the Leveson Inquiry into press practices come and go, despite the criminality and corruption it highlighted, was because the so-called Fourth Estate is a major part of their post-truth armoury. I am in little doubt that Johnson would never have made it to the top if so much of the media had not ignored or covered up what they knew him to be. Nor, I believe, would he have survived so long without the press supporting him as they did; both those parts of the press which were overtly biased on a scale that would not look out of place in North Korea – yes, you, Paul Dacre, and you, the *Daily Express*, with, on a bad day, the *Daily Telegraph* and the *Sun* not far behind – and those parts of the media which all too often allowed themselves to be influenced by that bias, chief among them much of our broad-cast media, not least – despite the right's constant decrying of its supposedly 'woke' tendencies – the BBC. It is not that the broadcasters become brazenly politically biased in the way that many of our newspapers are, but that the weight of the press bias impacts hugely on their assessment of the news agenda.

Time and time again, the press covered Johnson's abnormal government as though it was all too normal. Think of the count-less scandals, which had they been on the watch of a Labour government would have been major news, and yet were pre-sented almost with a shrug of the shoulders. Think of the lies that went unchallenged, the policy failures that were ignored. I lost count of the number of front pages heralding how 'Boris' was going to get the economy roaring, seal a US trade deal, end

Covid without huge loss of life, fix the NHS, fix social care, level up. Slogan after slogan was turned into 'news' stories, stories being the operative word. Fairy tales in the main. Not normal. We have, in the *Daily Express*, a newspaper that can run four near identical front pages heralding the arrival of four successive prime ministers from the same party within six years as the answer to all the nation's ills. Again, not normal.

Talk to journalists from most parts of the democratic world – those who cover the UK for overseas media – and, in the main, they will tell you that they view the entire relationship between politics and media in Westminster as abnormal. The close friend-ships between politicians and the people who cover them, who socialise with them, who get up to all sorts of stuff with them. The journalists who are completely embraced as part of a political circle (hands up; that was me with some Labour politicians when I was at the *Mirror*, but, my God, I was outnumbered by those on the other side of the political fence). Newspapers which help exaggerate success and cover up failure; and then, when experts criticise the government, attack the experts and their motivations, rather than covering the issues they raise. Johnson was blessed to have several on his side when it came to playing that game, and they undoubtedly helped him cling on longer than he would have done had we had a more normal press that was genuinely moti-vated by the idea of holding power to account, rather than being part of the pursuit and maintenance of power itself.

There's a visceral nastiness to what they're prepared to do, too. When John Major called out Johnson, his reward was an ava-lanche of abuse. 'Revenge of the Remoaners', screamed the *Daily Mail*, whose editor-in-chief Paul Dacre was at the time desper-ately pursuing a peerage from Johnson – an award which in other democracies would be viewed as not merely inappropriate, but corrupt, as should Johnson's attempts to install Dacre as head of OFCOM, the broadcasting regulator. The *Mail* seemed unable to engage with the arguments Major was making – including the not exactly revolutionary view that prime ministers should obey the law, and tell the truth, and that it is dangerous if they don't – so went for the man and the motives instead. There's a certain poetic justice in the fact that ultimately such craven behaviour helped bring their man down. Johnson's willingness to listen to *Daily Telegraph* journalist Charles Moore – a fellow Old Etonian ennobled by Johnson alongside a clutch of Brexiteers in 2020 – who wanted rules changed to help their mutual friend Owen Paterson MP avoid investigation for breaching parliamentary standards on lobbying was, for some MPs, a shameless step too far. It led to the kind of rebellion Johnson had assumed, having survived so much already, he would not have to face. It was an important step in the draining of his authority, and a wonderful irony that Moore, one of Johnson's most slavish supporters, was central to it.

What happened under Johnson in the UK is, depressingly, what is happening in many countries where populist political parties have gained a foothold. In France, Marine Le Pen's move to soften her image has been aided by much of the media, which has helped normalise policies that remain as hard right as they were when her party was seen as a pariah. Given that French presidents can now only serve two consecutive terms, Emmanuel Macron won't be around to oppose her at the next presidential election, and I certainly wouldn't write her off yet. In Italy, too, Giorgia Meloni has become prime minister because the media focus on the phrase 'post-fascist' has centred more on the 'post-' than the 'fascist'.

When people such as Johnson fall from power or experience a setback, it's tempting to breathe a sigh of relief. But I think that's precipitate. Don't forget that Johnson was not ultimately dispatched because of what he'd done, but because he no longer looked like a winner. I have no doubt – again I can cite Dominic

Cummings in support of the same view – that Johnson backed Truss over Rishi Sunak, partly because the former chancellor's resignation confirmed his downfall, but also because he believed Truss would be more likely to screw up more quickly. Which would have meant a grateful, desperate party turning to Johnson once more. It backfired, and though he tried to throw his hat into the ring when Truss fell, too few MPs wanted to pick it up and run with him. I would love to think Johnson has been banished for good, but we cannot be sure of it. The ludicrous Churchill complex extends to the belief that his party and his country will come to see the error of their ways, and one day welcome him back. Also, much of the politics Johnson represents lived on in his immediate successors and their party. That is the reason I felt no great joy when he went.

The depressing fact of the matter is that these days we can take nothing for granted, perhaps not even democracy itself. Who, for example, can seriously say the Conservatives' two leadership elections across the summer and autumn of 2022 reflected a healthy politics? Each time, the choice made would have an impact on every single person in the UK, and millions beyond. Yet the process, routinely described as 'democratic' by those engaged in it, and those covering it, consisted of Tory MPs – who had spent three years telling us how marvellous Boris Johnson was, then defenestrating him, before telling us as he left what a great job he had done – whittling down eleven candidates to two in a debate every bit as superficial, dishonest and delusional as the one that led to Brexit and Johnson becoming PM in the first place. The final two were then voted upon by just over 140,000 mainly elderly, almost all white, middle- and upper-class Tory Party members, who are about as representative of the whole country as a herd of elephants is of all animal life, or a didgeridoo is of all music. And when Sunak replaced Truss, even they were excluded.

It was also evidence of the continuing grip of the populist virus

over the Conservative Party that every one of the eleven contenders to replace him pledged to back Brexit come what may,
supported breaking international law to carry on peddling the
fantasy that a hard Brexit won't undermine the peace process in
Northern Ireland, backed the policy of sending asylum seekers
to Rwanda, and indulged in a whole series of fantasy economic
promises to make the members, the only ones allowed to decide
on our prime minister, feel better. The virus had spread to every
single one of the candidates, including those described as 'sensible' and 'moderate'. When a survey of members had climate
change as tenth of a list of ten in their assessment of priorities
for the new prime minister, little wonder it barely featured in the
debate.

Much of the damage caused is more insidious, more hidden,
and therefore perhaps even more shocking. I find it incredible,
for example, that a British government has followed the example
of some Republican-controlled American states in trying to make
it harder for poorer people to vote by introducing the require-
ment to show personal photo ID when casting a ballot. They
have cited a virtually non-existent problem – there was just one
conviction for this kind of ballot box fraud last time – in defence
of this policy. And yet they know full well that there are some
forms of identification which can be used by the old but not
the young, and that it costs money and takes a record amount of
time to secure a passport. Add in, too, the continuing relentless
populist attacks on everything that stands in their way – civil servants pointing out inconvenient facts, the legal system pointing
out inconvenient laws the government may be minded to break,
the people exercising their right to protest – and the comparison
between Trump's America and Tory Britain becomes stronger.

This part of the book is very much part of the analysis of what
has gone wrong. The 'But what can I do?' stuff comes later. But
here is an early element of what you can do. In the battle for

democracy, and against the undermining of the institutions which maintain and support it, stay alert. Be aware and actively attentive to important facts and issues . . . be aware and actively attentive to the nature of the world around you, what is right and what is wrong . . . what is true and what is false . . . be aware and conscious of the realities of political debate . . . We need to be more alert not less in the face of the rise of the polarising post-truth populist, not least because we need to be worried about where it can all too easily lead. Fascism.

5.

The Threat of Fascism

British film-maker David Puttnam – a Labour peer in the House of Lords until he resigned in disgust at what he called the UK government's assault on decency and freedom – once interviewed the Nazi architect, armaments minister and former inmate of Spandau prison, Albert Speer. As they spoke, he later recalled, 'I came to understand what we now call "the fascist playbook" – the way democracy can be corrupted and overturned by a few malevolent but persuasive politicians, those who are prepared to exploit divisions in society with simple populist messages.' Speer explained the extent to which any society or system is vulnerable, and the importance of developing the 'moral vigilance' required to recognise nascent evil for what it is.

Decades later, former US secretary of state Madeleine Albright urged the same point in her final book, *Fascism: A Warning.* The Czech-born daughter of a Jewish family which fled Nazism for England in the late 1930s, she had been planning to write the book even before Donald Trump was elected. His occupancy of the White House made it not just timely, but terrifying.

I read Albright's book not long after reading Laurence Rees' masterpiece, *The Holocaust.* What is noteworthy about his book is not the account of the gas chambers and the deaths of six million Jews, a story whose broad outlines most know well. Rather, it is the descriptions of the build-up: the normalising of the abnormal; the creeping acceptance of what was once deemed unacceptable, not least by foreign governments and domestic

media; the little things that Hitler got away with, which emboldened him to chance his arm for more. Then I read *The Rise
and Fall of the Third Reich*, by an American journalist, William
L. Shirer, who covered Germany for the *Chicago Tribune* during
the Hitler years. On virtually every page there is something,
large or small, that makes you think of today. Things happening
that conventional wisdom had once deemed 'impossible'. The
turning against elites in the wake of financial crisis. The sense
that institutions are failing to meet people's needs. Politicians
exploiting grievances, rather than engaging in the hard graft of
policy development that is needed to address those grievances.
Weak personalities, in politics, business and the media, allowing themselves to be bullied, intimidated and silenced by those
perceived as strong. The failure of political colleagues at home,
and fellow leaders abroad, to speak real truth to power. The
desire to believe things will turn out fine despite overwhelming
evidence to the contrary. Cultism. Politicians endlessly spewing
lies about themselves and their opponents. A relentless focus on
propaganda. Nationalism. The deliberate creation of social and
cultural division. The vile othering of those deemed not to be
somehow truly German.

Then look at the kind of messages that Trump so forcefully
projected during his term in office. Ultra-nationalism ('America First' as a governing strategy comes to mind). Authoritarian
tendencies (consider his relentless attempts to undermine a free
press). Demonising minorities (the Muslim travel ban, the caravan
of 'rapists and criminals', the caged children). Promoting a cult
of the leader and of self above party (if it is good news, stand by
for 'thank you Mr President' tweets – from the president; if it's
bad news, shift blame – both tactics he repeated about Republican
fortunes ahead of the 2022 midterms). Being 'for the people' and
'against the elites'. Attacking the judicial system if it puts obstacles in your way. Showing contempt for political institutions (like

Congress). Broadcasting slogans that promise huge success without saying how that success is going to be achieved. Loving big shows of loyalty (remember the toe-curling filmed Cabinet meeting where everyone at the table had to tell Trump how marvellous he was), and big parades (such as the one he had for Independence Day, complete with tanks: we can blame President Macron for that – Trump saw France's Bastille Day parade and said: 'I want one! I want one!').

Would Trump have imprisoned political opponents if he could have? The incessant chanting of 'lock her up' during the campaign against Hillary Clinton offers a fairly good answer to that, as does his view that his vice-president, Mike Pence, deserved all that was coming his way if he dared to certify that Biden had won the 2020 election fair and square. Would he, if he could, do the same as Xi, Putin, Sisi, Erdoğan, Saudi Arabia's Mohammed bin Salman, and others, in whose countries journalists risk imprisonment, torture and, in some, death, for trying to do their job of speaking truth to power? Well, he regularly attacked the press, dismissing great American newspapers like the *New York Times* as 'fake news' and applying the same label to anything broadcast on CNN. When it started to turn against him, even Fox felt his ire. He castigated any critical voices as liars, and issued regular expressions of support for 'tough guy' leaders. Giving serious policy and administrative roles to family members, whose qualifications did not seem to extend beyond being related to him, likewise smacks of activities Americans would usually condemn when perpetrated by African, Asian or Latin American despots. And what to say about the attempted coup on 6 January 2021, and the shocking evidence that later emerged of what Trump said and did during the days leading up to the assault on the Capitol, and the effect, up to and including loss of life, on those who had to deal with the chaos he unleashed?

★

Trump may seem an extreme case – an aberration – but the fact is that the political landscape, on both sides of the Atlantic, resonates in every page of Shirer's account of Nazi Germany, and of Albright's wider exploration of fascism in the past. I never knew that Mussolini was the first to coin the slogan 'drain the swamp', which Trump and his global cheerleaders would also adopt. Or that the right in 1930s Germany called judges 'enemies of the people' for upholding the law, just as headline writers in contemporary Britain have done. There are other parallels with the past, too: parliamentarians being labelled traitors by their colleagues in the House because they dare to veer from the party line; anyone with a view contrary to the one held by this newspaper or that, this broadcaster or that, this president or that, is abused, derided, dismissed, labelled as a liar or hostile to their own country. Make no mistake, these are the seeds of fascism. The extent to which they have been sown, in Trump's America, but also in Europe, was never clearer than when Hungarian prime minister Viktor Orbán was given a hero's welcome as Trump's warm-up man at the Conservative Political Action Conference in Texas in 2022 – think Glastonbury for right-wing fanatics. Orbán delivered a message so extreme, at one point warning against the mixing of racial blood, that even one of his own senior advisers resigned in disgust. Anti-fascist education and campaigning is needed more than ever, especially as the Second World War recedes further and further into history's rear-view mirror.

And while Italy's past provides us with a historical context within which to view the rise of far-right leader Giorgia Meloni, what to make of a far-right party, with overtly neo-Nazi roots, becoming a major force in Sweden? Gone, perhaps forever, is the comfort that liberals and social democrats could take in the idea that, whatever forces may swirl around Europe, at least we could count on the Scandis to keep flying the flag for sensible, centrist, decent politics. The rise of the Sweden Democrats, from 1.4

per cent in the polls when a young man named Jimmie Åkesson became leader in 2005, to a potentially king-making 20 per cent in 2022, felt seismic. (To those who have grown used to respecting Swedish social democracy, don't be confused by the word 'Democrats' in the name of this nationalist far-right party.) It followed an altogether too familiar playbook that we had seen in many parts of Europe: with Marine Le Pen in France, Vox in Spain, the Finns Party in Finland, Meloni's Brothers of Italy, and the populist Swiss People's Party, which managed to secure an amendment to the Swiss Constitution to ban the construction of minarets in Switzerland.

The constituent parts of Åkesson's campaign were standard and fairly simple: modernise the far-right ideology; appear to make it less toxic by purging some of the more violent elements; secure support from the working class in former industrial areas; enjoy the fact that media and tech companies' business models are boosted by extremism; exploit grievances and also the fact that too many in the centre and on the left play into the hands of the extremists by denying the seriousness of those grievances rather than seeking to address them.

The outcome in Sweden was another triumph for populists and polarisers. Social Democrats, Greens and left parties won overwhelmingly in major cities; the right and far right made huge gains in working-class areas that had once been solidly aligned with parties of the left. The Sweden Democrats combined technically sanitised far-right politics with provocative language and behaviour typical of fascist-minded populists. In 2020, Åkesson stood at the border of Greece and Turkey with leaflets telling Syrian refugees, 'Sweden is full; don't come to us', much as Nigel Farage had stood in front of his 'Breaking Point' poster during the EU referendum. Farage's poster had featured migrants crossing the Croatia–Slovenia border in 2015, the only prominent white person in the picture obscured by a box of text. That the Nazis had used similar images of snaking queues of 'parasites and vermin' was not lost on those opposed to Farage's world view. But, of course, the angrier one side of the polarised debate got, the happier the other side was at the fuss being generated, ensuring that the poster became one of the most talked-about events of the Brexit campaign.

The left can and should beat itself up about its failure to recognise and combat the rise of the far right. But responsibility also lies with the conservative mainstream, which has failed to stand up for what it believes in, and so has allowed the parties it encompasses to drift ever further to the right, most notably in the UK and the US.

Key to this has been the constant linking – amplified incessantly in right-wing media – of immigration and broader social concerns. A rise in violent crime – blame the immigrants. Shortages of housing stock – it's because there are so many immigrants. The NHS overwhelmed – because the immigrants are adding to the pressures upon it. The economy is weak – and immigrants are weakening it. If the right-wing populist is looking to find someone or something to blame for all our ills, immigrants and immigration are the perfect target. Blaming immigrants removes culpability from the populists and their supporters. It avoids placing blame at the feet of a rival political party which could refute the populist's claims and stand up for itself. Instead, it directs the blame at people who have next to no political voice, at a time when many are struggling to survive and have no real means of defending themselves.

Because the problems immigrants are blamed for are so diverse, when populists bring polarisation into the mix, they are able to harness a substantial body of anti-immigration feeling which they can then groom for their own purposes. Handled well, the group of people who believe that the populist has the solution to society's biggest problems can swing elections. That those who win power in this way don't actually care about that group of people is neither here nor there. Once they're in, they're in, and free to wreak havoc, all the while persuading supporters to credit them with everything good, and blame anyone else for everything bad. Classic Trump. Classic Johnson.

In the Swedish elections, even worries about the impact of the war in Ukraine on the cost of living – and bear in mind that the war led Sweden to break its decades-long neutrality and declare its wish to be part of NATO – played second fiddle to the central driving narrative of the right: that Muslim migrants were responsible for a wave of violent crime. The election campaign showed what we had already seen in Italy, Spain, the UK and the US: that moderate mainstream conservatism, far from standing up to such rhetoric and argument, played into it instead. Instead of containing the far right, they helped boost them. The end result is that in several parts of Europe, we now have around one in five people who seem prepared to vote for politicians and parties who essentially build their electoral strategies around the notion of fighting proto-civil wars against minorities.

In the course of an interview I did with Tony Blair for *GQ* magazine when Trump was in power, I pointed out the many parallels with the 1930s, and my worries that Trump had dangerously fascist tendencies. Tony felt I was going over the top.

AC: So you don't share my terror that this guy is president of America and the comparisons with Hitler and Stalin are not overdone. It took Hitler a long time to go for journalists and judges. He did it in the first week.

TB: The comparisons with Hitler and Stalin are ridiculous.

AC: Are you sure?

TB: Yes.

He was less sure after the insurrection on 6 January 2021.

In her book, Albright actually went a lot further than I do in drawing parallels between Trump and both Hitler and Mussolini, and between both those dictators and contemporary trends in world politics. 'Mussolini called on his followers to believe in an Italy that would be prosperous because it was self-sufficient and respected because it was feared,' she wrote. 'This was how twentieth-century fascism began: with a magnetic leader exploiting widespread dissatisfaction by promising all things. Il Duce, Italy's prime minister from 1922 until 1943, said that his mission was 'to break the bones of the democrats . . . and the sooner the better.'

Hitler, she argued, projected himself as the leader capable of acting in a way that conventional politicians could not. As today's populists do. He 'lied incessantly about himself and about his enemies'. As the populists do. 'He convinced millions that he cared for them deeply when, in fact, he would have willingly sacrificed them all.' As one or two of the populists around today would no doubt do. Of today, she wrote that 'anti-democratic leaders are winning democratic elections, and some of the world's savviest politicians are moving closer to tyranny with each passing year.' She spared Putin the label of 'full-blown fascist' – the book was written some years ago, and she has since died – but added: 'He has flipped through Stalin's copy of the totalitarian playbook and underlined passages of interest to call on when convenient.' The world has seen plenty of that since her death, as the Ukraine war has dragged on, and Putin's journey to full-blown fascism has advanced.

Trump was not a new Hitler or Stalin. He did not want to invade other countries, or murder millions, and I think it would show an unforgivable lack of respect to those who perished at the hands of those monsters to suggest some kind of moral equivalence between them and the former US president. I do strongly believe, however, that he has dangerously fascist tendencies, was shaking loose the guardrails of democracy even while, as president, he was charged with the task of upholding them, and continues to do so now that he's out of office. Only last December, falsely claiming once more that the election had been stolen from him, he argued that this allowed 'for the termination of all rules, regulations, and articles, even those found in the Constitution'.

Fascism doesn't start with gas chambers, or systematic persecution, or ethnic cleansing – surely one of the most disgusting phrases humanity has ever produced – or the Nuremberg trials. It ends there, or at least did in the case of the German variety that led to the Second World War. History does not repeat itself exactly. But we do not have to imagine the very worst that fascism can lead to, the pure evil that Hitler and Stalin came to represent, in order to worry about where those fascist tendencies might lead. I am writing this at a time when Putin is bombing hospitals, and the US Congress is investigating Trump's role in the January 6 riots. As we looked on while the rioters stormed the Capitol, how many of us said to ourselves: I cannot believe this is happening in the USA? I certainly did. So, even though the investigation ought to see Trump banished from public life in disgrace, or even jailed, as many think he should be, he and many of his supporters remain convinced he can return; just as Boris Johnson and his true-believer supporters believe he can return to the power in the UK, liar or not, law-breaker or not. That Trump should even have indicated his intention to run for the presidency again in 2024 underlines the fragility of the rules and institutions on which the world's most powerful democracy is built. Having had one or two difficult conversations with her father, former vice-president Dick Cheney, I have been moved by the courage of his daughter, Congresswoman Liz Cheney, who has calmly and consistently, in the face of organised campaigns of intimidation, called out Trump and his unfitness for any public office.

★

It's worth bearing in mind, too, that there is not a single playbook for fascism. It comes in different guises. Not all fascist leaders are empire-builders, for example. Some are exponents of 'populist nativism' – seeking to turn their countries in on themselves rather than goading them to attack other nations. Trump obviously comes to mind here, but one also thinks of the likes of alt-right strategist Steve Bannon and Nigel Farage. And while many of the central messages and tactics of the hard right have stayed much the same down the years, changes of emphasis are apparent, as are new ideas and weapons in their armoury.

In this context it's worth considering what is arguably the bible of the sado-populists: a book called *The Sovereign Individual*. It is possibly the most important book you've never heard of. I myself had never come across it until August 2018, when a man chased me down a railway platform at Marylebone station, thrust a dog-eared copy into my hands, and pleaded with me to read it.

'Even the first chapter,' he said, putting his hands into praying mode. 'Even if you just read the first chapter, please, I promise, you will see straight away why it matters.' It was something of an Ancient Mariner moment, in that the intensity with which he approached me led me to believe that I should take him seriously. I later learned he was a committed anti-Nazi campaigner, who believed that Brexit was but one part of a highly orchestrated attempt by very right-wing conservative forces to increase their power and wealth.

A few days later, I did read the first chapter. He was right; I saw straight away why it mattered, and read it, spellbound, and horrified, to the end, on a long train journey from London to Aberdeen.

Published in early 1997, amid the New Democrat, New Labour, Neue Mitte era, *The Sovereign Individual* makes clear why the political right fought so hard for Brexit's disaster capitalism opportunities, why authoritarian populists have enjoyed considerable ascendancy around the democratic world, and why they relish the chaos unleashed.

The subtitle, *Mastering the Transition to the Information Age*, is instructive. It is a book written *by* Masters of the Universe, *for* Masters of the Universe, also known as Sovereign Individuals. One of the co-authors, James Dale Davidson, is American; the other is British, very British . . . Lord William Rees-Mogg, ex-editor of *The Times*. Younger readers are likely to be more familiar with his son, Jacob, another Etonian who rose to the UK Cabinet, and who has been a leading light of the Brexit revolution.

The book is prefaced by a quote by Tom Stoppard, from his play *Arcadia*. 'The future is disorder . . . It is the best possible time to be alive, when almost everything you thought you knew is wrong.' To most people, disorder is threatening, scary. To Rees-Mogg and the radical right it is the chance for the Sovereign Individual to rise above tedious constraints imposed on lesser mortals: tax, regulation, government, even politics and democracy itself.

From their 1990s vantage point, Davidson and Rees-Mogg forecast that the information revolution will 'subvert and destroy the nation-state, creating new forms of social organisation. It will be faster than any previous revolution, and not without pain.' In their view, government is nothing more than a drag on ambition and success, and welfare something the rich are forced to fund for the less bright, successful and ambitious. There are strong, disturbing hints of a belief in a master race throughout.

A profound loathing of democratic politics runs through the book. It explains why the populists project themselves as anti-politics, anti-elites, even as they seek political power to further the interests of the elites of which they are part. Government is constantly equated with organised crime – then US president Bill Clinton portrayed as something akin to a gangster – but, as the modern nation-state 'decomposes', they say 'latter-day barbarians like the Russian mafia, other ethnic criminal gangs, drug lords,

and renegade covert agencies will be laws unto themselves . . .
They already are.' Indeed.

Sovereign Individuals, like the ancient gods, will enjoy a kind
of 'diplomatic immunity' from political decisions. Meanwhile,
the capacity of nation-states to raise money for redistribution
will collapse, and members of 'the information aristocracy' will
move their wealth to wherever they are least troubled by politicians, whose capacity for taxing will fall by 50–70 per cent. 'The
twentieth-century nation-state, with all its pretensions, will starve
to death as its tax revenues decline.'

Herein lies the authors' breathless excitement. 'Payment will be
rendered in cybercurrency. Profits will be booked in cyberbanks.
Investments will be made in cyberbrokages. Many transactions
will not be subject to taxation . . . Extraterritorial regulatory
power will collapse . . . Control over money will migrate from
the halls of power to the global marketplace . . . Cyberspace is
the ultimate offshore jurisdiction. An economy with no taxes.
Bermuda in the sky with diamonds.' How dare they co-opt the
genius of the Beatles into their sordid plans?

The book is written somewhat in the manner of a memo to
investors, a guide for disaster capitalists. Privatisation of services
heralds 'the ultimate form of privatisation – the sweeping de-
nationalisation of the individual'. (That's you they're talking about,
dear reader; you are to be left on your own, to fend for yourself,
so God help you if you can't afford to live.) In their vision, the
Sovereign Individual will not be the asset of any state, nor even a
citizen, but a customer of competing jurisdictions. He/she (probably he) will benefit from this commercialisation of sovereignty
by choosing jurisdictions, in the same way they might choose
their insurance companies or their religions. Jurisdictions that fail
to deliver will face bankruptcy and liquidation, just as incompetent commercial enterprises or failed religious congregations do.

And how is this for a radical right-wing view of public services, one in which the idea of the cooperative pooling of resources for common goods like roads and hospitals is clearly anathema? 'If you went into a store to buy furniture, and the salespeople took your money but then proceeded to ignore your requests and consult others about how to spend your money, you would quite rightly be upset. You would not think it normal or justifiable if the employees of the store argued that you really did not deserve the furniture, and that it should be shipped instead to someone whom they found more worthy. The fact that something very like this happens in dealings with government shows how little control the "customers" actually have.'

There will, Davidson and Rees-Mogg admit, be 'left-behinds,' and they will become 'increasingly jingoistic and unpleasant'. The authors predict violence, especially in America and Europe. 'The more psychopathic of these unhappy souls' will strike out against anyone with more prosperity. The rich and immigrants will be most at risk. 'A furious nationalist reaction will sweep the world,' we are told. 'One of the crucial challenges of the great transformation ahead will be maintaining order in the face of escalating violence, or alternatively escaping its brunt . . . Our guess is that the recriminations will intensify when Western nations begin to unambiguously crack apart in the manner of the former Soviet Union.'

Again, though, Sovereign Individuals must fear none of this, because every time a nation-state cracks up, they enthuse, it will facilitate further devolution and encourage the autonomy of Sovereign Individuals. In that light, the possibility that Brexit could herald the break-up of the UK, in two places, Scotland and Ireland, and the seemingly relaxed attitude to that prospect from Conservatives who claim to be Unionist, becomes more comprehensible. So, too, are a couple of Rees-Mogg junior's more controversial moves: his decision to shift millions in his hedge fund from the UK to Ireland (yes, he was at one point 'Minister for Brexit Opportunities' but the Sovereign Individual always puts self-interest first); and his observation that it may be fifty years before we see 'the full benefits' of Brexit (Sovereign Individuals are exempt from that long wait, because, as Rees-Mogg senior makes clear, 'Market forces, not political majorities, will compel societies to reconfigure themselves in ways that public opinion will neither comprehend nor welcome'.) Rees-Mogg junior is not the only would-be Sovereign Individual in the Brexit project, of course. Such figures as media owners Rupert Murdoch and the Barclay Brothers, to whose clicking fingers Johnson and Michael Gove jumped so often without being asked to, come to mind, too.

Much as I might recoil from the Rees-Mogg senior vision, I cannot but admire his acute intelligence and some of the fore-sight involved in his analysis. Vladimir Putin was a little over two years off becoming president of Russia, Mark Zuckerberg was just thirteen, and Dominic Cummings in his twenties, when Rees-Mogg senior wrote this: 'We believe the Information Age will bring the dawn of cybersoldiers, who will be heralds of devolu-tion. Cybersoldiers could be deployed not merely by nation-states but by very small organisations, and even by individuals. Wars of the next millennium will include some almost bloodless battles fought with computers . . . The result will be a massive problem of data corruption that will provide an accidental illustration of a new potential for information warfare. In the Information Age, potential adversaries will be able to wreak havoc by detonating "logic bombs" that sabotage the functions of essential systems by corrupting the data upon which their functioning depends.' The authors describe how it will be easier to bring down an aeroplane by corrupting the software that controls it than by aiming a mis-sile at it, and then make the broader point that data corruption can disrupt a country almost as much as physical weapons can.

And as we all scratch our heads today and wonder what to do about 'fake news'. perhaps we should have paid more heed to

WRM. Having argued that, 'for a variety of reasons', news coverage will become ever more unreliable, he goes on to suggest that 'There is no reason to suspect that reporters and editors are any less prone to corrupt consideration than building inspectors or Italian paving contractors . . . They will see little and explain less.' See little and explain less . . . the media's motto for much of their political coverage in recent years.

He foretells the algorithmised echo chambers of today, predicting a world where technology improves to the point where 'you'll even be able to order a nightly news report that simulates the news you would like to hear'. 'You'll see any story you wish, true or false, unfold on your television / computer with greater verisimilitude than anything than NBC or the BBC can now muster.'

Indicators of the commercialisation of sovereignty and the death of the nation-state pile up. They include economic upheaval caused by the computer revolution; the decline in reputation of governments, unions, professionals and lobbyists; the decline in the power of traditional elites; the decline in respect for symbols of statehood; widespread secession movements in many parts of the globe; intense, violent, nationalist reaction from those who lose income, status, power; suspicion of and opposition to free trade and globalisation; hostility to immigration; hatred of the 'information elite', the rich and well-educated; acts of ethnic cleansing to restore nationalist identification; neo-Luddite attacks on new technologies, especially from the poor; the ultimate collapse of the nation-state due to fiscal crisis.

In its more unpalatable central messages there are some parallels between Rees Mogg's work and the thinking of arch libertarian Ayn Rand, whose philosophy has something of a hold on the Tory right. There are parallels, too, with a more recent libertarian treatise, *Britannia Unchained*, published in 2012 as Britain basked in the glow of the London Olympic and Paralympic

Games – this huge success, perhaps the high point of UK soft power, was a project planned under the Labour governments of Tony Blair and Gordon Brown, and delivered under Cameron's Conservative-led coalition. The book's authors Liz Truss, Kwasi Kwarteng, Chris Skidmore, Dominic Raab and Priti Patel had only relatively recently become MPs. If their aim in writing the book was to establish themselves as the coming generation of right-wingers, they certainly succeeded. Four of them went on to become senior Cabinet ministers and holders of one or more of the great offices of state. One of them, of course, even made it to 10 Downing Street, and another to Number 11, albeit briefly.

The central messages of *Britannia Unchained* are right out of the Rees-Mogg playbook. Tax bad. Regulation bad. Free market economics wonderful. Employment laws a brake on growth. We should be looking to Singapore, Taiwan and Hong Kong, not America and Europe, for our economic lessons. The 'Singapore-on-Thames' vision. If we don't, we risk 'an inevitable slide into mediocrity'. The whole text is permeated with an indifference to income inequality and a contempt for the average worker, who is regarded as inherently idle. The focus, the authors argue, should be less on workers' rights and more on getting them to labour harder for longer, and to take any job they are offered.

Once installed in Downing Street, the promoters of this world-view, Truss and Kwarteng, swiftly revealed their right-wing populist credentials: for example, showing hostility to anyone who could be characterised as 'them', whether they were migrants, immigration lawyers, the BBC, or civil servants (note the sneers at 'Treasury orthodoxy', symbolised by their immediate sacking of the Treasury's permanent secretary and the sidelining of the Office for Budget Responsibility ahead of their first budget). Liz Truss even came up with a non-existent group of conspirators she termed the 'anti-growth coalition', of which, as a North London podcaster with woke views, I was proud to be identified as a member. Then there were the usual attacks on the 'metropolitan elite', even as Kwarteng, her chancellor – yet another bloody Old Etonian posing as an anti-elitist – sought to make the rich richer by scrapping the 45p top tax rate and removing the cap on bankers' bonuses. Needless to say, his intellectual justification for this – that the benefits would somehow trickle down to the less fortunate – has never found support among the vast majority of economists. Needless to say, too, the markets took fright, the Bank of England had to step in to prevent mere carnage becoming cataclysmic calamity and their forty-nine-day tenure in charge blew a massive hole in the economy.

Nor is Kamikwasi Trussonomics what the vast majority of the electorate want. Of course, most people like the idea of paying less tax, and having to abide by fewer rules and regulations. But they also want decent public services. And they know that if tax revenues fall, growth is low, and borrowing costs are high, they will have to settle for inefficient, underfunded public services. They know that they have to contribute significantly if they want to see improvements in education, the health service, public transport, social care, the legal system – all of which are felt to be going backwards. The alternative is government borrowing that leads to even more debt – debt which the taxpayer has to repay eventually anyway, and with interest on top – or austerity, which is not only unpopular but actually deadly, it turns out. A report by academics at Glasgow University and the Glasgow Centre for Population Health, published in the *Journal of Epidemiology and Community Health* last autumn, attributed 335,000 excess deaths to the effects of austerity, and the cuts the government insisted were required to public services and benefits. And while inflation (which on Sunak's watch rose to its highest in more than thirty years, and has risen even further since, thanks in part to the war in Ukraine) may be manageable for the affluent, it's a very tough proposition for the poor.

I'd go further. If people really understood the world view of the likes of Truss, Kwarteng and Rees-Mogg, they would recoil in horror. Most of us, I believe, want a society where there is genuine equality of opportunity. We believe we can achieve more together than we can individually (after all, that is what humans have demonstrated since time immemorial), and that therefore there is such a thing as society. We believe we have a sense of obligation to one another, and most people don't want to see fellow citizens discriminated against or left behind. We also know (as endless research has shown) that more equal societies are more productive ones and that they are more at ease with themselves. This is all the very opposite of the neo-Darwinian, elitist view of the Sovereign Individual, or, for that matter, of the populist who pitches elites against 'the people'. Civilised politics is pluralist politics, where different groups are embraced and brought together rather than pitted against each other.

Truss's forty-nine days in office represented classic right-wing libertarianism in fast forward. Once a Lib Dem, formerly a Remainer, she was a convert to radical right-wing economic views. Kwarteng, for his part, was a lifelong believer with an arrogance to match that of his fellow Old Etonians Cameron, Johnson and Rees-Mogg, if without the charm of Cameron or the political cunning of the other two. Neither prime minister nor chancellor had a reputation for listening to advice. Both doubled down when they were shown to be wrong. Talk to anyone working at senior level inside the Bank of England at the time: it was as close to economic collapse as a single government event had ever taken one of the advanced economies of the world. Yet, even as the pound was slumping, and the Bank had to intervene amid the markets taking fright at what they considered to be a cavalier disregard for serious economic discipline, sums that add up, and tax and spending decisions that can be justified by economic reality, Kwarteng could be overheard outside the Groucho Club insisting 'so what?' If sterling slumped, it would come back. When one considers the calamitous economic and social impact of Kamikwasi Trussonomics – estimates of their hit on the economy vary, but start at £30 billion – it's worth calling to mind the subtitle of the book they co-authored. Are you ready for this? 'Global Lessons for Growth and Prosperity.'

The architects of this disaster are gone from Downing Street. Boris Johnson suddenly had an immediate rival in the 'worst PM in history' stakes. And Truss's defeated rival for the leadership, Rishi Sunak, was at least able to say: 'I told you so.' He had after all warned that the economic plans Truss set out in their leadership battle would spark a run on sterling, send the gilt markets into freefall and see the FTSE tumble as global investors took fright. It should not, however, be forgotten that while he did not support the idea of unfunded tax cuts which were central to the Truss-Kwarteng fiasco, he is very much on the right wing of the Conservative Party, and a true believer in Brexit and the disaster capitalism opportunities that he sees it as offering.

I am writing this shortly after the Queen's death in September 2022. She saw fifteen prime ministers in her seventy years on the throne, while King Charles is already on to his second. But the radical right will keep on keeping on with their radical right 'vision'. They believe in the Sovereign Individual view of the world, because they are the Sovereign Individuals, or at least Sovereign Individual wannabees.

It should come as no surprise, then, that among the goals of today's libertarian right – aggressively pursued by well-funded and well-connected think tanks, like-minded politicians, academics, media and business tycoons – is a redesign of the world's economic, political and data systems along lines that are wholly free market and almost wholly unaccountable to outside scrutiny. The debate over so-called 'non-doms' goes to the heart of this issue. Labour want to close the loophole that allows residents of the UK not to pay tax on any earnings made outside the country. The Tories insist that it is good for the economy that the super-rich choose to live here, so leave them be, a view that sits very oddly with chancellor Jeremy Hunt's argument, when seeking to clear up the mess of Trussonomics, that those with the broadest shoulders should take the biggest share of the burden. (His predecessor, Nadhim Zahawi, clearly did not get the broad shoulders memo, his attempts to avoid tax resulting in a fine from HMRC, for which he had ministerial responsibility at the time.) The brutal fact of the matter, though, is that non-dommery fits perfectly with the reality of a world in which the richer you are, the better supported you are in your efforts to keep a greater share of your wealth, a benefit from which Rishi Sunak's non-dom wife, and so the prime minister himself, have benefited enormously. Theresa May sought on one occasion, cosying up to her Brextremist fringe, to divide us between 'citizens of somewhere' and 'citizens of nowhere'; the suggestion being that those of us who were continuing to fight for our place in the European Union were very much in the latter camp. However, the real citizens of nowhere are the Sovereign Individuals: those who live here, yet, with full government support, end up being subsidised by the so-called citizens of somewhere as they avoid full taxation on the vast wealth they've secreted in various friendly tax regimes around the world.

The freeports and charter cities that these individuals vigorously promote are perhaps the most obvious manifestations of the Sovereign Individual campaign for a world free from such petty annoyances as labour law and codes on corruption. The UK government defines freeports as 'special areas within the UK's borders where different economic regulations apply'. Charter cities are defined by their backers as 'geographic zones within a country that operate under government-approved free market-oriented charters, rather than under restrictive national laws'. Rishi Sunak, in conjunction with the right-wing think tank the Centre for Policy Studies, enthusiastically adopted the notion of freeports and then promoted the setting up of ten new ones when he was chancellor · of the exchequer (needless to say, his ideas have been widely criticised for their low standards of regulation). During the leadership battle that followed Johnson's fall from power, Sunak and Truss competed with each other to see who could be more supportive of the notion of freeports, investment zones and charter cities.

I mentioned earlier how in a post-truth world, sado-populist politicians reverse reality, winning campaigns on one basis whilst delivering their objectives on another, the promises of the campaign trail quickly forgotten once the campaign is over, as we saw with Johnson and Brexit. There is a similar gap between the publicly stated objectives behind this free enterprise push, and the actual goals. The Charter Cities Institute is, on the one hand, backed by many of the same people who have backed the fossil fuel lobby in resisting the realities of climate change; on the other hand, it has the nerve to pretend its goal is to address the challenges of climate change and global poverty. In much the same way, Rees-Mogg junior not only moved effortlessly overnight from membership of a Cabinet that had banned fracking to one that supported it, but – in an act of populist polarising Putin would have been proud of – condemned as Luddites opponents who sought to promote cutting-edge renewable energy, and suggested they were funded by the Russian president.

It's time to introduce you to the Norwegian word for cheese. I only know it because a few years ago I used it inadvertently in a talk I was giving in Oslo about my book *Winners: And How They Succeed*. I was telling the audience about my habit of writing quotes, tips and acronyms on Post-its, and sticking them on the wall of my office on the top floor of our house, so that I can nudge myself back on track if I am veering off it. I said that my most important Post-it had just three letters on it, which I proceeded to write in thick black marker pen on a big, shiny whiteboard:

A huge O.

A huge S.

A huge T.

Even before I had begun to state that OST was the key to progress and essential for the success of any meaningful venture, my thus far serious audience appeared to be having a fit of the giggles – always disconcerting for a speaker in full flow.

'What's the joke?' I asked.

'OST means cheese,' I was told. Ah.

Still, I stand by my cheese . . .

O = Objective.

S = Strategy.

T = Tactics.

I will address the all-important subject of strategy in more detail, and so return to Norwegian cheese, later in the book. I mention it here, however, to explain that when you view the Sovereign Individual and the Brexit project through the prism of OST, it is possible to put Brexit as an O, an S or a T, depending on how wide you want to go.

O – Brexit.

S – Get a referendum, win it.

T – Populist messages, Take Back Control, more money for the NHS, Facebook ads, Cambridge Analytica.

O – Create opportunities via disaster capitalism.

S – Brexit.

T – Get a referendum, win it.

O – Shift the democratic dial to the right.

S – Populism and polarisation.

T – Brexit.

Brexit is just one element of the Sovereign Individuals' O. Ultimately, they want to ensure they are not subject to the rules and scrutiny of governments. They want a world where laws and rules are for the little people, not for those who shape and make them. And they embrace disruption and destruction to get them to their goal. If that seems far-fetched, note how the same people who fought for Brexit are now part of the so-called Net Zero Scrutiny Group, which seeks to persuade us that warnings about climate change are alarmist, and that business should be allowed to let rip without regulation from government.

While we all too often focus on the culture war distractions of the radical right, they are making enormous change, much of it elitist and anti-democratic, with consequences, as with Brexit, that will have a greater reach on the young than any other section of the population. That is why we need to wake up.

When reading all those books on 1930s Germany, with their focus on the big figures in politics, business, culture and the media, I kept wondering what the so-called 'ordinary' people were doing. All too often, they were absent from the narrative. But I suspect they were divided into similar groups to those we have today: true believers in the political cause and its leaders; media voices ventilating the cries of the powerful, and gleefully turning on the enemies created by them; followers who were happy to trust that the people in charge knew what they were doing, or else how did they get there?; the indifferent, who thought politics was about and for other people and who, as a result, just sleep-walked towards whatever future was shaped for them; and the helpless, who knew what was happening was wrong, and dangerous, but as its force grew, didn't know how to arrest it. I bet there were plenty of people in 1930s Germany asking the question: '*Aber was kann ich tun?*' But what can I do? Too many ended up doing nothing to stop what was happening. Let's hope, ninety years on from Hitler becoming chancellor of Germany, that we don't make the same mistake and assume that we are all powerless in the face of forces we know are both dangerous and wrong.

6.

The Perils of Disengagement

If things are this bleak, should we really be surprised that so many are giving up on politics altogether?

One of the questions I get asked, perhaps as often as any other, is why the quality of politicians appears to be so low. The answer lies in the fact that a great number of those asking that question might, in a previous era, have thought about going into politics themselves and so raised the bar. But now they don't. It is not just politicians who turn them off, but politics itself. This adds to the danger we will find ourselves in unless we do something to put things right. More than ever, we need good politicians, because the challenges we face are so enormous, and yet so many of our current leaders seem to add to the world's problems rather than solve them.

As you will have gathered by now, and will see even more as we move into the more optimistic parts of the book, I set great store in the ability of younger people to make sense of the mess we are in, and help take us out of it. But I am not blind to the fact that all too many are disengaging completely. Generation after generation has grown up to be better off than their parents . . . until now. No wonder, then, that younger people in Britain are turned off when they hear the politicians in government endlessly boasting about how good they are, and how the decisions they make are always 'the right thing to do'. Today's younger generation have to cope with wages and living standards that are at best stagnant, and a housing ladder that is effectively out of their reach unless they have wealthy parents. They've been entering the world of work either during a systemic financial crisis, a Brexit that the majority of them opposed and which took away so many of their rights and opportunities, or a global pandemic. And though I can give the economic, political and intellectual arguments for university tuition fees – and did so many times when working for the government – I accept that political and social engagement might drop down a list of priorities for today's young when the obligation to repay student debt is added to all these other factors. Offering time for free is not easy for the student who has chalked up £50,000 or so of debt. I totally understand, therefore, how hard it is for those who are struggling just to keep afloat to find the time and the energy even to think about trying to create real change. The other big generational change is that today's young people are living through a period of world history defined by enormous economic, social and political transition. All my life, there has been change, important and defining events and movements. But most of it took place within parameters easily understood by the generation that went before us. Can we really say the same of the world our children are living in? The parameters are changing so fast. Think of the pace of technological change, the advance of the climate crisis, the widening of inequality, a seeming shift among so many leaders away from commitments to global solidarity, human rights and the rule of law. Generations like mine could afford to rely on the previous generation to act as 'caretakers' and wait until our forties or so to start worrying about making a difference. The paradox for this new generation is that, although they really cannot afford to wait that long, they are also all having to cope with so much in the here and now that there is little or no space for that much-needed early involvement.

These factors have conspired to create a paradox. In general, young people today, as defined by any serious analysis of their views and attitudes, are the most socially conscious on record. They are, however, the least civically engaged. Indeed, research completed in 2021 showed that just 29 per cent of people aged eighteen to twenty-four would be 'willing to work together with others on something to improve my neighbourhood' – a substantial decline on the 50 per cent who responded positively when asked the same question in 1998. And while young people may still volunteer, they do so less now than previous generations did, and this volunteering is generally through big organisations, where they will often not feel the impact of their contribution, rather than smaller local groups where they are more likely to.

The research also showed that younger generations – particularly Millennials and Generation Z – are much more likely to have narrower social networks than in the past, despite – or perhaps because of – social media being a constant presence in their lives. The impact of this disconnect – widened by the lockdowns of Covid – is stark: in the first six months of the pandemic, the share of 18–24-year-olds who said they trusted their neighbours fell from 57 per cent to 47 per cent. By contrast, social trust among people aged between fifty-five and sixty-four increased in the same period, from 53 per cent to 65 per cent. Such a trend suggests that power and powerlessness will end up concentrated even further.

As for disengagement from the voting part of democratic participation, in every continent in the world, the decile least likely to vote in national elections is the 18–29-year-old group. A survey of thirty-three countries showed that 44 per cent of young adults aged 18–29 years 'always vote', compared with almost 60 per cent of the whole adult population, and over 70 per cent among those over the age of fifty. In Europe, an analysis in 2015 of the then twenty-eight member states of the EU showed that almost 60 per cent of eligible voters up to the age of twenty-four years old opted not to vote in their country's most recent national election. Just looked at in raw political terms, it means politicians inevitably worry much more about pensioners than they do about students. In a sane world, focused on building a better future, it should be the other way round.

A vicious circle has thus been established: younger people feel disaffected, unengaged, uninvolved and unheard, and therefore withdraw from the political arena. But in so doing they leave the way open for the special interests of an older generation who make their presence felt at the ballot box. Politicians seek office under the system that is presented to them, and so court that older generation, leaving younger people feeling even more left out in the cold. Look at the Tory party leadership election to replace Boris Johnson, where 0.3 per cent of the country made up the electorate. When it was time to replace Liz Truss, even that 0.3 per cent was excluded, lest it make another disastrous decision. The process that led to Truss becoming Tory leader, and so prime minister, made for grim and grisly viewing at times. The contestants focused all their attention, rhetoric and policies on those people among the 0.3 per cent, pandering to their narrow views. But, to be blunt, those people were simply being rewarded for their activism, just as the disengaged young were being penalised.

Occasionally, another scenario plays out. According to the think tank Onward, some young people become so disillusioned with the perceived failure of current politics and political structures that they move away from democratic values altogether and end up 'flirting with authoritarianism', in numbers greater than those similarly tempted among older age groups.

It's perhaps worth exploring in a little more detail the reasons why young people are more socially conscious but less socially engaged than previous generations. It is definitely not for lack of empathy, because so many young people are fiercely passionate about myriad social causes. Nor is it for lack of skill: they continue to be brilliantly innovative, endlessly creative and tooled-up with attitudes, experiences and technical abilities that any cause would find valuable. Indeed, I wonder if their superior digital skills might be one of the reasons for a sense of disengagement. Are they the right skills for building collaborative campaigns across the generations? They are certainly not the only skills required. There has to be collaboration between young and old, and an understanding that operating solely in the Twittersphere isn't doing anything for anybody.

The bigger problem, though, as I see and sense it, is the feeling of powerlessness I've just highlighted. It's a feeling that stems in part from an experience of mental or emotional overload (which is why I put such focus on the importance of looking after our mental health, and developing resilience as a force for good). It is also caused by practical barriers to participation and effecting change. And it has much to do with the space between reality and perception – or what Barack Obama calls the gap between 'the world as it is and the world as it should be': the space in which all change should happen. In this final space, there is an expectation gap: in the context of the magnitude of the problems we face, we fail to see that a small step forward, however incomplete or incremental, is still progress. Climate change in particular lends itself to that sentiment. 'I can't do everything, the problem is too big, so I'll do nothing.' Down that road lies despair and destruction. Thank God for Greta. More later.

At various stages in writing this book, I have sent drafts to a number of people whose opinions I value – in the main people a lot younger than I am. I wanted to be sure there would be an interest among them in what I was trying to say. I wanted to make sure I wasn't doing too much Dadsplaining, or speaking ignorantly about some of the issues I address, many of which impact younger generations more than mine. Above all, I wanted to have their ideas and experiences to help illustrate the challenges they face. The feedback, both general and specific, was excellent, and has helped to shape the final result, for which I am very grateful. From it three themes emerged particularly strongly. The first was a sense of exhausted despair, brought about by the pressures – financial, social and psychological – of the way so many live now. The second was a frustration, in some cases distaste, and even revulsion, at the way politics currently operates. The third, more hopefully, was the feeling that 'we have to do something!'. And they are.

The basic economics of disengagement was well articulated for me by one of my draft readers, Mete Coban, a young social entrepreneur who founded My Life, My Say, a charity which seeks to engage young people in active citizenship, enterprise and political engagement. 'I was speaking the other day to one of my junior staffers who studies a part-time master's degree at Cambridge,' he wrote. 'He feels really disheartened by life because he was doing everything that he was told to do from a young age but still struggles with the cost-of-living crisis. Worked hard at school, got a job, moved to London, went to a top-class university, but he is still earning just enough to keep him surviving. The reason why this point matters is because young people don't often feel like the system works for them.'

So, he has taken the difficult choice to work in a poorly-paid but socially valuable job 'to do the right thing', rather than just work in the well-paid private sector. But given his advanced degree from Cambridge, it can only be a matter of time before the private sector comes calling . . . and if he is feeling overwhelmed by financial concern he may be tempted to accept their offer and then find it financially difficult to reverse course. It would be such a waste if Mete's colleague were to leave his rewarding and impactful job at some point simply because he can't afford to pay the bills, or wants to start a family.

Similar exhaustion and frustration come across from my

nephew, Jamie Naish, who has a full-time job, part-runs a business he founded with his brother Graeme, is recently married to a hospital doctor, and is also a dedicated Labour Party activist and local councillor who, by the time of the third draft of this book, had become leader of his council. I know from experience, when he worked alongside me for the government of Albania a few years ago, that he is incredibly committed and hard-working. I was conscious of him being a very political animal from a young age, and I have always hoped – and believed – he would one day end up in Parliament. But his initial response when I sent him the draft underlined how even the most committed and hard-working can find their commitment challenged. I can feel his pain! You will too.

Will read with interest. Had a rough week myself trying to fit everything in. The day job is very busy, as we've had a couple of big projects go live recently, so councillor work and meetings have had to wait until the evenings. One meeting didn't finish until just before 11 p.m.! And then to top it all off, there was a party campaigning session at 10 a.m. today. Laura is on nights, so I dropped her off at Barnsley last night, so I had the car to get there this morning, but no one turned up. Arghhh!! Four hours of canvass-related driving, completely wasted . . .

I think it is very hard being actively involved when you have other full-time commitments as a young person – which our greying party members don't always get. For you, activism was always in and around your job with Tony Blair, at the top of the tree. For someone like me, however, it is a completely separate commitment to my job and, therefore, needs active planning and thinking about, day by day.

So, I would say there needs to be a focus on how you manage your involvement once you are involved. Politics doesn't change anything overnight . . . it's a long-haul slog in most cases. Managing yourself and those around you is key to sustaining interest and activism, and it's hard . . . especially on days like today when you feel like you've wasted your time!

Might not be relevant once I look at the book – but I'm sure there are lots of faded activists out there who started well and quickly found it hard to manage their situation.

It really is relevant. His point about grey-haired activists with more time on their hands is well made. Political parties are not always the most welcoming places, and at a time when politics needs the energy of young people, they should be doing a better job at engaging them in real activism. Many will not naturally see knocking on doors in the rain in that light. Being told, 'Ah, but we've always done it this way', is one of the most common, and most obstructive, barriers to people with drive and energy who want to make a difference.

Jamie's other main point is spot on, and echoes what so many young people say: there is a huge disconnect between the desire to make things happen quickly, and the reality of the political process. We cannot afford for activists to become faded and jaded, because their activism ends up feeling like a drag on the rest of their lives, where things can and do change speedily. I am pretty sure Jamie will keep on keeping on, because that is his nature, but it would help if people like him had better support and political systems to help them to do so. Too many of the young people I speak to who *try* to get involved in politics feel they are patronised, taken for granted, aren't invested in, and are seen as threatening because they might be better educated or faster on social media. They feel their older counterparts don't fully appreciate the difficulties they experience in balancing political and non-political commitments, and don't see how much harder it is for a thirty-year-old to be politically active than a seventy-year-old. This means that campaigns and institutions get run as though everybody involved was a pensioner. Before you know it, the light of activism is dimmed.

In 2019, Jamie took a 56 per cent pay cut to move from the private to the public sector (going from a salary of £90k plus bonuses to £40k). 'That is a huge sacrifice which I was happy to make at the time,' he said. 'But then when I was faced with hierarchical problems that meant I couldn't effect change as I had hoped, and my skillset wasn't valued or developed, I switched back to the private sector. It only took nine months for me to see that I was making a personal sacrifice to "do my bit", but the system wasn't capable of absorbing my aspirations and rewarding these in any way, so I left.'

Tarik Salih, a 23-year-old account manager with a PR company, who had contacted me through my website to ask me for my views on what his generation could do to make a difference, expressed a similar frustration with traditional activism. 'If I want to say that such and such a politician is an absolute pillock, I can unlock my phone and tweet in an instant. The same can't be said for building a political party, or a campaign to unseat the Tories. To have the motivation and determination to pursue a long-term goal and delay gratification requires it to be executed by someone with ambition. As a young person, I often worry about where my time and focus are being allocated. There's always a fear that if I spend X number of years building a political career or party and it doesn't work, then I've wasted X number of years when I could have built a career elsewhere.'

I think those of us who have spent our lives in and around political parties underestimate sometimes how alien politics looks to a lot of outsiders. As Holly Morgan put it to me, while we were filming *Make Me Prime Minister*: 'I am interested but most of the time I don't feel they are talking about the same world as the one I'm living in.' It's that sense of alienation and distance that comes across very powerfully in the reactions of another of my draft readers: Alex Smith, founder and former CEO of The Cares Family, an organisation which twins young people with old people in an attempt to combat loneliness and strengthen communities. Alex has considerable experience both of charities and of politics and campaigns. Having worked as a volunteer on Barack Obama's first presidential election campaign, he then worked for Labour, including for former party leader Ed Miliband. In 2018 he was appointed one of twenty inaugural Obama Foundation Fellows, selected from 21,000 applicants from around the world.

He was in part inspired to work for Labour by his experience in the States in 2008. However, he was shocked by what he discovered on returning home to the UK. 'I'd seen in Brooklyn and across the US how a neighbour-to-neighbour approach could work, and how community organising could tie bonds of trust long before elections came,' he told me. 'I felt I had some practical learning that I could contribute.' His first encounter with a Labour Party meeting, however, 'couldn't have been more different'. 'Instead of planning vibrant campaign events that would bring local people together to build trust,' he said, 'the meeting focused on procedure and arcane rules that seemed to stymie all action. Instead of being a space to plan creative community outreach events like open mic nights that could inspire and engage for the future, this was a discussion about socialist philosophy and the relative merits and demerits of figures from the past. Instead of asking how people on doorsteps really thought and felt about the world, door-knocking was simply about asking people which way they were likely to vote – and those who might think of voting differently were quickly moved on from. Instead of thinking of ways to harness the Internet to drive mobilisation and real-world connection, my local party obsessed about forthcoming committee meetings that apparently had the power only to plan further committee meetings.'

What he found most alien, he said, was that only Labour members were welcome at meetings and campaign events, and everyone insisted on calling everyone else 'comrade'. 'They even sang "The Red Flag" at meetings, which I'd only known as transposed to football chants. It was a far cry from walking in off the street in Brooklyn and being entrusted with a clipboard and flyers to go out and tell my story and listen to the experiences of others. To a newcomer, nothing at that first Labour Party meeting echoed the culture of campaigns as I'd learned it on the Obama campaign: "respect, empower, include". On the contrary, although this was apparently the party that believed in the more equal distribution of power and opportunity, it felt like another closed shop – part of the problem, not the solution.'

In terms of the wider world of public service, I fear that charities all too often share some of the off-putting characteristics of political parties. Charities are an obvious home for people asking themselves 'But what can I do?' and there are some great charities which do wonderful work, and some great people either on their payroll or working as volunteers. But most do not speak to young people, or to the pace of change which has defined their lives. Many are bureaucratic in the extreme, in an age where even banking is instant and at the touch of a button. They require long-term or day-time commitments that are anathema to young people, particularly in a time of such inequality and insecurity. Most are very top-down: they can be managerial, centralised, apply the clinical language of service-provision rather than the inclusive language of community, and are competitive rather than collaborative. While two-thirds of employees in charities are women, only a third of charity leaders are. These are cultures and practices that most young people do not relate to. There is a new generation of bottom-up and entrepreneurial charities that are bucking the trend – The Cares Family, GirlDreamer, Home Girls Unite, Cysters, Little Village, all of Ruth Ibegbuna's projects – but they remain the exception rather than the rule.

At a time when fewer young people are voting, joining parties, standing for election, and generally involving themselves in social and volunteer enterprises, we need the trends to go in the opposite direction. But those currently in charge do not make it easy, and with all the other pressures on their time and in their lives, the danger is that people find their commitment, when it comes to activism, tested to destruction. As New Labour, we talked the talk on party reform, and mass membership, but with all the pressures that come with being in government, we did not maintain the momentum needed. David Miliband's leadership campaign in 2010 centred on the idea of 'Movement for Change'. He wanted the Labour Party to become adept at bringing four goals together: mapping power in a locality; listening, genuinely listening, to people who wanted change; then allying with them to achieve change; thus boosting the prospect that come election time they would be allies of Labour. Famously, David lost to his brother Ed, who as Labour leader also put the principle of community organisers at the heart of his leadership. But Alex Smith, having experienced Obama's campaign and then Labour's, was clear that Labour as a party simply wasn't set up, culturally and organisationally, to make the same kind of breakthrough as the Democrats made under Obama.

The factors that support the status quo are fairly obvious. Tradition. 'Old-boy' networks. Focus on seniority and experience ahead of talent. Outmoded recruitment and development capacities. And, of course, lack of both time and confidence among the young. Conversely, the older generation have too much confidence and too much time, and some would rather feather their CVs by holding positions and power than nurture the next generation with advice and encouragement. Some countries are doing better than others, but around the world, politics is largely dominated by middle-aged and old men. It is true that in 2019, the year in which we had the highest number of nations led by women, there were six times as many as thirty years earlier, when Margaret Thatcher became prime minister. But a 600 per cent increase seems less impressive when you consider that the jump was from three to eighteen. The Biden–Trump choice in America in 2020 exemplified the sense of a male older generation being in charge. Given the option, not many young people would pick their elderly grandparents to be leaders of their country, but this was the choice presented to America in 2020, and might well be the choice again in 2024.

If young people are not joining parties as they used to, it is all too easy to blame them for being uninterested, or even to call them shallow and selfish. In the main, they are not. It is the parties which need to look at themselves, and how they attract young people. They need to help the young develop the skills and motivation to engage in politics. We often hear that part of the problem with politics is that there are too many 'career politicians'. It is in the main intended as an insult, as if somehow the very desire to be a politician should be viewed with suspicion. One thing you don't hear too often, however, is that politics is too competent, too professional, too well run. That benefits the chancers and the charlatans, and makes it all the more important that people currently excluded find a proper way in. It's therefore vital that young people fight their cynicism about the prospect of constructive change. If they don't, they are leaving the field wide open for those responsible for the mess we are in in the first place.

I did warn you that Part 1 might be a bit depressing, and scary. But, frankly, I think we need to be scared, so that the fear wakes us up to do something. Despite all the good in the world, when it comes to power, and those who have and hoard it, there is an awful lot of bad in the world right now. Every generation faces its own challenges, but has any generation had quite so many that feel quite so big, and quite so existential? If Part 1 has been somewhat dark, I make no apology for that, because unless we face the world as it is, rather than the mythical version sold to us by populist politicians promising the earth, or biased, superficial media operating under instructions from political and commercial vested interests at the top, how do we even begin to face those challenges?

I just want to revisit some of the themes I've addressed so far, before I try to raise the mood.

- There is a populist virus around, which thrives on the divisions found in contemporary society.

- This has to be challenged, and a cure found.

- The extreme form of populism, sado-populism, needs to be recognised, understood and taken seriously.

- The real motivations of the radical right need to be understood and challenged far better than they have been so far.

- We need to be ever vigilant to the underhand destruction of the guardrails of democracy, because the signs of creeping fascism are all too evident in too many parts of a divided, confused and challenged world.

- The systems on which our democracy depends have to be made stronger and more resilient, and the barriers preventing good people from getting into politics have to be torn down.

- We must not only want to make a difference, but believe that we can.

It's a lot to be getting on with. The good news is, that for all the power of money and technology to do good and bad, the answers are in people. We just have to understand that we do have power and agency, and decide to use them.

So, if Part 1 is about the problems, Part 2 is about the attitudes we need to hold and the approaches we need to develop, in order to become part of the solution.

The mood lifts from here on in, honestly . . . and, remember, when I first thought about writing this book, Trump was president, Bolsonaro was president, Johnson was prime minister. They now carry two important letters before them . . . EX. Change can come, if people *make* it come.

PART TWO

How You Can Help Fix It

7.

Resist Cynicism

When the problems we face are so large and so varied, it is all too easy to be cowed by them, assume that there is nothing we can do to fix things, and opt to leave it all to someone else. I have days like that too, plenty of them, when I think we're all doomed (though even on the road to doom, there can be plenty of good along the way). On a good day, though – I have more of those than bad – I really do believe that the challenges we face are surmountable, and that the next generation will make a better job of running the world than their predecessors. Either way, I don't accept what I call the 'It-is-what-it-is-ology . . .' 'It is what it is' – five tiny words deadened by defeatism. They carry the frustration that comes when we know something is wrong, but are also convinced that there is nothing to be done to fix it. They allow us to turn away and embrace apathy. In embracing apathy, we embrace cynicism too, by rewarding the cynics. They want us to turn away from the wrong they do. That way, they get to keep doing it.

It's fine to look at Leader A or Leader B, Company C or Business D, and say: 'I don't believe you; I don't trust you, I am not convinced you are even trying to do the things you say you are.' But the question then is what you do with that negative view of that person or institution, who has power over you through the decisions they are making. Do you use your scepticism as a motivator to do something good yourself? Or do you allow it to drive out hope, create apathy, add to the globalisation of indifference, become a cynic yourself? Using it as a motivator has to be the better way.

We have to believe that things can be better, or we give up. We have to do whatever we can to bring about that positive change. And the first step on that road is to believe that we can. That means you too! It means that on bad days we reject cynicism in favour of optimism, and on good days we embrace both our idealism and the idea that there is only one answer to the question of whether you have it within you to do something to help sort out the bloody mess we're in, and change the world.

Three letters. Begins with Y. Ends in S. Channel your inner Obama. Yes we can. Yes *you* can.

As the man himself said: 'Hope is not blind optimism. It's not ignoring the enormity of the task ahead or the roadblocks that stand in our path. It's not sitting on the sidelines or shirking from a fight. Hope is that thing inside us that insists, despite all evidence to the contrary, that something better awaits us if we have the courage to reach for it, and to work for it, and to fight for it. Hope is the belief that destiny will not be written for us, but by us, by the men and women who are not content to settle for the world as it is, who have the courage to remake the world as it should be.'

Look up the video online. It sounds even better with the soundtrack of his voice!

Here are three statements that I have heard all my life, and I suspect you have too. You might even have said them. They are all wrong, really irritating, and they help the cynics.

1. It doesn't matter who I vote for, because nothing ever changes. So I might as well not bother voting.

2. Politicians are all the same – they're only in it for themselves. So I might as well not bother being interested.

3. It's impossible for one person to make a difference. So I might as well not bother trying.

Let's focus for now on the first and second of those three infuriatingly cynical, and wrong-headed, statements.

Honestly! 'Nothing ever changes!!' How can anyone even begin to say that? Do they never look at pictures of their parents at the same age, and observe how different everything about those pictures looks? Has their dad never bored them, as I have bored my children, with stories about what it was like having a black-and-white telly with just three channels, and with a button for each that you had to rise from your chair to 'turn over'? My brother Graeme used a snooker cue to do it, to save him having to get up! Or how the phone used to be a clunky thing that sat on a small table, plugged into a wall? 'What? No remotes? No mobiles? You're kidding me!'

Have their grandparents never told them of the days when not only was there no TV and no phone, let alone the Internet, but no instant hot water, and no inside toilet? And have they never read of their great- and great-great-grandparents' generations, for whom putting food on the table was often a struggle, infant mortality was at terrifyingly high levels, and average life expectancy for men and women was under forty-five? Amid the mood of negativity that seems so all-pervasive at times, and in the face of the myriad challenges besetting the world, it is sometimes easy to forget that in so many ways our lives are immeasurably richer and more secure than those of our ancestors.

Also, as we look on in despair at the lack of solidarity in global politics right now, the undermining of international organisations, the divisions ripping through the structures of the UN, the wars – there are currently forty-five armed conflicts in the Middle East and North Africa, thirty-five in Africa, twenty-one in Asia, seven in Europe, six in Latin America – we should remember that even when the world is divided, great global change can come. Helen Clark, who went from being prime minister of New Zealand to heading the United Nations Development Programme, says: 'Because we can't fix everything doesn't mean we can fix nothing. We are well off target on a lot of the major development goals, and the world is divided. But we know that whether it is better pandemic preparations, climate, getting a new treaty on the oceans, across a whole range of shared interests, we have to work on them and we have to do it together, whatever the obstacles.' To underline that no matter what the state of geopolitics in the world, change can still come, she reminded me: 'We recently celebrated the fortieth anniversary of the eradication of smallpox. That was achieved at the height of the Cold War.'

So, before anyone is tempted to echo the nonsense that nothing ever changes for the better, so there is no point trying, and no point taking an interest in politics, reflect on this great quote from Nelson Mandela: 'Everything is impossible – until you make it happen.' Now write it on a Post-it note, and stick it to your wall, your laptop, or the inside of your wallet or notebook.

Of all the people I have met in my life, Mandela is the one who made the hair on the back of my neck stand up every time I was in his presence. It wasn't just that I knew that both his name and his role in history would be remembered for ever. It was also that I was acutely aware of the scale of the change he had played such a central role in achieving.

'Everything is impossible – until you make it happen.'

Absorb that, then reflect on this:

Once upon a time, the slave trade was legal, and profitable for those who ran it.

Once upon a time, women couldn't vote, or own property.

Once upon a time, gay people had to live a lie. All the time. Everywhere.

Once upon a time, there were no controls on pollution.

Once upon a time, education was the preserve of the privileged.

Once upon a time, everyone had to pay for health treatment.

Once upon a time, there was no lower limit on what workers could be paid.

Politics was central to changing all of the above. Change may have taken too long. But it did come in the end, with a lot of people power en route, a lot of protest, argument and campaigning.

Turning to more recent times, I would argue that the government I worked for, led by Tony Blair, made significant change across a whole range of economic, social and constitutional issues. National Minimum Wage. Bank of England independence. Devolution in Scotland, Wales and Northern Ireland. Record NHS investment leading to the shortest waiting times since records began. Over 42,000 more teachers. More young people attending university than ever before. Crime down, police numbers up. Civil partnerships giving legal recognition to same-sex partners. Debt cancellation for the world's poorest countries. I could go on and on. I often do.

'What have the Romans ever done for us?' indeed.

Two of those advances, the minimum wage and the Scottish Parliament, were among the three founding policy goals of the Labour Party when it was founded in 1900. A free beer or whisky for the first person to guess what the third was? Too slow. It was abstinence from alcohol. Not exactly a vote-winner, but not a bad idea for many!

And what about sectarian violence in Northern Ireland? That

was another problem deemed impossible to tackle. There was no way you could stop the violence, no way you could get Catholics and Protestants to co-exist within democratic institutions, no way that you could hope that a new generation would grow up without the fear and terror that had defined the lives of their parents and grandparents. But it happened. Step by step. Endless, patient negotiations. First a broad acceptance that there would be no change to the constitutional position of Northern Ireland without the consent of the people, alongside an acceptance of equality for Nationalists. Then, after more negotiations, speeches, arguments, deadlines, initiatives, meetings, new processes and structures, the Good Friday Agreement. Then referendums in the North and the Republic of Ireland. Then legislation, more negotiations, more attempts at reconciliation. On and on and on.

I accept such changes take time. There is always so much opposition to overcome. There are so many people and organisations and arguments that have to come together to persuade, cajole and build the case. It always takes time. But change does come.

'Everything is impossible, until you make it happen.'

It saddens me to say so, but the Brexiteers are entitled to have that one on their walls too! The people who wanted to make it happen, made it happen. They fought for it – a tiny minority at the start, some dead by the time it happened – for years. They laid the ground for it. They persuaded powerful people to their side. They never gave up. They knew they needed a referendum, so fought for years for that. They got it. And then they won it. They didn't much care – certainly the campaign leaders didn't – whether what they said was true or not, what they did lawful or unlawful. They didn't much care about the consequences, or whether the promises they made to win failed to materialise when they won. Winning was all that mattered.

Like it or not, they won. They won on the politics. They pushed the law and the rules as far as they could go, and beyond. Politics.

They played hard and sometimes dirty. Politics. They won. They won because of the votes of those who could be bothered. By the same token, of course, they won because of the apathy of those who couldn't. So, I can blame Cameron for holding and failing to win the referendum, Johnson and Farage and co for the lies told to win it. But I also blame the people who couldn't be arsed, didn't think it mattered, didn't appreciate just how much was at stake for them and their children, didn't care about the scale of change that was potentially on the ballot, thought, 'nothing ever changes', and 'they're all the same anyway', so 'what's the point? . . . It is what it is.'

The current situation with Brexit, albeit in a depressingly negative fashion, shows how change once thought unthinkable can become the status quo. With the populist virus affecting Johnson's successors in the same way it affected him, with Labour insisting they will 'make Brexit work', and the Lib Dems also largely silent on the issue, and only the SNP, Plaid and the Greens really calling out the Brexit realities, it would appear to be the settled will of our politics that the Brexit decision cannot be revisited. 'Going back' is never the most exciting campaign cry, though, my God, the Tories have taken us backwards on so many fronts in the years since they 'took back control' (*sic*). It is quite something that once upon a time leaving the single market was a red line that even the most extreme Brexiteers said should not be crossed. Now, despite all the damage, it is a return to the single market that is a red line not just for the Tories but also Labour, even though most of their MPs, members and voters know in their hearts that such a hardline stance is making things worse.

But, of course, if converting the country to Brexit was possible, so is restoring it to sanity. The realities will mount, and eventually those realities will force politicians to face up to them. There are the ones that could be termed frustrating inconveniences (when I was on a break in France in the summer it took me forty minutes at the local post office to complete all the paperwork needed to send a good-luck gift to our comedian daughter Grace ahead of her opening night at the Edinburgh Fringe). But there are also the ones that are having, and will continue to exert, an existential impact. Former Bank of England governor Mark Carney has pointed out how the UK economy fell from being 90 per cent the size of Germany's economy in 2016 to 70 per cent in 2022. The Tories immediately responded by condemning Carney as a bitter Remoaner – that one again – and blaming Covid and the war in Ukraine, dodging the obvious fact that Germany, and all other countries, were hit by those events too. At a time when the focus is increasingly on the state of global and national economies, Brexit is our elephant in the room.

So, those who believe Brexit was an appalling mistake, masterminded by Sovereign Individual ideologues, should take comfort from that 'Everything is impossible, until you make it happen' mantra. I for one am not moving on until the lies and the crimes have been fully exposed and understood. I will not stop calling out the damage Brexit is doing to our economy, our society, our culture and our standing in the world. I will continue to point out that Brexit was a decision made by one generation, in response to a campaign led by a now utterly discredited leader, that will affect all generations to come. Those younger generations have every right to fight to have the decision revisited. At the absolute minimum they deserve to have the specific problems Brexit has created revisited in a way that will help promote the prosperity the politicians promise. If change can be for the worse, it can also be for the better.

If the 'It is what it is' philosophy encourages people to be cynical about change for the better, it also makes them highly sceptical about the people whose responsibility it is to drive that change. Time and time again I encounter the view that politicians are 'only in it for themselves', that they're at best career opportunists and at worst corrupt politically, financially and morally. After all, we live in a world where Donald Trump and Boris Johnson can make it to the highest office in their respective countries.

But are all politicians really the same?

Consider these pairings of names:

Donald Trump and Hillary Clinton

Donald Trump and Joe Biden

Bolsonaro and Lula

Boris Johnson and Jeremy Corbyn

Liz Truss and Keir Starmer

Scott Morrison and Anthony Albanese

Emmanuel Macron and Marine Le Pen

Vladimir Putin and Alexei Navalny

All the same?

There are, of course – and always have been – rogues and charlatans in public life. Given recent events, I can completely understand where my headteacher friend, Andrew O'Neill, from All Saints Catholic College in west London, is coming from when he says: 'How the hell are we supposed to teach children right and wrong, and that it is never good to lie or cheat, when we have seen our prime minister and Cabinet caught lying on multiple occasions and also playing fast and loose with the truth day in day out?' I also find it deeply alarming for the country, and the future of our politics, that it took a Labour leader, Keir Starmer, amid Johnson's Covid law-breaking, to remind Tory MPs that it was Margaret Thatcher, in the 1975 speech I mentioned earlier, who said: 'Any country or government which wants to proceed towards tyranny starts to undermine legal rights and undermine the law.' The fish rots from the head.

However, judging from my days both as journalist and political adviser, and having known and worked with many, many politicians, I would strongly argue that the corrupt, the cynical and the selfish are in a minority. Most MPs I have known are decent people. Some are unbearably dull, some are not very bright, some are both, and as a journalist wandering around Westminster you develop the skills to avoid those ones, alongside the skills needed to find the ones you want to see. Some have very bad breath, but seemingly nobody to tell them. Some can be pompous, a trait not helped by getting those two letters after their name, or the word 'Lord' or 'Baroness' before it. Some can be unutterably vain and self-important. Given how important communication and public speaking are in politics, it is sometimes shocking to reflect that many cannot communicate effectively, deliver a decent speech or make sense in an interview. Some have had an empathy bypass, others a charisma bypass, others seem hopelessly out of touch with the real world.

But many are thoughtful, passionate about their politics and the places and people they represent, reasonably and sometimes very intelligent, and interested in the world around them. Most are ambitious, and that is not a bad thing, though typically their ambitions will never be entirely fulfilled – a remarkable number assume themselves to be prime minister or chancellor material. Most want a profile for themselves, and that is not a bad thing either, provided they are using it for good. Most work hard, don't make a fortune, never will, and are genuinely motivated by the idea that politics can and should be a vehicle for making life better for the people who sent them to Parliament. I would say the same for the elected members of the Scottish and Welsh

Parliaments, the Northern Ireland Assembly, mayors, councillors and elected members of other democratic bodies around the UK – and for elected politicians in many democracies worldwide.

I am sure many of you will remember the scandal of MPs' expenses in 2009. A small number of MPs went to jail. Others charged the public purse for the most ridiculous of claims and were rightly condemned in the court of public opinion. But would it surprise you to know that the overwhelming majority did *not* fiddle their expenses? We hear a lot about bullying and sexual harassment in Parliament, and it is absolutely right that where it exists it is properly exposed and tackled. It is right, too, that the media focus on those breaches of acceptable standards. But it is again worth reflecting that whatever disgust and anger you feel when you read about an MP's misconduct is shared by the bulk of their colleagues, who do not indulge in such behaviour. There is a risk, if we convince ourselves that Parliament really is a cesspit of humanity, that good people who might think of politics as a career are further deterred.

I don't say this in a partisan way, either. I can think of plenty of politicians with whom I profoundly disagree who I nevertheless regard as essentially decent and honest people. When I think, for example, of politicians motivated by those Nolan Principles – Honesty, Openness, Objectivity, Selflessness, Integrity, Accountability, Leadership – I would definitely include Neil Kinnock, the Labour leader who played a big part in inspiring me to switch from being a general news reporter to becoming a political journalist. But I would also include the politician he faced across the despatch box, Margaret Thatcher. As a political reporter for much of her premiership, I disagreed with a huge amount that she did, found her manner overbearing and patronising, and felt she was insufficiently cognisant or caring of the social implications of her economic policies. I therefore wrote hundreds, indeed thousands, of negative stories and comment pieces about her.

But if I match her against those seven principles, and then do the same for Johnson, Truss and Sunak, I would say she wins seven nil. And when she died, I found myself reflecting that irrespective of her faults and the policies that I had strongly opposed, she was a leader who had courage and beliefs, which she used to drive enormous change, cared passionately about the UK's strength and standing in the world, and was in public service to serve the public as she saw best, not to serve herself.

Not only do I dispute the line that all politicians are the same, I also think it's a very dangerous view to take. It encourages disengagement – which is a gift to malevolent people like Trump and Johnson, and people blatantly not up to the job like Truss, because it provides them with a clear path to the top. It also suits the interests of populists in power, because if the public think 'they're all as bad as each other', they're likely to come to the passive conclusion that they should 'stick with the devil we know'. It's worth bearing in mind the dictum of the nineteenth-century philosopher and parliamentarian John Stuart Mill that 'Bad men need nothing more to compass their ends, than that good men should look on and do nothing.' Or, as he also put it: 'A person may cause evil to others not only by his action but by his inaction, and in either case he is justly accountable to them for the injury.' A message never more relevant than today, I would argue. We must engage. We cannot stand by.

The other great mistake of believing the 'all the same' charge is that it can lead to so many people assuming that there is no place for them in politics. I am, for example, always amazed at many school students' assumption that you have to have a degree to be an MP, simply because so many of the more vociferous politicians currently at Westminster happen to possess one. We have had several prime ministers who never went to university, notably Winston Churchill and, more recently, Jim Callaghan and John Major. There is a lot wrong with politics, not least of which are the barriers of class and clique that allow Oxbridge (especially Oxford), as well as Eton, Harrow, Westminster, Winchester and the other top private schools, to act as a kind of conveyor belt for a certain type of person who has their eye on Downing Street and other citadels of power. However, despite that, the truth is that you absolutely do not have to come from a particular class or background to find a way into politics and become an MP. Limiting your own horizons in this way is a terrible mistake. Though there is a lot of focus on privately educated MPs, not least in the Cabinet, the fact is that around 70 per cent of MPs were not privately educated. Ninety-nine of the MPs elected at the 2019 general election did not have a university education.

Here is the thing . . . there was nothing in my background to suggest that I would do the kind of job I ended up doing in politics. My father Donald was a vet, my mother Elizabeth, who not only had the same name as the Queen, but was born in the same week, called herself a 'full-time wife and mother, the two hardest jobs in the world'. They watched the news a bit, they read a paper from time to time, and had the *Sunday Post* sent down from Scotland every week, but it was not what I would call a political household.

If you had said to the eighteen-year-old me that one day I would be running election campaigns that changed the government of the country, I would have worried for you. If you'd said back then that I would be part of a tiny audience in the White House treated to a Stevie Wonder–Elton John duet organised by Bill Clinton, I would have given you odds of many millions to one. If you'd suggested I would ever have seen Nelson Mandela in the flesh – at the time he was thirteen years into his 27-year imprisonment – let alone discussed with him how to reconcile the hatreds of the past in South Africa; or met other presidents and prime ministers, kings and queens, and been asked my advice on issues they were dealing with; or that I would be in the room when peace in Northern

Ireland was made; or be seconded to NATO to modernise their strategic comms, I would not even have been able to compute why you were saying it. Nor would my parents. (As it was, they found it hard to understand. 'Can you not get them to stop talking about you on the radio, Ali?' my mum once asked me in the aftermath of the Iraq War, 'If I lose any more weight worrying about you, there'll be nothing left of me.')

And if you had said that because of the profile and notoriety I would develop, I would end up, at forty-nine years old, playing football with Diego Maradona and several other World Cup winners in front of 72,000 people for the first UNICEF Soccer Aid at Old Trafford, I would have said: 'Oh please, please, make that happen.' It did. I have mentioned it to someone every day since, and shall do so till the day I die. When great things happen to you, treasure them. As I say whenever someone says to me: 'You people are just all the same' . . . 'Oh yeah? Find me someone else in politics who has played football with Pelé and Maradona!'

Helping Labour win three elections in a row . . . impossible, until it happened.

Playing, aged almost fifty, with Diego Armando Maradona . . . impossible, until it happened.

I'll leave you to guess which gave me the greater pleasure . . .

So, if I am speaking in schools or colleges, I always say to students: do not feel limited by your own background or upbringing. John Major was from a very poor family. He became a Tory prime minister. Margaret Thatcher sounded like the Queen having elocution lessons. Her dad was a grocer. Rishi Sunak may be married to one of the wealthiest women in the world, but he served in a Cabinet (and later resigned from that Cabinet) alongside Sajid Javid, whose dad was a bus driver (as was London mayor Sadiq Khan's father).

Some of the most inspiring politicians I know are those who have overcome particular obstacles to make a career in politics.

To take three of my favourite Labour MPs of all time: David Blunkett was blind, Jack Ashley was deaf, and Anne Begg was in a wheelchair. Very different people, in very different circumstances, but they were all able to see off prejudices and practical difficulties to live a life of public service, to make a real difference and bring about change– not just in the example they set but in what they achieved with the platform and the influence they developed.

We can't all be – and may not choose to be – MPs. But we can all be change-makers, and we can all make a positive difference, if we decide to. Making the decision to make change happen – that can be the most important step of all. Then it's all about what you want the change to be, and how you intend to make it happen.

8.

Develop a Campaigning Mindset

So much for two of the three lazy and cynical statements I find so irritating: 'It doesn't matter who I vote for, because nothing ever changes' and 'Politicians are all the same – they're only in it for themselves'. Now for the third: 'It's impossible for one person to make a difference, so I might as well not bother trying.'

It's just not true. 'Am I bovvered?' was a brilliant comic line made famous by comedian Catherine Tate. However, it is the worst possible philosophy for life. Being bovvered matters, now more than ever.

Think about it: if no one person could ever make a difference to the world, nothing would ever change. The belief that change can come, and that you as an individual can make it happen, is essential to what I consider to be one of the most important insights I can offer you: campaigning is a mindset. As to what that means in practice, that depends in part on the nature of the campaign, and the nature of the individual, or team, involved.

Last November, as the Truss implosion saw the Labour Party steam ahead in the polls, the senior management at party HQ asked me to go in and talk to the staff. Both they and I were happy to overlook the fact that I had been expelled from the party under previous management. They wanted me to talk about the New Labour campaigns, the new political landscape since then, other campaigns I had worked on, and generally gee up the troops. So, I found myself picking my Post-it notes off my office wall and taking them in, to use as the basis of my talk. 'Campaigning is a mindset,' I said, inevitably, given it is one of the most important of my sticky messages to self.

As I left the building, a young woman was waiting for me by the lift on the ground floor. I recognised her from the meeting. She asked if I minded if she put a question to me that she had felt embarrassed to ask in front of her colleagues.

'Not at all,' I said. 'Go ahead.'

'When you say campaigning is a mindset, what do you mean?'

As I answered, I realised that what I was telling her was about my own mindset, when in campaign mode. Reflecting on our exchanges later, when I sat down to write a more considered reply, I realised that this would not necessarily apply to everyone. So I tried to boil it down further, to principles which might apply to anyone. In asking me what I meant, she forced me to try to answer that very question: what do I mean when I say that campaigning is a mindset? She made me think in ink. You will hear that one again later.

The answer I came up with, for me and the way that I tend to campaign, is that you need to be a little bit, or even very, obsessive. I said I would be very worried if there had *not* been a number of obsessives among the Labour team I had been speaking to. However, I recognise that is not possible, or healthy, for everyone to be obsessive. Indeed, the young woman, who had read my diaries, said she could not imagine herself ever working as hard as I seemed to do, nor dealing with so many complicated and stressful issues at the same time. In the course of my life, I have had full-time campaigning jobs which not only allowed me to be obsessive, but required this quality of me. Most campaigners, however, have lots of other personal and professional commitments, and finding the right balance is not easy. Also, as my partner Fiona will testify, my obsessiveness, whilst I hope it can be an asset in terms of the energy, commitment and creativity I can bring to a cause when in campaign mode, can also be a danger to my health, and to the well-being of those around me. That, too, is obvious from my diaries, though I was less aware of that at the time. Again, getting the balance right is not easy and I often failed to do so. My GP once told me I was operating at normalised stress levels that most people could not cope with for a week, let alone a year or a decade. He believed my various ailments – depression, ulcerative colitis, asthma, recurring nasal polyps and chest infections – were all at least in part fuelled by my work. Interestingly, the colitis, which on diagnosis I was told would be with me for life and was likely to morph into Crohn's disease, vanished – 'miraculously', said my bowel specialist – a few years after I left Downing Street.

What I wrote to the young Labour staffer was that she might or might not have the character and capacity for the kind of full-on obsessiveness that I felt, and still feel, is important to the way I campaign. But if she does not, that is fine, because though you want some full-on obsessives in a campaign, if that is all you have, it could be a recipe for disaster. I suggested, therefore, that in her case a campaign mindset might simply mean that she ensures that there is always a part of her mind that is in campaign mode: alert and alive to opportunities that present themselves, keen to persuade anyone she can, always thinking about new and creative ways of fighting for the cause she believes in. For her, in practical terms, this meant seeking ways to bring about the re-election of the Labour Party and, alongside that, pressing for the devotion of more resources to voter mobilisation among the young (a cause, she told me, she felt particularly strongly about).

I told her that when I was a young journalist, an old mentor of mine, Syd Young, who became one of my closest friends and sadly passed away during the Covid pandemic, said to me: 'There is a story in everyone you meet.' That insight came to occupy a place at the centre of my journalist mindset. 'Everyone is interesting. Everyone has something worth hearing to say. Everyone is worth engaging with.' I take that same attitude to campaigning. If I meet someone who tells me there is no point getting involved, or that all politicians are the same, or that no one person can make a difference, I try to persuade them they are wrong. If I meet someone who is really wealthy, I try to probe their philanthropic tendencies, work out their interests, establish whether they might be interested in backing any of the campaigns and causes I am involved in. It might be as simple as trying to get money out of them for a campaign. Or, it might be about mining their ideas, experience, energy and contacts.

More important than anything in the campaign mindset, I believe, is the point about being alert and alive to opportunities in whatever set of circumstances you find yourself. The reason I never stop 'banging on' (a phrase used disparagingly in the main, but which I take as a badge of pride) about things I really care about – Labour, Brexit, mental health, political and media standards, the Tories getting away with stuff the other parties wouldn't – is because when I meet people, and I spot opportunities to boost campaigns I support, the conversation has effectively already begun if they know what my basic standpoints are.

I can mention my football club, Burnley, in the same context. We are doing very well in the Championship just now, having had a long spell in the Premier League, and at the time of writing we are on course to be back there by the time the book comes out, the season ending in the same week as publication. But not that many years ago we were close to administration. I helped put together a fundraising campaign to save the club. The fact that those I contacted knew about my love for the club, because I'd 'banged on' about it privately and publicly all my life, was a benefit when it came to calling in favours from friends, generating media, asking for money. I did not 'save the club'. But I was part of a campaign that did, and I like to think my campaigning mindset helped in that.

The young Labour staffer wrote back a couple of days later, just to thank me for taking the trouble to write, and then again after about ten days. She said she had heard two people on her bus home complaining about the government. One of them had then said that Labour were no better, and that all they ever did was complain. 'I had been at a meeting that morning and we had been working on a broadcast about the economy. I had the script in my bag and got it out and started talking to them. Is that a campaign mindset?'

'Yes, it is,' I replied. 'And I hope by the end of the journey you had got them signed up as members!'

I study change-makers not merely because they tend to be interesting, but because of what I can learn from them. There are so many examples of people, both those you've heard of and those you haven't, who have single-handedly made real and lasting change, because they fought for it until they won. They had that campaign mindset! Role models can come in so many different forms – young and old, dead and alive – and we should never underestimate either our need for them, or their capacity to be part of the change we try to make.

I suspect that many among my daughter's generation may not be familiar with the name of former Liberal MP David Steel. And it is possible, of course, that whether he had been in Parliament or not, the law on abortion would have evolved from the highly restrictive form that drove so many desperate women to seek back-street abortions (in the 1920s, 15 per cent of all maternal deaths were due to these) to the infinitely more liberal law we have today. But we can't know that for sure. What we do know is that the big change was secured by Steel's Private Member's Bill in 1967. He drove it, securing sufficient support in government and across Parliament for the changes he was proposing. And, after a passionate, often heated, political, ethical and moral debate in Parliament and across the country, he saw passed into law an Abortion Act that legalised abortions – funded by the NHS and carried out by registered practitioners – with certain restrictions and in particular circumstances. That act remains the basis of our abortion laws today.

When David Steel leaves us – he is now in his mid-eighties – the obituaries will doubtless focus on the fact that he led the Liberals for twelve years, including through several elections. They may also mention that he resigned his seat in the House of Lords in 2020, after an independent inquiry into child sexual abuse criticised his failure to investigate allegations of abuse against Liberal MP Cyril Smith. The Abortion Act, however, represents a real legacy. It's a shining example of an MP taking up an issue and building a campaign to get legislation passed to make the change he believed in; displaying an unrelenting campaign mind-set; having the willingness and capacity to endure all the abuse and brickbats that came his way; having both the political and communications skills to develop and win complicated, difficult arguments through passion, conviction and knowledge.

Recently, Fiona and I attended a reception hosted by Commons speaker Lindsay Hoyle to celebrate Harriet Harman's fortieth anniversary as an MP. As first the speaker, then Keir Starmer, and, finally, Harriet's friend and colleague Margaret Hodge laid out the political milestones in Harriet's life, it became clearer and clearer just how much she had achieved: as a constituency MP, a women's rights campaigner, a minister legislating for some of New Labour's most important advances, and in two spells as interim leader of the Labour Party. It was Harriet's idea to establish the Low Pay Commission, which built support from both employers and unions for the introduction of a minimum wage. Maternity rights, paternity leave, childcare support, Sure Start, broader welfare reform – Harriet was at the forefront of all of them. She led campaigns to change people's attitudes to domestic violence and people trafficking, as well as helping to introduce tougher laws to combat both. I remember her fighting for a commitment to the Equality Act in the 2005 manifesto, which updated existing legislation and brought in greater protection against discrimination with regard to age, disability, gender reassignment, marriage and civil partnership, pregnancy and maternity, race, religion or belief, sex, and sexual orientation. When you look at how far to the right Tory home secretaries Priti Patel and Suella Braverman have moved the dial on some of these issues, coupled with justice secretary Dominic Raab's dismissive attitude to the European Convention on Human Rights, I think it is fair to make the case that the Act has helped take the edge off some of the worst excesses of Tory legislation since Labour lost power.

However, it was in her leadership role in the battle for women's rights and representation that she really shone. There was a time when there were no women's toilets in Parliament, let alone women MPs, women Cabinet ministers or women prime ministers. Arriving in Parliament in 1982, seven months pregnant and one of just ten women Labour MPs, she really was a trailblazer. Today, more than half of Labour's MPs are women, and I am sure all will testify to Harriet's support and inspiration.

Harriet and I had a few difficult episodes down the years, both political and personal, but what I saw at the reception was a very special woman and a very special parliamentarian, who really will have a remarkable legacy to look back on when finally, at the next election, she leaves the Commons. A good MP can make an enormous difference to their constituency and also to the world beyond. Harriet Harman is one such MP. And she is not the only one.

If change can come from individual politicians deciding to prioritise particular campaigns, it will almost always involve people outside the system working in tandem with them. Paula Sherriff was a Labour MP when, in 2016, she led and won a parliamentary fight to secure an amendment to the Budget finance bill that removed VAT on feminine hygiene products, so ending the so-called 'tampon tax.' But many outside Parliament were active in making the case for that reform, among them student Laura Coryton, who launched a change.org campaign that was crucial in gathering support. Ending the tampon tax may not have been a revolution per se, but thanks to a coalition between concerned members of the public and a determined backbench member of Parliament, it did change many people's lives for the better. Also, if I can be allowed a 'proud dad' moment, one of the proudest for me was when I stood in the crowd in Whitehall as one of a few men among hundreds of women listening to a succession of speeches by politicians and campaigners fighting to end period poverty, including one by my daughter Grace, who with her friend Scarlett Curtis had kickstarted the campaign. Paula Sherriff was there. 'You should be proud of her,' she said. I am.

In much the same way – people working with politicians – a key change to the legal status of civil partnerships came about through a seemingly unlikely alliance between campaigners and a Tory MP. This is a story that has a particular resonance for me, and that went to have a big effect on my life.

My partner Fiona and I have never wanted to get married: she for feminist reasons, me because I see marriage as a religious institution, and both of us because we don't 'do God'. One day seven Christmases ago, as we were driving to Scotland, we heard a young couple on the radio being interviewed about a legal challenge they were mounting to what Fiona had always felt to be a strange anomaly in the law governing relationships: legally recognised civil partnerships had been secured by gay couples, but they had not been extended to their heterosexual equivalents. Consequently, Charles Keidan and Rebecca Steinfeld told the interviewer, when they had gone to Chelsea Register Office to try to register their civil partnership, they had been refused.

So began their long legal and political campaign to take the government to court on the grounds that the law as it stood was discriminatory. Marriage was, by then, open to same sex and opposite sex couples, they pointed out, but civil partnerships were available only to the former. There's no doubt that Keidan and Steinfeld's willingness to share their story with the public helped their cause. So, too, did their crowd-funding campaign and their success in attracting organisational support – in this case the Joseph Rowntree Foundation. Fiona made contact with them and joined a small campaign steering group seeking to get the law changed.

With the Conservatives in power (whose leader David Cameron had legislated for same sex marriage), it was particularly important to get support from Conservative MPs. Help duly came in the unlikely form of Tim Loughton, generally thought to be on the right of the Tory Party. He felt strongly that if gay couples could be married *or* have a civil partnership, a man and a woman committed to each other should have the same choice. His support was vital. Charles and Rebecca took the case to the High Court, where they lost, then the Court of Appeal, where they lost again. But then they took it to the Supreme Court, where they won. Their victory paved the way for the government to change the law, the argument already having been advanced by Tim Loughton through a Private Member's Bill. The twin strategy, legal and parliamentary, worked. Fiona and I signed our civil partnership into law on a lovely sunny day during the Covid lockdown of March 2021, with our children, Rory, Calum and Grace, as witnesses.

Lib Dem MP Wera Hobhouse played a similar role to Loughton in a campaign led by a woman named Gina Martin. The story starts in June 2017, when Gina is at a festival, surrounded by a group of men, and sees to her horror that one of them has taken a picture of her up her skirt. She grabs his phone, and reports him to the police, with his device as evidence. The police, however, say he has not broken any law. There is nothing they can do. She goes public with the story, which attracts a lot of attention. Lawyers want to help. Wera Hobhouse also wants to help and tables a Private Members' Bill. However, a Tory MP, Christopher Chope, uses arcane parliamentary procedures to block it. By now, though, the campaign is sufficiently strong for the government to feel they have to take it up. I don't know if she does, but Gina should have a copy of the Voyeurism (Offences) Act 2019 on her wall, because she was the person who inspired it and secured the support of those in Parliament who could steer it through.

Or, across the Atlantic, look at Amanda Nguyen. Raped when she was studying at Harvard. Discovered that the rape laws were not fit for purpose. Fought to change them. Helped propose and draft the Sexual Assault Survivors' Rights Act, passed unanimously – rare in US politics – by Congress. She didn't stop there. She campaigned on other issues. Like many Asian Americans, she had been a victim of racism. She produced a video that received worldwide coverage and provided a huge boost for the Stop Asian Hate movement. And, in addition to training to be an astronaut, she then founded and is now CEO of Rise, a non-profit campaign that teaches grassroots organising, something that always has been, and always will be, so important in the world of activism and making change. She named her organisation Rise, she said, 'to remind us that a small group of thoughtful, committed citizens can rise up and change the world'.

There are also numerous cases around the world where new laws that are passed are known by the name of the person whose personal experience led their family to fight for change. Take Kristen's Law in the US, for example. It's named after Kristen Modafferi of Charlotte, North Carolina who disappeared aged eighteen, in 1997. Because she was an adult, her family couldn't use any of the nation's kidnapping resources to try to track her down. When it was signed into law in 2000, Kristen's Law created a National Center for Missing Adults. Sometimes even cats can get in on the act, as with Buster's Law. In the same year that Kristen Modafferi disappeared, a young thug from Schenectady, New York, Chester Williamson, doused a cat named Buster with kerosene before setting him alight. Amid the outrage that ensued, and the campaign it led to, Buster's Law made animal cruelty a felony within New York.

Powerful campaigns often arise from causes close to people's personal experience. That was certainly the case for Gina Martin and for Amanda Nguyen. For his part, Marcus Rashford took up the cause of food poverty among children after having grown up in challenging economic circumstances. As a famous footballer, he was able to use his fame to help mount a campaign which the media embraced, the Opposition backed and the government, ultimately, found harder and harder to ignore. Helped by a small but savvy team, he ran rings around the government by finally getting them to admit to the reality of children's food poverty. He shamed them into taking action they did not want to take, and he continues to do so. Gina Martin, Amanda Ngugen and Marcus Rashford all demonstrate one of my favourite Post-its in action. GGOOB: Get Good Out Of Bad.

Check out Amir Ashour, persecuted into exile for his beliefs; founder and executive director of IraQueer, Iraq's first and only LGBT+ human rights organisation. This is a culture where you will find doctors promoting the view that homosexuality is a mental illness, something rarely challenged by politicians or the media; and where a climate of hostility towards gays puts them at risk of discrimination, violence, torture and murder. The situation for trans people is even worse, he argues. Amir may have fled Iraq for Sweden in 2014, but he is still fighting for change. 'I try to channel the anger I have about what I experienced in Iraq into my work. One day, I will return to Iraq – despite the trauma and difficulty – because I want to change things in politics and law from the inside. I am very passionate about going back and hopefully helping to make it a place where those who violated our rights don't have space to operate.'

Check out Nathan Law, elected aged twenty-three to the Hong Kong Legislative Council (its youngest ever member), then expelled because he used the oath-taking ceremony to protest against the erosion of democratic rights. 'You can chain me, you can torture me, you can even destroy this body, but you will never imprison my mind,' he said. Later jailed for his role in organising protests, he is also now living in exile, in London. But the Chinese have not heard the last of him, or his activism.

That Amir Ashour and Nathan Law are so determined to Get Good Out Of Bad is even more praiseworthy given the personal risks they have run as a result. Campaigning is never easy, particularly if you come from a marginalised background or community (I love the honesty of Gina Martin when she asked: 'Would the coverage of my campaign have been the same had I been a black woman below the poverty line?'). But under dictatorships, or in repressive democracies, it is not merely difficult but positively dangerous. It's impossible not to be awed by individuals who risk their freedom and their lives to promote the causes they believe in. Think of the young women in Iran who in 2022 took to the streets, many shedding their hijabs and cutting off their hair, in protest at the death in custody of Mahsa Amini, a 22-year-old woman who had been arrested for wearing an 'improper' hijab. That the initial protests led to a deadly security crackdown, and yet the demonstrations continued despite it, underlines their courage.

Such campaigns don't always succeed in the short term, but that does not negate their importance. One always hopes for a positive and measurable result, such as those achieved by the likes of Charles Keidan and Rebecca Steinfeld, or Gina Martin.

Sometimes, though, it's more than enough to start shifting the debate in the right direction.

Think, for example, of Greta.

Isn't that remarkable? I just say her first name, and I reckon you immediately know who I am talking about. How many teenagers have ever been known the world over by their first name alone? OK, maybe I could think of a few pop stars, child actors, fictional characters . . . but Greta Thunberg is an environmental activist, for heaven's sake. She is living proof that it is cool to care! And caring – being 'bovvered' – is a big, big factor in any attempt to change the world for the better.

I doubt that when she first sat outside the Swedish Parliament in Stockholm on 20 August 2018, aged fifteen, with her 'Skolstrejk för Klimatet' placard, she ever imagined she would become the phenomenon that she has. So it is worth reflecting on how she's achieved this status, and so quickly.

First, the issue was crying out for new and more relatable voices and role models. Greta is authentic, interesting and unusual, having been diagnosed with Asperger's syndrome, OCD and selective mutism. She speaks with passion but also clarity and simplicity. She is strong in the face of criticism and fearless in the face of opponents. And she knows her stuff; she does detail. She was the *right person*. Second, she started her campaign in a country that has a broadly positive reputation in the world and that is not so large or polarised that an individual voice might simply be drowned out. *Right place.* And, finally, she marshalled support with a simple call to action when the evidence for her cause had become overwhelming. *Right time.*

It is virtually impossible to quantify the number of people around the world who have been inspired by the example she has set since she posted a picture of her solo protest to her relatively small number of followers on Twitter and Instagram (I was in Germany recently, listening to a local radio station, and heard someone being introduced as 'Bavaria's version of Greta Thunberg'). Today, she has close to five million followers on Twitter and almost fifteen million on Instagram. And, although she is barely twenty, she has spoken at the UN, addressed several parliaments, been nominated three times for a Nobel Peace Prize, been showered with awards around the globe, and has had four new species named after her: a beetle from Kenya, a land snail from Borneo, a spider from Madagascar and a New Zealand freshwater snail, *Opacuincola gretathunbergae*. If her many (often male, often old or middle-aged, often right-wing) detractors had done even a tiny fraction of what she has managed to achieve in her short time on earth, they might be worth listening to. She is my go-to example whenever anyone says: 'But it's impossible for one person to make a difference.'

Closer to my own generation, I would put the development double act of Bono and Bob Geldof in the same category, even if some among Greta's generation of campaigners think they are too close to the political and business elites they seek to influence. The fact is, they have influenced the world's decision-makers, and continue to do so, with a mix of conviction, knowledge and nous.

I also credit Bono with one of the best lines I ever heard about how to campaign. It was in Cologne, Germany, in 1999, where G8 leaders were meeting. The writing off of Third World debt was high on the agenda. But it was not high enough for Bono and Geldof, who came to Tony Blair's hotel room to demand more and faster action. Tony said that the leaders were making massive steps in the right direction, but his rock star visitors had to understand that in terms of what they were asking for, 'We are looking at Mount Everest.' To which Bono replied: 'When you see Everest, Tony, you don't look at it . . . you fucking climb it.' Now that, ladies and gentlemen, is a campaign mindset.

Of course, the cynics, particularly those with a vested interest in maintaining a status quo which helps their political and economic interests, want you to believe that such people as Greta or Bono cannot bring about big change on their own. Part of their battle is to stop you from thinking about making small changes too. 'What can I do to stop climate change? Is it really going to make that big a difference if I put that light out, recycle that bag, don't drive that car, don't go on that plane?' Well, no, set against the CO_2 being pumped into the atmosphere by big business, or the sewage poured into the rivers by water companies, it probably won't make a massive difference. But that doesn't mean it makes no difference at all. Just because you can't save the whole world, it doesn't mean you can't play your part in helping to save your bit of it. Just because you can't be Greta, it doesn't mean you can't be inspired by her to do your own bit too. The more people make conscious efforts to think about doing environmentally-friendly things, the more they become the norm in society. If you avoid single-use plastics, sooner or later someone will notice and ask about it. They might end up doing the same as you! Eventually, shops will realise that drinks in plastic bottles are not selling as well as cans, and they will start ordering fewer of them. That's one way change can happen. It's in our hands.

Not that many years ago, it was almost impossible to buy free-range meat in mainstream supermarkets. Now they all sell it. That's because a steady flow of people asked for it, refused to buy factory-farmed alternatives, and shopped elsewhere until it became available. It's a slow-burner in campaigning terms, but it can still be effective. I would argue that when you live by your own standards, and are true to your own beliefs, your confidence will soar, which is especially useful when you start spreading the word more widely. Living your life in a way that reflects the values you believe in and campaign for? That, too, is a campaign mindset.

So here am I, a 65-year-old man with a lot of experience of campaigning, who fairly regularly, believe it or not, gets messages from young people telling me I am their 'role model'. And yet I am, frankly, in awe of Greta Thunberg. I see her as a role model by whom I can be inspired and from whom I can learn: what she does and how she does it; how she deals with all the hate; how she just keeps going; and how she never loses the campaign mindset that is absolutely vital if you are to provide leadership in making real change.

Let me turn to another personal role model, someone I suspect most of you have never heard of, and someone I never met: Miep Gies.

Throughout the German occupation of Holland during the Second World War, Gies was one of the tiny number of non-Jewish 'helpers' who knew that hiding in an annexe concealed behind a bookcase in Prinsengracht 263, Amsterdam, were Anne Frank and her family, the van Pels family, and a dentist who ended up sharing a room with Anne. Gies's 'campaign' was to keep the Frank family alive. She would source and deliver food as well as books – which Anne devoured – and organise others to do the same. But it is for her role in bringing Anne Frank's diary to the attention of the world that Gies deserves perhaps the greatest admiration, and indeed a place in history.

On the day in August 1944 that the eight hidden inhabitants of the secret rooms were betrayed, Gies went back to the house on Prinsengracht after the police had left, and discovered the notebooks in which Anne had been recording her thoughts and experiences. Anne and her sister Margot died of typhus in Belsen a few weeks before the war ended. Only one of the eight – their beloved father Otto, who was sent to Auschwitz – survived. When Gies learned he was still alive, and Anne dead, she found him and handed him the books. Stunned when he read them, he effectively devoted the rest of his life to promoting the story his daughter had told, for more than two years, in letters to an imaginary friend, Kitty. One particular line in the diary of this girl who had ambitions to be a writer or journalist takes my breath away: 'I want to live on, even after my death.' That she has is down to Miep Gies, who died a month short of her 101st birthday on 11 January 2010, proving that the good don't *always* die young.

Gies's example reminds me of a concept introduced to me by Alex Smith, founder of The Cares Family, who uses it in his work linking young people with old, to the benefit of both. It is called the '200-year present' and it embraces the notion that there are people with us now who were alive 100 years ago, and there are people here today who will be alive another 100 years from now – and that in the course of that 200-year span the world will transform many, many times.

I take a lot of comfort from that thought, for several reasons. First, although it may make us feel insignificant, I also believe that it can give us hope that, at a time of division, the future remains in our hands. We still have the power to shape our fate, just as previous generations shaped theirs. Second, it is another great weapon in the fight to dispel the myth that nothing ever changes. How much did the world change in the lifespan of Miep Gies? How much more will it change in the century after her death? Who makes that change? We do. People. It's up to us. We can innovate and campaign to make change for the better, or just sit it out.

Third, it is possible to be so consumed by everything that is going on, day by day, hour by hour, even minute by minute, that our sense of long-term change gets obscured to the point of invisibility. Stepping back and thinking of the 200-year span can provide a clearer perspective. And fourth, it allows you to reflect that, often, history is not defined merely by those who make the headlines, but by those who are doing great things we do not even know about at the time. Can you remember the name of the Dutch monarch, or the head of the Dutch government-in-exile at the time Anne Frank was writing? No? Me neither. But we all know Anne Frank. And now you know, and I hope you will remember, Miep Gies. Is it too much to imagine that when the history of the period we are living through is written, it will be defined less by the Trumps, Johnsons, Netanyahus, Putins and Bolsonaros of the world, than by people yet to come to public prominence?

Maybe it is. But it won't stop me hoping that, out there right now, there are people, possibly some reading this book, of whom we are largely unaware, but who are thinking, saying, writing, campaigning and doing things that ultimately will help to set the world on a different and better course. Bizarrely, for all the horrors of the context, and the knowledge we have from the very first page that Anne Frank's life will end so young, her diary somehow leaves you feeling more hopeful.

In January 2022, to celebrate the seventy-fifth anniversary of the publication of the diary, I attended a wonderful event in London, a fundraising lunch for the Anne Frank Trust. My personal highlight of the event was a presentation by fifteen school pupils, from Rotherham, Ilford and Dundee, who read extracts from the diary, interspersed with accounts of prejudice, bigotry and ignorance from today – and also their hopes for the future. A girl bullied for wanting to play cricket; a young girl of Asian heritage confronted by white youths who told her it was 'beat up a Muslim day'; a boy with autism constantly teased and told he was 'weird'. It was all incredibly moving, sad at times, but hopeful, because they had hope, and because they found their hope strengthened by the message of Anne Frank's diary, and the story of her life. A role model who died aged sixteen, never knowing how famous she would become, now inspiring others, decades after her death, to take up campaigns on issues of which she would barely have been aware.

At the event, I was on a table right at the front, with a close-up view of the guest of honour, the then duchess of Cornwall, as she lit a candle with Holocaust survivors, including Anne Frank's 92-year-old step-sister Eva Schloss, and other victims of hatred, and made a speech. I was impressed, both by its content and her delivery – and I speak as a lifelong republican who had a major swoon for Princess Diana, her rival for Prince Charles' hand and heart.

Camilla spoke of her visit to Auschwitz in 2020, saying she would 'never forget' a speech given by Marian Turski, a Holocaust survivor who had talked about the laws discriminating against Jews in Nazi Germany in the 1930s, and the relevance of this to our own time. 'He described how people – victims, perpetrators and witnesses – can gradually become desensitised to the exclusion, the stigmatisation and the alienation of those who have previously been friends. Marian warned us that this can happen again. But he gave us, too, the answer to preventing it. "You should never, ever be a bystander." Let us not be bystanders to injustice or prejudice. After all, surely our personal values are measured by the things we are prepared to ignore.'

I love that line. It should inspire us all. It is at the heart of the campaigning mindset. Be like Miep Gies. Never be a bystander. Don't ignore. Fight for the change you believe in.

9.

Be a Leader

Anyone who decides to fight for the change they believe in needs constantly to bear in mind the following trinity of campaign essentials.

Campaigns need leaders.

Leaders need teams.

Teams need strategies.

None of the three – leaders, teams and strategies – can exist without the other two. All three draw strength from each other. Leadership, teamship, strategy. My Holy Trinity.

But let's start with leadership.

Some years ago, I was at a conference on leadership in Canada, making a speech that drew on my experience of working with different leaders in politics, sport and business. As at any big conference, there were different speakers and panels, lots of stories and concepts to digest, and, frankly, by the time I was home, I had forgotten most of what I had heard. But one thing stuck in my mind, and I have thought of it many times since.

On one of the panels, a Canadian maritime historian said that when he was growing up, his father told him that the reason for the '-ship' suffix in 'leadership' was that the word was first used many years ago in the context of ice-breakers. Not ice-breakers as in team-bonding exercises, or conversational openers, but ice-breakers as in ships that smash through ice when the water has frozen over. 'The ships needed to get out to sea,' his father told him, 'to fish, to transport people and goods, to keep the wheels of the economy turning. But ships cannot sail on ice. So the ice-breaker was the lead ship, and that is where the word leadership comes from. It is, literally, the lead ship. It cut through the ice, and as it did so the waters opened and widened behind it, and the other ships could follow.'

The historian said that that image had helped inspire his passion for the subject to which he would devote his professional life. He also admitted that he could find very little factual evidence to back up his father's story.

Maybe that is why this account of the word's etymology so appealed to him as a child, and to me as an adult interested in the concept of leadership, and intrigued by words and where they came from. It is just a *story*. But there is power in the myth. Reflect for a moment on the imagery. Waters frozen over. The 'leadership' cuts through the ice, showing strength, purpose and a clear sense of direction, as leaders must. It sails on, displaying calm and determination in overcoming obstacles, as leaders must, to open up space for others to follow, as leaders must, so that the followers too may contribute to, and benefit from, the change the leader is making. Those followers then go about their own business, make their own way.

Like the historian, I, too, have failed to find historical evidence to back up his father's account of how the word 'leadership' came about, but it remains one of my favourite stories and images of the concept. And when I think of great leaders and great leadership, from Lincoln to Mandela, from Queen Victoria to the recently departed Queen Elizabeth, that ship leading the way through troubled waters, destiny and full steam ahead, often comes to mind. Perhaps that's why so many ships are named after great leaders.

An entire industry has built up around leadership. Whole librar-
ies are full of books and academic studies devoted to the subject.
This is a reflection both of how much it matters, and also of how
multifaceted it is. Most of the books available are, like the Canadian historian's dad, trying to distil this complex idea in a simple
way, and pass on clear, obvious lessons.

Yet although the history of humanity is substantially written
through the life stories of people we identify as leaders, such as
those I list above, the word leadership itself dates back just two
centuries, to 1821. Variations of the word leader go much further
back, though, interestingly enough, there is no ultimate Latin or
Greek origin for the words lead or leader. The Latin word that
gets closest in meaning is '*ducere*', which translates as 'to lead,
consider, regard'. It survives in modern Romanian (a language directly descended from Latin) as '*conducere*', which means leading
and leadership. '*Conducere*' summons up images of conducting,
as in leading the orchestra. At the same time, the 'con' element,
which derives from the Latin for 'with', reminds us that the leader
needs other people. He or she cannot do it alone.

Dig a little deeper into the history of the words attached to
leadership, and you start to see why it has bred that industry
analysing its complexity, because it contains so many tasks and
challenges. It is about setting goals. Steering a course. Giving direction. Giving guidance. Encouraging and exhorting. Hiring and
firing. Orchestrating and, at times, manipulating. Enabling and
facilitating. Inspiring and motivating. The great leaders take their
teams with them, head and heart.

Leadership cannot just be about power. The leaders who rely
purely on the power and status their position gives them are
unlikely to succeed in the long term. It's why most dictatorships
eventually end in disaster, not just for the dictated, but the dicta-
tor too – even if it can take a long time for the disaster to unfold.
It's why, perhaps today more than at any time in history, high EQ

as well as high IQ is required for a leader to maximise his or her own potential as well as the potential of their team. Just as we should consider physical and mental health to be two sides of the same coin, so intellectual and emotional intelligence work hand in hand. The best leaders have both.

People we might define as unintelligent are unlikely to make good leaders, even if they might be able to make up for some of their analytical and intellectual weaknesses through high emotional intelligence. But, equally, there are plenty of very clever people who make terrible leaders, because they lack the emotional intelligence required to lead, to inspire, motivate, organise.

People with high EQ are good at sensing, appreciating and understanding the feelings and interests of others. They are also good at understanding and, where necessary, regulating, their own feelings and interests. The self-awareness point is every bit as important as the ability to relate to others. Leaders who are able both to recognise and assess their own strengths and weaknesses, while genuinely relating to other people, are likely to make better decisions, build stronger relationships and teams, enjoy work more, and reduce stress and conflict among others. Leaders who are able to recognise and assess their own emotions – the ups and downs we all experience – are less likely to allow them to affect their judgement and therefore more able to provide consistent, stable leadership. For example, a leader with high EQ experiencing stress or anger has tactics to help them deal with those feelings, rather than be overwhelmed by them, and so risk overwhelming the team.

Emotional intelligence is so much more than empathy, important though empathy is. It is also about a familiarity with our basic motivations, the things that move us to do what we do, and to keep wanting to do them even when we face setback, failure and defeat. No campaign worth winning is ever going to be easy, and when the setbacks come, it can be hard to stay motivated. That is when emotional intelligence reserves get called upon. We have to remind ourselves why we do what we do – the campaign goals and values – rather than focusing on the setback in the moment. People with low motivation are more likely to give up quickly, or undermine the work and ideas of others, to the detriment of what the leader is trying to do. So they need to be re-motivated. Motivated people like to work, have new ideas, love feedback and debate, are always looking to improve. Leaders have to set that example. Motivation, like confidence, can be contagious. There's another benefit of a developed or high EQ: the ability to predict the likely actions and reactions of opponents and others outside the team. This is valuable, if not crucial, for planning good strategy and for knowing how and when to introduce new policy. And, even if we might get set in our ways with age, the brain's plasticity means we can always add to our emotional intelligence skills if we work at it. Some are lucky, and are born and raised with high emotional intelligence. But it can be learned, too, not least by studying those who use it well.

'Incredible leader, very ordinary coach.' That's Peter Schmeichel, one of the greatest goalkeepers in football history, describing his former Manchester United boss, Alex Ferguson, one of the greatest managers of all time. I am sure most football fans, and others, would assume that it would be impossible to be simultaneously a great manager and an indifferent coach. Not according to his goalkeeper. 'He wasn't a very good coach,' Schmeichel told me.

> Brian Kidd, who was my coach for seven and a half of my eight years, was a brilliant coach. Oh my God. Love him. Absolutely fantastic. And Steve McLaren for the last six months. And when they weren't there, which wasn't often, Sir Alex would start the sessions and players would laugh and he'd go: 'Aaargh – you take over.' The thing about good leadership is managers should never

coach. A manager should always just observe. The manager's responsibility is not just to the first team, it's to every player in the club. So, what he always did was start training with us. He was there, he observed, and then he would wander off to the other teams. Connect with the coaches, connect with the players. Then he would come back to us. But if you coach, you cannot do that.

The mythology that developed around Ferguson's leadership often centres on the so-called 'hairdryer treatment' meted out to players who let him down – the hairdryer a reference to how close he got to the faces of players with whom he was angry, as they felt his wrath in the heat of the air coming from his mouth. He did have a temper, and could lose it. But the reason I call it mythology is that if you talk to the people who played for him, as I have with Schmeichel and many others, that is not how they define his leadership. They speak of his ability to make big, bold decisions, and live by them; to motivate different people in different ways; to know when to praise, when to exert pressure, when to let go; to manage the players' emotions and anxieties so that they could get the best out of themselves under pressure; to move on from setbacks; and always to be thinking of the future, the next game, the next team he was building.

'He basically had two brains going at the same time,' said Schmeichel. 'He'd have one brain for the current, here and now, and one brain for the future. He was always looking at the bigger picture for himself and bringing that to the squad.' Another quality Schmeichel defined as helping make Ferguson a great leader was that he was 'brilliant in defeat'. 'He didn't brood too long,' Schmeichel added. 'He didn't take it out on the players. He always made sure that you could move on to the next game. The thing about Fergie and the hairdryer is overdone.'

Ferguson himself learned a lot of his football and leadership skills from one of his heroes – and former boss – Jock Stein, a true legend in Scottish football who led Celtic to become the first British club to win the European Cup, in 1967, one of my earliest sporting memories. Ferguson said of his mentor that whether in public or private, whenever he was asked what made him successful, 'he always talked about the players, Jimmy Johnstone this, Bertie Auld that, never about himself'.

Ferguson, though, is just one type of successful leader. You need only to look at José Mourinho, another of the most successful managers of modern times, to realise that there is no one style, no one approach. The self-anointed 'Special One' is very much someone who talks about himself. Critics might charge that it is because he is a narcissist, who underplays the importance of the players, and overplays his own role. His admirers argue that drawing the attention to himself is a way of taking pressure off the players. So, while you might prefer the Stein approach to the way Mourinho does things, or might be more enamoured by the evident love for their players shown by Manchester City's Pep Guardiola and Liverpool's Jürgen Klopp, it is important to remember that there is no single right or wrong style of leadership. There is just different, because there will be as many leadership styles as there are leaders.

It's the same in politics. Winston Churchill and Clement Attlee. One a barnstorming war hero, the other a self-effacing creator of the modern welfare state. Both were great leaders. Clinton and Obama. Similarities, for sure, but so many differences. Heath and Thatcher. Blair and Brown. No two personalities the same. No two back stories the same. No two voices the same. Angela Merkel was no great orator. She would watch Barack Obama make a speech and, like most of us, be lost in the beauty of the voice, and the richness and poetry of the language. Yet Obama would watch Merkel work a room of leaders, managing a difficult impasse in a negotiation, say, and marvel at her patience, her attention to detail, her ability to broker compromise. From a very difficult start, in which their differing styles tended to irritate each other, they became close partners on the world stage. And they were both in awe of Mandela, of course. Partly because of the personality, the voice, the warmth; but above all the life story and what it had come to represent. I remember Tony Blair once saying to him when they were arguing about Libya: 'The trouble is, Nelson, you can come out with any old nonsense, and because it's you, everyone has to listen and agree.' Mandela laughed, enjoying both the point, and the truth of it.

To revisit the 'politicians are all the same' myth, you only have to attend a European, NATO or G7 summit to see the absurdity of such a view. They are all very different. But they are all leaders, and if we are trying to learn about leadership, it is important at least to try to assess the qualities that they share: the good and, sometimes, the bad.

Let's start with bad.

Last summer I was invited to the Army Leadership Centre at Sandhurst Military Academy, where I was interviewed by Lieutenant Colonel Henry Llewelyn-Usher for the academy's podcast series on modern leadership. I have enough experience of, and respect for, our armed forces to know that I had to leave my political views out of our exchanges. Even so, as I later read through the latest iteration of the Army Leadership Doctrine, a Ministry of Defence publication setting out military principles of leadership, it was political leaders who constantly came to mind.

The Army Leadership Doctrine is heavy on values, standards, ethics, moral courage and integrity. It also painstakingly identifies what it calls the 'characteristics of toxic leaders'. Autocratic. Narcissistic. Manipulative. Intimidating. Overly competitive. Discriminatory. Obviously, the document is talking about military leaders who might tend that way, but it's not difficult to compile a lengthy list of recent political leaders who embody some, or all, of those vices. The army's determination to identify both good and toxic leadership perhaps helps to explain why several among the first Tory MPs to call on Boris Johnson to move on were ex-military – including Johnny Mercer, Tom Tugendhat and Tobias Ellwood. Shaped by what they had seen of their leaders when they were still in uniform, they were appalled at the way Johnson expected others to follow him, whilst trashing the principles on which real leaders should operate. When Mercer resigned as a minister in 2021, he described Johnson's government as a 'cesspit . . . the most distrustful, awful environment I've ever worked in.' 'In government,' he went on, 'almost nobody tells the truth.' You can feel his rage, but also the sense of contrast with his time in the military, in virtually every word.

Autocratic. Narcissistic. Manipulative. Intimidating. Overly competitive. Discriminatory. Was I alone in thinking immediately of Donald Trump on seeing those words? Trump, who assured us that if Abraham Lincoln and George Washington came back from the dead and ran against him, he would beat them by forty points. This is a man seemingly incapable of reflecting upon any person or situation without making it all about himself, and his own self-regard. Only he could have seen protestors out on the streets in London and said that they had come out to say how much they liked him. 'The Queen is a great lady, she was nice to me,' was about as high as his EQ score ever got. The churn in his senior personnel while he was in the White House says much more about the former president than it does the people who generally either quit in disgust, or discovered via Twitter that they'd been sacked. As both he and Johnson found to their cost, it is hard to develop a positive and effective culture once the team senses that their leader is constantly looking to take credit if things go well, shift blame if they go badly, and is willing to sacrifice others for his own mistakes.

Let's compare Trump's White House to George W. Bush's.

Bush may not have been in the Lincoln league of American presidents. He couldn't get near Obama for oratory, Clinton for detail, Biden for empathy, or Reagan for his relaxed positivity. But I was always struck by how he dealt with people: not just the senior advisers, but the drivers, security men, cooks and bottle washers, whose names he always seemed to know, along with little details about their lives. I saw that characteristic for myself when I mentioned to him that I was running the London marathon to raise money for research into leukaemia. He told me that his sister Robin had died of the illness when she was four, and immediately sent for his chequebook so that he could sponsor me. His impulsive generosity prompted Tony Blair to do likewise (I still have both cheques – uncashed! – because I reckon one day they might raise a lot more in a charity auction). Equally impressively, on every occasion I met him thereafter, he would ask about the marathon, training, timings, the day itself. With some politicians you sense the 'people person' thing is a bit fake. I never felt that with Bush, and I think that approach is vital to effective leadership and team-building.

The role of leaders in motivation is vital. I have never understood how leaders think they are likely to get the best out of people in the long term by subjecting them to fear, abuse, bullying and intimidation. You get a completely different level of effort, loyalty, forethought and care from people who feel that they are valued. If people sense their leader barely knows they exist, and cares less, they're less likely to be as committed and effective as they could be.

If we turn to the qualities which define good leadership, the most important, for me, are: the ability to make decisions; the ability to fit them within a framework of clearly understood beliefs and values; the ability to communicate and build support for them; the possession of a vision for their organisation, their country and, where relevant, for the world; and a clear sense of their own role within it. Leadership is not just about management, or delegation. It is not just about problem-solving. It is about knowing where you want to lead to, knowing how to achieve this and how to take others with you, focusing on all the opportunities, and using them to proceed to your stated goals. And being able to distinguish what's important and what's not.

It's making the big decisions that really separates the true leaders from the rest. The good ones take responsibility for them, too. If you're a football manager faced with the choice of picking Player A or Player B for the cup final, you can discuss the pros and cons with staff and anyone else you want; you can analyse endlessly the mass of data now available about every player on the planet; but ultimately, you, the leader, have to decide. In politics, when it comes to whether to cut or increase Tax A or B, whether to increase spending for Department C or D, ministers, advisers, researchers, pollsters, MPs, and the media will all have their say, but in the end the prime minister and the chancellor have to decide.

Much of my time with Tony Blair was spent on planes travelling to and from meetings with other heads of government. On many of those journeys, especially the return flights, I would be seated next to or opposite him as he worked his way through his red boxes. These are the boxes, lined with lead and black satin, in which papers for the PM are organised by his team. Some were simply for him to read. But most required some kind of decision, large or small. Occasionally there would be a suggested decision for him at the end, which he could simply tick and initial 'TB'. More often, there would be options. He might want more research done, or want to speak to people when we landed, but ultimately he had to come down on one side or the other. And he was having to do this dozens, hundreds of times every day. Sometimes – particularly if something else major was happening – he would have very little time to ponder. But he would still have to make the decision. And, once it was made, he had to move on to the next one.

The ways in which a national leader operates here may be particularly pressured, but the basic principles and stresses apply in all fields. Businessman John Browne, who once led BP, one of the biggest companies in the world, described the experience to me like this: 'It is not quite as fast as a tennis player in a grand slam final, but the decisions come at you all the time, and you have to make those decisions, knowing you cannot always predict the outcome with absolute confidence.' 'Leaders,' he concluded, 'are the ones who can handle that, handle all those decisions coming at them from all angles.'

No leader can see every letter, every email, every research paper about every decision that has to be taken. It all has to be curated to match priorities and time pressures. Good leaders accept this is the case, and so recognise the importance of having able people around them who can take the smaller decisions themselves and do the research and heavy lifting required on the bigger ones so that the leader can make all the decisions he/she has to make in an informed and confident way. Bad leaders generally lack the self-confidence to have strong and talented people around them.

Good leaders also understand the vital importance of not being blown off track by day-to-day distractions. This is a particularly vital skill in the political sphere where, thanks to the relentless nature of modern media, shortened attention spans, and widespread addiction to breaking news and clicks, there is constant pressure to shift one's focus from the important to the newsworthy (they can be the same thing, of course, but often aren't). Bill Clinton said to me after he left office: 'Too many decision-makers define their reality according to that day's media. It is almost always a mistake.' He is right. There are plenty of high-profile leaders today who fall into that trap. They are fixated on day-to-day, even hour-to-hour coverage, flitting from issue to issue. Everything is a 'priority', and everything seems to require their attention. The result is that they rarely engage with issues fully or join up their various responses into a considered overall approach. The media's pressure pushes leaders and governments to act more reactively. The response should be to be more strategic.

Of course, no leader will ever get every single decision right, so another important facet of leadership is knowing when to reverse a decision, when to change course, and how to do so without too many reserves being drained from the credibility bank. I would argue that one of the reasons Boris Johnson ran out of ministerial support was because ministers were constantly being asked to defend positions which then, as facts emerged or political situations changed, were totally undermined. The media love a 'humiliating U-turn' story. That said, the public are far more tolerant of them, provided the U-turning politician is clear about the reason, and prepared to admit to the mistake or poor judgement in the first place. Do it every day, however, and you're in trouble.

Sometimes it is possible to make mistakes by being a victim of your own success. In New Labour's first term, we could not have been prouder of keeping, as promised, inflation and interest rates low, not least thanks to some major decisions made by Gordon Brown in the early days after the 1997 election. But that success gave rise to another problem, namely that pensions were linked to inflation, which we had kept so low that it meant pensions would rise by just 75 pence a week. We believed pensioners would understand why, and appreciate the big-picture economic success. We were wrong. Gordon found a number of other ways to help pensioners and deal with the political problem we had caused for ourselves. The overall strategy remained unchanged, but it's fair to say a considerable measure of tactical adaptation took place.

One of the most mulled-over questions in the academic and publishing industries surrounding leadership is whether it can be taught. The short answer is yes. The longer answer is that, although not everyone is capable of being a president or a CEO, a football manager or the conductor of an orchestra, everyone can benefit from learning *about* effective leadership, and *from* studying different leaders and different approaches to leadership. Of course, just as some people have a more natural talent for certain subjects or sports, so some will have the qualities we associate with leadership in more abundant natural supply. But that doesn't mean those qualities can't be encouraged and honed. If you learn to play the piano, you are probably not going to be a concert pianist, let alone a modern-day Beethoven or Mozart. If you play cricket at school, the likelihood is that you will never play for England, or any other country, or county. But study and practice will help. The same is true of leadership. Learning about it, studying how a good leader leads, or led, is never a waste of time . . . if only to allow you to recognise bad leadership when you see it and do something about it!

Having a coach or a mentor can certainly help here. I have coached leaders in sectors about which I know next to nothing. There is no way I could do their jobs. But I can help offer candid analysis of how they operate, how skilful they are at communication, empathy, team-building, strategic development and implementation and so on. Many businesses have formal mentoring and career counselling systems, usually but not always involving people who are older who can give guidance to younger colleagues outside traditional HR frameworks. Given how much politics matters, it ought to be the same there. It rarely is.

Outside of the monarchy, nobody is actually born to take on

a leadership role. But I believe strongly that everyone has some capacity for leadership within them. Prince William and Prince George have been raised and educated since birth for the role that King Charles has just stepped into after serving perhaps the longest apprenticeship in history. For everyone else, high-profile leadership doesn't automatically lie in our future. It may happen. It may not. That will depend on our characters, how our lives progress, whether our experience and learning allow us to maximise our potential. But even if we cannot be 'the' leader, we all have it within us to be 'a' leader. We all possess leadership qualities. Indeed, some of the best and most inspiring leaders I have ever worked with have been people who didn't see themselves as leaders, who would run a mile if you offered them a job with 'leader' or 'director' in the title, but showed true leadership in their work ethic, their empathy, their energy, their ability to motivate, and their ability to stay calm under pressure and keep others calm around them. One thing all schools should be able to take from the private sector is the emphasis you find there on teaching pupils about leadership (I would argue that it's because they teach leadership at private schools, as well as focusing on self-confidence, that so many emerge with both those strengths. Although it is also about privilege, it is not simply about that).

When we come on to the other two parts of my Holy Trinity of effective activism – strategy and teamship – you will see that I have fairly fixed views. When I apply my rules for them to successful strategies and teams, I find a series of ticks. The fact that we all have such different personalities makes me rather less absolute about what constitutes a good leader. There are certain qualities they have in common, not least a strong sense of what they want to achieve and an ability to take tough decisions. But, as I acknowledged earlier, good leaders come in many forms, which is why the following list of principles is quite lengthy. While the majority of good leaders will tick most, if not all, of the boxes, some might not, but have other skills and personality traits to compensate. Nonetheless, I hope it is a useful guide to the qualities that the best of the best appear to possess, and use effectively.

Rules for leadership

- Good leaders are good team-builders, and set a clear course for the team.

- Good leaders strive to have the brightest and the best people around them. They do not surround themselves with yes-men.

- Good leaders avoid the blame game. They take responsibility when things go wrong, and share the credit when things go well.

- Good leaders listen to their team members, and genuinely value the team at all levels.

- Good leaders make sure that if a team member has to be given bad news, they are the ones giving it.

- Good leaders are good communicators.

- Good leaders must be able to devise, execute and narrate a clear strategy.

- Good leaders lead by example.

- Good leaders wear their power lightly.

- Good leaders know when to be cautious, and when to be bold.

- Good leaders know when to be flexible and when not to bend.

- Good leaders never take trust for granted.

- Good leaders show rather than tell their authenticity.

- Good leaders value learning as well as teaching.

- Good leaders know their weaknesses, and work on them.

- Good leaders care little about day-to-day popularity or media currents.

- Good leaders can adapt to change, but seek to do so according to core strategic principles.

- Good leaders think ahead.

- Good leaders understand that one day they will move on, and that leadership succession matters.

10.

Be a Team Player

There is something a bit cringey when actors and musicians collecting a major award endlessly and often tearfully thank the people who made their triumph possible. But there is a truth being spoken there, too. None of them could have achieved what they did alone. Teams need leaders. But, by the same token, leaders need teams. The Oscar winners all needed a team. All leaders need teams to make meaningful change or deliver significant success. I am almost always the last to leave the cinema, because I enjoy marvelling at the sheer number of people involved in making a film, the vast array of teams and tasks involved, and so watching the credits go by is part of the night out for me.

In the same way, while sport may seem an even more obvious area for individual greatness – from boxer Muhammad Ali to tennis players Roger Federer and Serena Williams to athlete Usain Bolt and Formula One drivers Lewis Hamilton and Michael Schumacher – the fact remains that a team is critical to the success even of those who can lay claim to GOAT status (Greatest of All Time) in individual sports. These behind-the-scenes figures help devise career strategies, business strategies, training strategies, or strategies for an individual race or fight or match. Lance Armstrong – another GOAT in his field until his drug-enhanced fall from grace – surprised me once by insisting Schumacher was the sportsman he most admired, 'because he is a great leader of an enormous, complex team. He makes them all better.'

Within any high-performing team there are three types of

people: leaders, warriors and special talent. Leaders provide direction and guidance, though only one of them will provide overall leadership (as the sailor Ben Ainslie puts it: 'You need more than one leader in a team, but they can't all be leaders'). The warriors do the hard grind. The special talents provide the spark, the creativity and the strategic response. All three groups understand the nature and demands of their role, and they also know how to fit into the wider group to maximise its effectiveness. Any imbalance can be fatal. Too many warriors and there are insufficient ideas. Too much special talent – a team of Ronaldos and Messis – and you end up with egotistical mayhem. Leadership requires skilled management of that balance. Followership is a skill, too, requiring an understanding of how to fit in with the team to maximise its effectiveness, and how and when to assume a leadership role within it. In the sporting arena, team cycling in the major Tours offers the ultimate in followership. Seven Tour de France riders put themselves through hell in support of the lead rider who, if they win, gets almost all the glory, the fame and the big bucks.

Good teamship is what you get when you have successfully built a culture in which the team members feel valued and understood, have a broad understanding of the goals of the team and their role within it, an appreciation of the roles of others, and the ability to bring the best out of each other to maximum effect.

Think of checking into a hotel. The chances are you won't meet the manager, the actual leader on the ground, or the owners. Who is the first person you meet on arrival? If it is a swanky five-star place, it will be the doorman who spots your cab arriving, and comes forward to welcome you, help you with your bags and show you to reception. He – almost always he, which I think is a tactical error, hotels – is your first point of contact. He is a leader in two ways; literally leading you into the hotel, but also leading you by giving you your first impression of the place. You get an instant feel for the entire hotel, not merely through its setting and architecture, but through him. So, he needs to have a sense of what the hotel is about, what it is trying to achieve, how it is trying to operate, and the sense of itself it is trying to communicate. Its culture. The team has to buy into it all. That is a key job for the actual leaders higher up the chain of command, to lead in the creation of the culture, and help the team to become its embodiment. The good doorman will have effective communications skills, get on with people, pay attention to detail – all of which are leadership attributes. He may not see himself as a leader, but if the actual leadership has done its job properly, people will respond to and respect those attributes and they will help to communicate the culture of the organisation.

If you're in a less swanky hotel, your first contact is probably the receptionist. How he or she – now more often she – welcomes you will go a long way towards determining whether you have a positive or negative view of your entire stay. Are you kept waiting? If you are, it means you're already starting to doubt the culture. Can they pick up whether you are one of those people who likes lots of chat, lots of bonhomie, lots of information, or, like me, someone who just wants the key, the wifi info and direction to the gym or the pool if there is one? That comes from training and experience. My point is that they are your leader. Good bosses make sure they develop the leadership-cum-teamship skills of people throughout the organisation, not just the ones who get the big bucks.

A powerful intrinsic sense of purpose is crucial here. People often assume that it's all about money. But money only gets you so far. As former Arsenal manager Arsène Wenger says of those involved in his own sport, where, obviously, remuneration can be huge, 'If a player has the money and is only motivated by the money, where does he go?' Wenger goes on to stress the qualities that make a team cohere: respect for others, solidarity when people are in trouble, the ability to enjoy the success of others, not merely your own, to help people when they fail, rather than exploit the failure. He gets almost teary when he talks about the feelings individuals have when expressing themselves through the team. 'Like the Ryder Cup in golf. It becomes a different sport. It adds something by being together, the emotions, going for something together, and suddenly the interest becomes bigger, suddenly it is about "us" not "me". Human beings subconsciously understand that alone I am nothing, but in a team I can achieve great things.'

To my mind, nothing demonstrates the truth of this better than the extraordinary team Nelson Mandela built around him while he was in prison, most of whom, for obvious reasons, he never met.

Mandela was a leader. Even behind bars, he was a leader. Despite being able to do nothing himself while incarcerated in a tiny cell, other than be a symbol, he remained a leader. But it was the team he had put together that had to take on the work he was leading. Of course, the core team was in South Africa. It comprised prominent political activists who knew his work and knew his mind, and were aware of the strategy to be pursued. However, Mandela's team also included millions of people around the world who supported the cause. They, too, knew what needed to be done and, in their different ways, they did it.

Key to this international team were two people you've perhaps never heard of: Bob Hughes and Mike Terry. Bob died in January 2022, aged ninety. Mike died of a heart attack in 2008, aged sixty-one. They were two of the loveliest men you could ever meet. Bob was a Labour MP from Aberdeen, later a peer, who chaired the British Anti-Apartheid Movement from 1976 for almost two decades until it was wound up in 1995, mission accomplished. Mike Terry ran the campaign as executive secretary over the same period. I was a journalist for most of that time, before I jumped to the political side of the fence in 1994, but I learned so much about campaigning from watching how they did it, and being on the receiving end of their attempts to shape and shift the debate.

Mike was quite softly spoken, self-effacing, but relentless. Friends would complain that he worked too hard, often sleeping in the office. He was restless, forever trying to find new ways of communicating the same message, over and over, again and again. By the end, he had helped organise over a thousand AAM branches in the UK alone. These coordinated campaign events, marches and protests, and mobilised MPs and the public through letters, speeches, books, music – whatever helped. They arranged attention-grabbing stunts, too, such as the one they staged on 18 July 1978, Mandela's sixtieth birthday, when they got a group of Labour MPs to cut a cake with sixty candles: a good stunt that won attention. Above all, they kept the momentum going. Support grew, and they were able to move from their tiny HQ to a better space in north London, in what later became Mandela Street.

Both Mike and Bob had the conciliation skills needed to keep difficult characters and groups broadly on the same track. They were therefore able to resist pressures to be more avowedly left wing on other fronts, insisting that the AAM was a single-issue organisation that needed to build support across as wide and deep a spectrum as possible. My diary records Mike saying to me once: 'Our success wasn't built by securing the support of the institutions of the British state to switch sides against apartheid; we did it by mobilising millions of people, we showed that sometimes change really can come simply through the power of hearts and minds being moved. In doing that, we didn't just help improve South Africa, we improved Britain by persuading so many people to care as much as they did.' It would be fascinating to know whether they would have been able to help bring down the walls of apartheid even more quickly had they had access to the social media that we now take for granted.

When Mandela was released from prison, the UK was among the first countries he wanted to visit. Although the official UK government line had been to support the apartheid regime, and though many in the governing Tory party viewed him as a terrorist, he felt the AAM here had been vital to the success of the campaign to free him. Neither Bob Hughes nor Mike Terry ever sought credit for what they had helped achieve. Alternating between the roles of leaders, warriors and talents, they were first and foremost consummate team players. Sadly, that's not something that could be said of many political campaigns, parties and governments today. All too often, personal ambition, taking credit and passing blame get in the way of the collective endeavour. Many businesses are just as bad.

If great teams embody purpose – as the AAM very definitely did – they also know how to stimulate and encourage new ideas and approaches. And they do so by recognising that these can come from anywhere and anyone. Dave Brailsford, who spearheaded the transformation of British Cycling from also-rans to global dominance, has a neat formulation for this: 'Ideas,' he says, 'have value not rank.' 'An idea,' he clarifies, 'should be judged on its merits, not on the rank of the person it came from. Obviously, knowledge and experience count for a lot, but you cannot expect the CEO to come up with everything. I always wanted to hear what the mechanics and the junior staff had to say, and some of the best innovations came from them.' Everyone at British Cycling was encouraged to help the team achieve 'marginal gains': small incremental improvements that cumulatively transformed performance. Brailsford even went so far as to install a suggestions box on the team bus. Some of the team's best ideas came from there, he says.

Encouraging people to have ideas involves empowering them to offer them without fear of criticism. Brailsford's team knew their suggestions were always welcome, that no one held it against them if those suggestions were ultimately found not to hold water, that no idea would be humiliatingly rebuffed outright. They also knew that if a team is functioning as it should, ideas may well be passed around to be refined and developed by others, and that no one will feel proprietorial about the end result. There is a reason why we find 'brainstorming' with colleagues useful. Having a brainstorming session is an admission that we need new ideas and energy to address a challenge; it is an invitation to think creatively, without fear of being judged for having an idea that others don't appreciate; and it's something that can be practised, a mindset that can be developed.

I have always sought to engender an ideas culture, both when I was in government and now that I'm involved in campaigns outside. An ideas culture recognises that initial ideas don't have to be fully formed or even 'right'; that they will evolve and sometimes be transformed into something completely different. New Labour itself was an idea long in the planning, and long in the development. It didn't even have a name at the outset. When, ahead of Tony Blair's first party conference as leader, we suggested putting the phrase 'New Labour' behind him on the backdrop, even he baulked initially, fearful that it might provoke a reaction from more traditionally-minded Labour members in the hall. And yet, ultimately, 'New Labour, New Britain' became our driving strategy in opposition and in government. The risk we took paid off. There were no protests. His speech seemed to capture the imagination of party, public and media. The success we achieved bred confidence to do more. That confidence bred more success.

And since an ideas culture involves having terrible ideas as well as good ones, let me share perhaps the worst idea I ever had – one I was reminded of in the summer of 2022 when a stack of official papers relating to the Good Friday Agreement negotiations over two decades earlier was released. Among them was a note detailing my 'idea' that during the referendum on the agreement in Northern Ireland, we should ask Glasgow's two great football rivals, the historically Catholic Celtic and the historically Protestant Rangers, to play a match in Belfast. So far, so OK-ish, albeit an alarming prospect for the Royal Ulster Constabulary, which we were in the process of changing into the Police Service of Northern Ireland. But, deep in brainstorm mode, I wanted to go further, and get Celtic players to play in Rangers strips, and vice versa. In the room at the time – NB, this is always a danger when there is a strong and determined character in full-on mode chairing the meeting – there was very little pushback. But when I called two men with close Rangers links to help progress the idea – former Rangers player Alex Ferguson, and the club's manager during most of the 1990s, Walter Smith – it's fair to say that they worried I had taken leave of my senses. Then, when Northern Ireland secretary Mo Mowlam and Scottish secretary Donald Dewar got to hear of it, my bonkers idea quickly died a death. Thank God. Bad idea. However – in my defence – in that same brainstorm, I also had the idea that we should mount a poster campaign across the North, in which Tony Blair would make a series of hand-written pledges about what the agreement would secure. That was an idea that worked. I had remembered the latter idea and conveniently forgotten all about the former one until – shortly after the official papers were made public – journalists started to call me and ask questions beginning with the words: 'You didn't really, did you?'

The trust and mutual respect necessary to incubate new ideas cannot exist in a silo. They must extend across everything the team does. Loyalty depends on them. Not blind loyalty, which can lead us to overlook wrongdoing, excuse the inexcusable, defend the indefensible, become stale and complacent. But the loyalty that arises from an understanding of what it is the 'leader' wants from the team, an understanding of the role the team members are expected to play, and a willingness to play it.

The respect team members have for each other must be genuine for that spirit to form. I can see why, from time to time, I get lumped in with Boris Johnson's former adviser Dominic Cummings. We are both backroom people who 'became the story'; both people thought to be close to and influential over a prime minister; both have at times served as lightning conductors for our superiors; both are bogey figures for political opponents and parts of the media; we are both driven and determined and unafraid to fight our corner. But there are several points at which any comparison of the two of us has to diverge. First, in our own roles as leaders of teams. One of the things I am proudest of from my time in Number 10 is that none of the people who worked directly for me has ever joined in with all the political and media attacks that have come my way – even though they have had plenty of opportunity, and offers of decent money in the days when the media paid handsomely for such stuff, to do so. I was obsessed, as I think my team would agree, by the idea of building a genuine spirit of teamship inside the operation I ran. Sharing credit. Avoiding blame. Encouraging ideas from all quarters. Rewarding good people and good ideas. Appreciating, and showing I appreciated, the work of people at all levels. Also, being clear that I did not expect members of my team to put in the kind of hours I did; but that I did expect them to put a lot into the hours they were there.

True, Cummings inspired loyalty among the team he ran in the Leave campaign (and, dare I say, for some, given the lies they told and the laws they broke, that was often of the blind variety, defending the indefensible). I'm sure many of you will have seen the phone video footage of him being cheered wildly as he leapt onto a desk in the campaign HQ to celebrate their victory in the referendum. But, once he got into Downing Street alongside Johnson he opted for the Millwall Strategy: 'No one likes us, we don't care.' It was a strategy which, among other things, involved having a special adviser marched out of Number 10 by police, and constantly criticising ministers, civil servants and special advisers who failed to share his analysis of any given problem that was under discussion.

This approach went beyond him, and pre-dated and has post-dated him too. I find it unfathomable that the Tories have devoted so much time and energy over the last decade to attacking and undermining people who work for them. Does it never cross their minds that if they keep telling teachers they are all left-ies when they're not; that if they blame NHS workers for long waiting lists and poor treatment rather than underfunding, and accuse them of actively wanting to hurt sick people on account of the fact they have chosen to strike in protest at real-terms pay cuts; that if they accuse the police of being more concerned with 'woke' gender issues than with crime – which is such nonsense it is beyond parody; that if they suggest that members of the civil service are just trying to swing the lead if they work from home, they might just end up with deeply pissed-off people who seek work elsewhere or, if they stay, are not exactly motivated to give their all for the leader and the team? It's terrible leadership, and the antithesis of team-building. If you constantly tell the people who work in public services that they're not good enough, then don't then be too surprised if morale is low, staff retention diffi-cult and the likelihood of industrial action higher than it would be if people felt valued and respected.

The other big difference between me and Cummings, inciden-tally, relates to our relationships with our respective bosses. Tony Blair inspired loyalty in me and the key people around him in the same way we tried to inspire loyalty in the teams we led. We had a policy of maximum openness for maximum trust. Work was always testing, but often genuinely enjoyable, fun even. He wanted to be challenged by us, rather than simply be told he was wonderful, or right all the time. We argued a lot in private, but then projected a common purpose in public, and throughout the government. We respected his position as leader, understood that any 'power' we had came only because of our proximity to him, and therefore did not seek to pursue our own agenda – a big difference to Cummings – but rather tested him repeatedly on his. He respected our right to do that, so long as we understood that he had the last word on the major decisions and issues. When he asked for our views, it was not so that he could hear us agree with him, but in order to look for weaknesses in his argument, ways of strengthening it, or different ways of addressing problems to which he was drawing attention.

The loyalty that developed from all this endures to this day. I do not think it is of the blind variety, because I still argue with him about all manner of things. But I still respect him for what he achieved as prime minister, for the manner in which he continues to want to contribute to public and policy debates, and for the fact that his core personality has not changed as much as it might have done, given the pressures of the job, and the fear and loathing high-profile politicians tend to attract. We still meet to range far and wide over all manner of issues; we still call on each other if there are problems to address; we still trust each other to be absolutely frank and open; we still have a good laugh. Every year since he left office, there has been a pre-Christmas gathering of the original team that was with him from the early days of his leadership. It remains, in so many ways, a team, and he remains its leader.

Very little of the above can be said about Cummings and Johnson. Cummings' loathing of his former boss would appear to be visceral. That may say something about him; but it says even more about Johnson. A leader who fails to inspire loyalty in key people is a leader destined to fail – as he did, and Cummings played a not insignificant role in that failure. The culture a leader creates permeates their entire team – for good or for ill.

Amid the controversy around the lockdown parties in Number 10, one of the defences made by the nodding-dog ministers sent out day after day to defend Johnson in the media was that he was unaware of what was going on. Put to one side the fact that this was almost certainly untrue. If he genuinely wasn't aware, then that is just as big a failure of leadership – the consequence of a culture made permissible by the dreadful example set from the top. I can state with total certainty that those parties would not have happened on Tony Blair's watch, nor on the watch of his predecessors.

A good team culture emerges in other ways, too. Chatting one evening with the contestants and production team of *Make Me Prime Minister*, we got round to talking about the importance of the feeling of belonging to a team, in part because one of the contestants, Holly Morgan, had until recently been a footballer with Leicester City women's team. We focused initially on teamship in sport, then politics, and then moved on to business. One of the team described one of her first jobs after leaving school – at Marks & Spencer. 'They gave me a uniform and several days' training before I was given a shift on the shop floor,' she said. 'They looked after their staff really, really well. A hairdresser, a doctor and a dentist were available to staff. There was a heavily subsidised canteen which served really good food. The effect this had on me was to make me proud to work for M&S. It made me feel like a valued member of the team. It made me want to represent the company to the best of my ability. I was also empowered by the training I was given. On every shift, I was told which department I'd be working in and who my team leader was for that shift. That was important – it made me feel more confident because I always knew there was someone I could ask for help or advice. So, M&S got the best out of me by showing me how important I, a part-time seasonal shop assistant, was to the whole team.' Years – decades – later, she said her view of the M&S brand is wholly positive.

Even such an apparently random thing as punctuality feeds into team culture. If one member of the team is late for a meeting, it disrupts the meeting and it weakens the team. It also suggests a lack of respect for the other people in the room. I've often thought it indicates a culture that is under stress. Team members who feel unappreciated and unimportant are more likely to turn up late, just as they will leave things undone, work sloppily and miss deadlines. Team leaders who think they are more important than the team might believe they are entitled to be late, because they are in charge. Their lack of punctuality suggests they are not. Another point in favour of George W. Bush – his obsessive punctuality. If you were late for a meeting, you didn't get in. Fair to say neither his predecessor, Bill Clinton, nor his successor, Barack Obama, operated by the same rules. Both had many strengths, but punctuality was not high up the list.

When a team is really in sync it operates like a kitchen in a great restaurant. The pot washer and the kitchen porter know they are as much part of the team as the head chef. If there are no clean pans or knives, the chefs can't do their jobs and everything falls apart. The person preparing the vegetables that go with the main course knows that if he or she does not get them ready in time to be plated when the main is ready, the dish will go cold and can't be served. The person washing the salad knows that if grit remains in the lettuce leaves, no matter how good the rest of the food, the customer will remember the grit. The waiters knows that if they do not respond quickly enough when the food is ready to be served, its quality will suffer and the kitchen staff will feel let down. Everyone relies on everyone else. Everyone therefore respects what everyone else does.

And when a team really comes together with a common purpose, a willingness to embrace a range of views, and the discipline to agree to be bound to the decisions that are ultimately made, it can do pretty much anything it puts its collective mind to. I experienced that powerful feeling of agency at various points during the New Labour years. When we were on song, it felt as though we were Barcelona and the Tories were Hartlepool United. When we fell out, sometimes for political reasons but often, frankly, because of personal ambitions and personality clashes, it felt as though we were gifting goals to the opposition before we even got onto the pitch. I loved the Barcelona periods, and hated it when we weakened ourselves by failing to operate according to basic principles of teamship, such as openness, trust, tolerance and mutual respect across both government and the broader team.

During our Barcelona periods, we drew genuine strength from one another. It was Norman Triplett of Indiana University who discovered back in the 1890s that people ride their bikes faster if they are with other cyclists. It is the basis of team cycling to this day, where the lead rider is the talent, and his or her warriors are the 'domestiques' who do everything from fetching and carrying food and water to offering protection from the elements. Why do athletes going for a world record have pacemakers ahead of them? Because they run faster when they run with others. I have been fortunate enough to run on different occasions with Sebastian Coe, Brendan Foster, Haile Gebrselassie and Paul Tergat, four athletics greats. They were kind enough to slow down for me, but I don't think I have ever run better, or felt better doing it, than when I was out with Tergat and his Kenyan team-mates, high in the hills above Addis Ababa.

Clause 4 of the Labour Party's constitution – as amended after Tony Blair became leader following a debate launched in that speech made in front of the first outing of the 'New Labour, New Britain' slogan – contains a line that reads: 'By the strength of our common endeavour we achieve more than we achieve alone.' It's

what good teamship is all about, whether in countries, governments, political parties, trade unions, sports teams, businesses,
schools, hospitals, charities or families. The question in the title
of this book – 'But what can I do?' – begs a second question, 'And
who can I best do it with?'

Rules for teamship

- By the strength of our common endeavour we achieve more
  than we achieve alone. (Have I mentioned that already?)

- The team must have and understand a clear culture.

- The team needs more than one leader, but if everyone is a
  leader, it gets messy. (Messy, I said, not Messi.)

- Ideas have merit, not rank. Good ideas can come from anyone.

- The blame game is a loser's game. Losing teams turn in on
  each other. Winning teams support each other, including when
  things go wrong.

- Maximum openness builds maximum trust.

- Internal communication matters. The team should hear
  important news before anyone else.

- Special talent requires special handling.

- The boat gets rocked if someone's not rowing.

- Good team leaders tend to be good team players.

- In a real team, the instinct for individual self-promotion is realised through the pursuit of the team goal.

II.

Be a Strategist

I've opted to arrange my political Holy Trinity in this sequence: leadership, teamship, strategy. In fact they could be presented in any order. They're interdependent. You cannot have one without the other two. In any meaningful fight for meaningful change, all three need to be working together, all the time. Great strategy without a leader to spearhead it and a team to make it a reality is dead in the water. Equally, a leader cannot operate to the very best of their ability without a good team, nor the team without a good leader, and even if you have both a good leader and a good team, without a strong strategy, you're unlikely to succeed.

Most people know what leadership and teamship are, though they may find them difficult to master. Strategy, on the other hand, can seem trickily elusive. There's often disagreement as to what precisely it involves and the role it plays. But to my mind, even if it's often difficult to enact, it's a proposition that is relatively easy to grasp, provided you keep at the front of your mind the Norwegian word for cheese I mentioned earlier: OST.

Those three letters, in huge black Sharpie pen handwriting, comprise my most important Post-it.

O = Objective (what you want to achieve)

S = Strategy ('the big how': your definition of the overall approach)

T = Tactics (the detailed plans required to execute the strategy)

An example from everyday life might go as follows:

O: Lose weight.

S: Diet and exercise.

T: Exercise regime. Food diary. Calorie counter. Picture of over-weight self on fridge. Gym membership. Walk to work. Use stairs, not lift.

Or

O: Get that job.

S: Polish CV and do plenty of interview preparation (a major life lesson – and key Post-it note – from Benjamin Franklin: 'By failing to prepare, you are preparing to fail').

T: ABCD: Appearance (be smart). Behaviour (be polite, warm, engaging). Communication (speak clearly and thoughtfully). Doing (be clear what you have previously done that makes you right for the role).

As you can see, at the outset, your objective can and should be summarised in a phrase, your strategy in a sentence, and your tactics in as many bullet points as come to mind. The tactics for getting a job, for example, might well include not only ABCD but such additional elements as: make my CV stand out, find out what I can about the people who will be interviewing me, come up with some likely interview questions and practise how to answer them, go to bed early the night before, take deep breaths during the interview if I think I'm struggling.

If you don't work through OST in this methodical way, and in that order, it's all too easy to get confused. Many people seem to think that an objective is the same as a strategy. Margaret

Thatcher's famous injunction to a senior civil servant illustrates the difference between the two: 'I know the what. Don't tell me the what. Tell me the how.' Another common error is muddling strategy and tactics: failing to distinguish your general approach from your specific plans. The following four statements – or rather the sentiments contained within them – came from the leaders of businesses I have worked with, with a summary of my replies.

'My company's objective is to build a fantastic website.' That's a tactic, surely?

'My company's objective is innovation.' Sounds more like a strategy to me.

'My company's strategy is to be the best at innovation.' You mean objective.

'My company's strategy is to take our innovation on a tour of schools and colleges.' That's a tactic.

This confusion extends to those who, theoretically at least, ought to know better. As the Truss government sought to recover from the economic and political calamity of a mini-Budget that promised huge unfunded tax cuts, ministers were sent out to tour the TV and radio studios with the message: 'Our plan is to grow the economy.' 'Growing the economy', however, is not a plan or strategy. It is an objective. Truss and Kwasi Kwarteng's actual 'strategy' was low tax and deregulation – a policy of 'trickle-down economics' that was supposed to achieve the objective government apologists misidentified. To compound the muddle and magnify the self-inflicted wound, Truss and Kwarteng went haywire on the tactics – failing, for example, to consult the Office of Budget Responsibility or prepare the ground in a way that might have helped steady the financial markets. The result was economic mayhem. Old Etonian Kwarteng's performance confirmed my long-held view that there is often a chasm between 'well educated' and 'clever'. It is not clever to allow your good education to develop into hubris and a view that there is no need to listen to others because you think you have all the answers.

Objectives, then, need to be clearly defined. They need to be ambitious. However, they also need to be realistic. There is no point someone my age setting themselves the objective of running a sub-four-minute mile. It is physiologically impossible. Running a four-hour marathon, on the other hand, while ambitious, might be realistic. For a talented young athlete with real potential and a good coach, by contrast, a sub-four-minute-mile objective, while ambitious, might be realistic. In a similar way, Manchester City, Liverpool and Chelsea began this season with the objective of winning the Premier League. Ambitious but realistic. Teams such as Fulham, Bournemouth and Nottingham Forest would be more focused on avoiding relegation. Setting themselves the object-ive of a Manchester City is unrealistic, pointless and, ultimately, soul-sapping.

Objectives also need to be, in some way, measurable. At one level, it's commendable to say: 'My objective is to change the world.' But that statement begs so many questions. How? In what area? With what goal? It's much better to set an ambition that allows success or failure in achieving it to be measured. It also needs to be borne in mind that what precisely constitutes an O, S or T very much depends on the bigger picture. 'Be an MP', for example, could be O, S or T, depending on that bigger picture.

O: I want to be an MP.

S: Visibility as campaigner in party of choice.

T: Get on candidate list, target safe seats where I have personal connections.

Or

O: I want to help get rid of the Tories.

S: Become a Labour candidate in a winnable marginal.

T: Get on candidate list, target safe seats where I have personal connections.

Or

O: I want to lead the fight against climate change.

S: Full-time activism.

T: Try to win a seat in Parliament.

Fixing on an ambitious but realistic objective takes some thought. Formulating strategy, though, is the hardest bit, requiring honest debate within the team, and a willingness to engage in open, mutually respectful discussion. Without that discussion you will either come up with half-baked ideas or fail to spot inconsistencies and elephant traps. Strategy formulation also requires someone to be wielding a pen. If OST is my shortest Post-it, not far behind it is one that comprises the title of a poem penned by Marilyn Monroe, entitled 'Think In Ink'.

> . . . *what's on my mind.*
> *'Taint dishes, 'taint wishes, it's thoughts*
> *Flinging by before I die*
> *And to think in ink . . .*

I don't know what she had in mind when she wrote her poem many years ago, though we can be sure it was not Labour's election strategies. But ever since I read that poem, and saw that final line, I have sought to live by it. I think in ink. The anecdote from the chapter on the campaign mindset explains why, having felt I didn't answer the question from a Labour staffer well, I later sat down and wrote a more considered reply. It probably also explains why I write so many books, speeches, blogs and columns. Writing clarifies thought.

In my view, strategy is not strategy until it is written down, and the words and what they represent are understood and agreed upon by all who are involved in the execution of the strategy. If it is not rendered in that way, there is a risk of misunderstanding when it comes to the delivery of strategy. People leave the room armed with the views and attitudes they went in with, rather than a proper understanding of what has been agreed. Writing it down nails it down. What are we trying to achieve? Write it down. What are the key facts that form the basis of the argument we are having? Write them down. What are the options for the decisions we are seeking to make? What are the pros and cons? Write it all down. Make it all part of the discussion, all aimed at answering the key question: what is our strategy?

Strategies may at times be complex, with many moving parts. It is essential, however, that they can be explained simply. The best strategies, I would argue, can be expressed in a word, a phrase, a sentence, a paragraph, a page, a speech and a book. When we were in opposition ahead of the 1997 election, after a lot of discussion – and I mean a lot, what with the awaydays, brainstorms, and seemingly endless circular conversations – we settled on 'modernisation' as the word, 'New Labour, New Britain' as the phrase, 'we exist to extend wealth and opportunity to the many not the few' as the sentence, and from that strategic framing the policies, the pledges, the speeches, the core arguments all flowed. If you cannot sum up the strategy in a word or, at most, in a phrase, then the chances are it will lack coherence as you take it forward and your chances of success will be reduced.

Looking back to the beginning of New Labour, I think it is fair to say that many of the key people were inclined to 'think in ink'. Both when we were in opposition and in government, one of the most important pieces of internal communications arrived on Sunday evenings, after Tony Blair sat down to compose a 'note for the core team'. This was a mix of what was on his mind; what he saw as the difficult issues in the weeks ahead, and thoughts about how to address them; and, above all, how they fitted within the 'New Labour, New Britain' framing of our overall strategy. Gordon Brown hammered a typewriter and, later, a word processor harder than anyone I've ever met, usually with the caps lock on. His notes were vital to strategic development and its tactical application. Philip Gould, our pollster and a key strategist, wrote copiously about his focus groups and how they were reacting to our strategy. He wrote copiously about speech drafts. He just wrote copiously. Peter Mandelson was another 'thinker in ink' – in his case, literally so, because he found the process of using pen and paper much more conducive to thinking than using a word processor. As did I, and as I do still. That's why my weekly 'next week in strategic context' notes, an attempt to align whatever was happening in government with broader strategy, were handwritten, and typed up by my long-suffering, patient PA, the only person on the planet who could read my scribbles, Alison Blackshaw.

The purpose of those notes was not simply to set out priorities and to seek to maintain discipline around what we were trying to do; it was to ensure that everyone understood that we did not see strategy as theoretical, but as something from which regular and consistent actions, policies, announcements, events, all flowed. 'The grid', a constantly updated document which covered every day, every week, every month, every year and every parliamentary session, and allowed us to plan ahead, was the mechanism by which tactics were properly ordered to fit the strategy. Of course, the communication was important. But not as important as what we were actually doing.

We sought always to be proactive; we did not want to be sitting there waiting for our opponents to fail, or to show weakness. As the great chess grandmaster Garry Kasparov puts it: 'Hoping for your opponent to make mistakes is not a strategy.' It is a message I hope the current Labour Party fully understands and acts upon. As the next election nears, they are facing a Tory government that has failed on so many fronts. It might well be that the country has just decided that they have had their day, and want to replace them with a Labour government. But that requires the kind of swing that is unusual in our politics, and Keir Starmer is right when he orders his team not to take victory for granted simply because of healthy poll leads. I doubt such a huge swing will happen purely out of disregard, or even disgust, for the Tories. Labour must have a winning strategy, rather than depend on the Tories losing it for themselves. The country has to know and understand what they are for, not only what they are against. I also strongly believe that if an opposition party arrives in power without having loudly and clearly communicated the key pledges and policies at the heart of its manifesto, they will be in a weaker position in government. The reason, for example, that in 1997 we deployed a 'pledge card', with a small number of goals and policy outcomes that we sought to achieve across the economy and public services, was not merely to signal intent, or even to show focus, but also so that, once we were actually in government, we could point back to them as a way of showing that we had delivered what we had promised. This became important for the 2001 election as we reminded voters what had been achieved, and offered them a fresh set of pledges for the future. Then the same again in 2005. People, especially those who do not follow politics closely, need clear and repeated reminders of an opposition's plans, and clear and repeated reminders of a government's achievements, set in the context of further plans for the future.

Of course, strategies have to be flexible, and may need to be adapted in response to changing circumstances. But, again to quote Kasparov, 'If you change your strategy all the time you really don't have one . . . you should only change it when the fundamentals change.'

It is important, too, to understand that if devising strategy is a team game, so is executing it. If I asked the hotel doorman or receptionist from the previous chapter, 'How would you define the strategy of your company?', I would not necessarily expect them to be as fluent or detailed as the manager or managing director might be in explaining it. But in a proper, well-functioning organisation, I would expect them to give me a sense of it. 'We're all about helping you have a good time,' or perhaps, 'It's all about feeling you're getting value for money.' Strategy will only become a team game if the leaders make sure that it is understood and shared from top to bottom. Why do schools all feel a bit different from one another when you walk in for the first time? It's not just about architecture. It's about leadership, culture, strategy, and everyone having a sense of what the plan is. In the modern age, in which there is so much media, so much noise, so much misunderstanding and misinformation, strategies must be devised, then executed and narrated. You do what you do. You keep doing it. You keep saying you're doing it. Over time, you paint the big picture, on your terms.

Rules for strategy

- In my Holy Trinity, S is God . . . (sorry, believers).

- Don't think about T until you are clear about O and S.

- Never confuse S and T.

- Strategy is the place to have arguments, not avoid them. Don't pretend to agree if you don't.

- Write it all down. Think in ink.

- The best strategies can be expressed in a word, a phrase, a sentence, a paragraph, a page, a speech or a book.

- Strategies have to be devised, executed and narrated.

- Strategy is a team game and all levels of the team must be brought into it.

- Strategy is about action, not theory.

- The best strategies are consistent, but are flexible enough to adapt to events. Only change the overall strategy if the fundamentals change.

12.

Learn Confidence

It will probably not have escaped your notice that two of the last four UK prime ministers, David Cameron and Boris Johnson, went to the same school, Eton. What you may not know is that Eton has produced three times as many prime ministers as the Labour Party has in its entire 120-year-plus history. Here's another interesting fact. Five of the six people who put together David Cameron's 2015 election manifesto – the one promising that referendum that would settle the arguments on Europe 'once and for all' – went to Eton (the sixth went to St Paul's), as did Jacob Rees-Mogg (of course), Kwasi Kwarteng, Prince William and the Archbishop of Canterbury.

There are all sorts of reasons why people, especially men, from the 'top' private schools end up with a disproportionate share of wealth, power and the top jobs. Many are born into privilege so start with considerable advantages over the majority whose parents lack the cash or the desire to pay for their child's education on top of all the other financial pressures they face, or who don't choose to have them living away from home or kept locked away from people from different economic backgrounds. Privately educated children also benefit from better paid (if not always better) teachers, smaller class sizes, and access to the kind of educational, sporting and cultural facilities most of the rest of the population can barely dream of. 'We now have four floodlit artificial pitches,' Eton's website proclaims, 'and from 2022 to 2024 we will build new indoor facilities, including a new swimming pool and two sports halls. These will all complement our fantastic current outdoor facilities, which include approximately 40 football/rugby pitches, a 2km rowing lake, 19 cricket pitches and 50 tennis courts.' Then there are the three theatres, two concert halls, a recording studio, three music technology suites, drum suites, a music library, seven pipe organs, and a 'state-of-the-art symphonic concert hall'.

But perhaps more important than any of this is the fact that the development of each pupil's self-confidence is absolutely central to the ethos of such schools. What does self-confidence mean? It means having an inherent faith that you will be able to meet challenges set before you, large and small. It means feeling you have something to contribute, and that it will be of value. It means facing the world with little fear and with a firm belief that you will do well.

Those educated at the leading private schools are encouraged to project, radiate even, an inner confidence. At its best that self-confidence takes the form of the qualities I have just outlined which, provided they do not tip over into arrogance and entitlement, are good things to have. At its worst, it leads to a tendency never to say, 'I don't know', nor to admit to the possibility of ever being wrong. David Cameron is 'right' four times on the first two pages of his autobiography. The referendum that led to Britain's departure from the European Union was 'the right thing to do'. So was quitting after he lost it. 'He's so fixated on being right, I worry for how secretly wrong he must feel,' says privately educated Richard Beard in his book about the role of private schools in the ruin of England, *Sad Little Men*. If Cameron does ever experience dark nights of the soul, he certainly never lets on. Projecting unwavering confidence in his decisions is baked deep into him. There was something classically Cameron about his exit from office in the wake of the EU referendum defeat, humming pleasantly to himself, seemingly without a care in the world, as he walked away from the microphone and the massed ranks of media recording his exit from office.

So, can confidence be learned? The record of many private schools suggests it can. Obviously, many who attend such institutions already enjoy the in-built advantages that stem from their parents' affluence and connections. But they also benefit from a school environment where the development of self-confidence is regarded not merely as a useful add-on, but as a key objective. They grow used to being expected to speak up in class (helped by the fact, of course, that class sizes are small). They also join clubs and societies that make them familiar with performing in public.

By contrast, according to Tarik Salih, one of the young people who read an early draft of this book, children from less privileged backgrounds 'are born feeling there are many limits, and then educated to feel there are more limits'. 'If the government was serious about levelling up,' he adds, 'they would focus on confidence as something that can be developed.' The legendary American football coach Vince Lombardi had an interesting take on this. 'Confidence is contagious . . . so is lack of confidence.' This is why we should do more to spread the former and minimise the latter.

In everyday terms, a lot of self-confidence comes down to feeling at ease when asked to speak in public. Historically, Scotland has led the way here. Why has it produced a disproportionate number of top-flight politicians and orators down the years? I would argue that, in part, it's because of a tradition of debating not just in universities but in schools too – and not just the posh ones. One of my closest friends outside my own political tribe, Charles Kennedy, who became an MP at twenty-three and proved a popular and effective leader of the Liberal Democrats, put a lot of his success down to the skills he learned in debating, first at Lochaber High School and then Glasgow University. These are skills that all of us need, especially today, when communication plays a far bigger role in most of our lives than it used to. Effective communication, which requires confidence and competence in conveying ideas, is an essential item in all of our toolkits; but it is also a means by which tangible change is created. You need confidence to be able to communicate effectively; and effectively communicating builds confidence. Which is why it is worth working on.

Former Australian prime minister Julia Gillard, a shy child who often felt she lacked confidence, told me that it was partly school debating that helped her conquer that shyness, in addition to making her understand the power of a good argument. 'I remember doing a debate where we had to argue *for* the proposition that the man should aways be the leader,' she recalls. 'Clearly, I don't believe that, but it was interesting to try to think how that argument would be made. I am not a natural extrovert, I best refresh in my own company, but it gave me a sense of how you need to argue things out. That opened my eyes to more possibilities. I had wanted to be a teacher but I had two friends, twin sisters I did the debating with, and their mum said no, not teaching, be a lawyer, you'd be good at arguing and debating, so that opened my eyes even wider.'

Of course, it also goes much wider and deeper than schools. Alongside teachers, we need parents, relatives, sports clubs, community leaders, university tutors and others to promote and encourage this vital personal attribute. Together, we have a responsibility to instil self-confidence in the next generation, breaking down the barriers Tarik spoke of, not erecting more and more of them. Only by doing so will we be able to take on the many challenges that the world currently presents.

I did promise not to go all lifestyle guru on you, but, given how important self-confidence is to anyone who wants to campaign for change, I think it's worth sharing a few thoughts on the subject, based on my own personal experience.

It's essential, I think, to be able to master your nerves so that you do not become overwhelmed when feeling under pressure; to develop a sense of self-belief and self-esteem; and to get comfortable at both sharing your views and debating their merits.

I may come across as pretty confident, but 'nerves' can get the better of me all too easily. My clutch knee was shaking uncontrollably on three of the four – or was it five? – occasions I failed my driving test. I once had a psychosomatic asthma attack while competing in a junior bagpipe contest. As you might guess, bagpipe-blowing and a bad asthma attack are wholly incompatible. Unsurprisingly, I did not complete the performance. At school, I found exams a real psychological challenge, and still have recurring dreams about being in the exam room, opening the test paper, and finding I am in the wrong place, doing an exam on a subject I have never studied.

Even now, with all the experience I have behind me, I quite often have periods of bad anxiety – sometimes in public – when my stomach is churning, my mind feels woozy, and I find it hard to make the tiniest of decisions. Occasionally, that anxiety triggers draining repetitive loops in my mind, where I cannot stop ruminating about something that really shouldn't be troubling me, like whether to say yes or no to a social invitation, or how many shirts to take on an upcoming trip. Sometimes it gets to the point where I allow something spectacularly trivial to take on life-changing proportions in my mind. I have had quite bad panic attacks, too, when catastrophising pessimism convinces me something terrible is about to happen: to me, my partner or my children, or the entire world. I am rendered virtually immobile by the fear that doing anything to prevent this disaster will only make it more likely to happen.

Search online for 'Alastair Campbell Andrew Marr interviews', and, at or close to the top, will be clips from an interview on Marr's Sunday morning BBC TV show in 2010, when I dried up, live on air. I don't really know why. But I do know I was in the middle of a depressive episode, hadn't been sleeping, and that anxiety often accompanies my depression and sleeplessness. It was almost like an out-of-body experience. It felt as though I just wasn't there. I feared that I wasn't going to be able to control what I said or did. You can hear when I begin to speak again that I am struggling to find my voice. It was not a full-blown panic attack, but it was certainly a moment when my anxiety got the better of me. Something similar happened a few days later, in the very same studio, when I was about to be interviewed by Jeremy Paxman on *Newsnight*. This time my panic took the form of an asthma attack, allied to the same feeling that I was not fully located in the seat where I was sitting. Thankfully, I had a couple of minutes to settle myself as we waited for the programme to start and Paxman, a much kindlier man than his TV persona would suggest, realised something was going on and made sure I was OK before bringing me in.

During my Andrew Marr meltdown, I decided just to sit it out, breathe steadily, and wait for the moment to pass. It did. But when a few weeks after my Paxman encounter I had a similar attack – asthma plus the sudden fear that I was losing control of mind and feeling – in the middle of a speech at a college, I decided I needed help. I therefore turned to a sports psychologist, Andy McCann. Together we developed a very simple technique for coping with an oncoming panic attack, which involves rubbing the tips of my thumbs and forefingers together in a gentle circular motion. I have no idea why, but it worked, and does to this day. I still have times when I feel nervous or anxious, or I doubt myself, but I find that this technique invariably helps. On other occasions, so might other tactics such as deep breathing, visualisation, mindfulness or talking to a friend.

As a depressive, I know there are times when 'positive thinking' is a lot easier said than done. Yet I also know that it can work. If I tell myself I am not going to enjoy something I have to do, it is likely that I won't. If I tell myself I am going to enjoy it, then I probably will. Feeling positive, quietening nerves, anxiety and doubt, and building self-confidence all require effort. All grow with practice.

At the other end of the emotional scale, I need to be very careful when I get too much energy, and risk becoming manic. I also have to watch my temper. I don't deny having one, and from time to time, especially with hecklers or in Q & A sessions, I can feel my hackles rising and can sense the danger that I am about to go over the top. Sometimes, instinct tells me it's fine to do so, and I will give as good as I get and more. Temper is not always a bad thing. It's almost twenty years since I allegedly 'stormed' into the Channel 4 News studio and laid into the BBC over their handling of our dispute about Iraq, after one of their reporters had accused us of falsifying the case against Saddam Hussein. To this day Fiona – and she is not alone – thinks it was a dreadful error of judgement on my part. To this day, I don't. It is true that temper drove me there, but having rewatched the interview to refresh my memory for the purpose of writing this paragraph, I stand by every word I said to presenter Jon Snow. That display of anger showed the media and the public where I was coming from on an issue that was dominating debate. In the circumstances, I believed it was absolutely necessary. By the same token, I wouldn't generally recommend that politicians thump voters in election campaigns, but John Prescott's handy left jab into the face of someone who egged him in 2001 did no harm to his standing with the public. Authentic, no-nonsense . . . it fitted the image.

At other times, though, I know I have gone too far, and end up regretting what I have said or done. This predisposition of mine has led to my installing an imaginary 'W switch' inside my head. The W is for Wanker. It comes from a time I was doing a Q & A on stage with comedian Matt Forde. In a quickfire round where Matt had asked for short audience questions and short answers from me, someone asked me a spiky but reasonable question about Tony Blair's record. 'You wanted short answers . . . here's mine,' I said. '. . . Wanker.' Many found it funny. I didn't, and later I looked for the man to apologise. Now, whenever I feel the hackles rising, I say to myself: 'W switch – OFF.' It works, partly because it makes me smile. And it shows that, as with the thumb and forefinger thing, there are clever 'centring' tactics and techniques anyone can develop to deal with the stress of the moment, whether that stress takes the form of anxiety, panic or anger.

Visualisation can prove a similarly powerful tool. I promise not to drone on about playing football with Diego Maradona too long – although, as I've already said, I do mention it at least once every day: if you want the full account of the experience, get *Winners*. But one of the things that put taking part in the first Soccer Aid match right up there as one of the best experiences of my life was spending a couple of hours with him at Old Trafford on the morning of the game, just the two of us knocking a ball about. Despite all his years of experience, he wanted to get a feel for the pitch and the stadium and, above all, as I discovered, he wanted to 'visualise' what the encounter was going to be like. He waved at imaginary fans. He hit balls into the net and on one occasion celebrated as if he had won the World Cup Final. It was wonderful to watch the greatest player of all time still taking his trade seriously, years after he had retired, making it matter, using nerves to psyche himself up, imagining what was to come, especially the opportunities he believed the day would offer to him.

So far, I've talked about confidence in general terms, but I'm aware that for many people, and most campaigners, confidence – or rather the lack of it – is something that goes hand in hand with having to speak in public. There's even a word for it: glosso-phobia. Most people are fine with talking most of the time. The moment the public element rears its head, however, the classic anxiety signs can exert themselves: a dry mouth, trembling hands, dizziness, sweating, raised blood pressure, stiffened muscles, nausea – full-blown panic. Recent research suggests that glosso-phobia is a condition that affects up to 75 per cent of people.

It's not hard to understand why. When you talk in public, you're putting yourself on the line. You're likely to experience the understandable fear of being embarrassed or rejected. That's often enough to generate low self-esteem and a sense of failure. And, of course, if you happen to have a bad experience, your fear of having to speak in public again can grow to the point where it becomes debilitating.

As with general anxiety, though, there are things you can do to make the experience, if not exactly pleasurable, at least bearable. In extreme cases, of course, medication may help. On a more everyday level, I myself have found CBT (Cognitive Behavioural Therapy) useful because, done well, it trains you to recognise and manage symptoms. Relaxation techniques have similarly proved effective. Deep breathing really can calm your nerves! So, some-times, does telling yourself that you're going to enjoy getting up in front of all those people.

Another tactic I have developed is to imagine that there is a switch inside my mind – just next to the W switch – that I can turn on and off by moving my head up or down. As I am being introduced to make a speech, I fill my lungs with air, tell myself to smile – not a big teeth-flasher, but just a nice positive smile – nod my head forwards, and say to myself: 'Light bulb – ON.' Then I let out the air from my lungs, and walk on, feeling energetic, and welcoming the attention of all eyes upon me – an experience which, in other circumstances, can be a source of huge anxiety. I say to myself, silently, inside my head: 'This is going to be good. You're on, and you're on form.' One head of government I work with now does the same and told me it had transformed his sense of confidence about 'filling a room', something leaders are expected to do, or at least think they are, which amounts to the same thing.

I also find it useful to be on the look-out to learn new things that I can use in both conversation and public speaking. One of my Post-its reads: 'Never go to bed at night without having learned something you didn't know in the morning.' The more you know, I would argue, the more confident you will feel about arguing or simply expressing your views.

But, ultimately, a lot of it comes down to being willing to put in the practice and the preparation. Just like Maradona, you should want to see the stage where you are about to perform. If you're making a speech or doing a presentation, practise it, in front of a mirror or with friends and colleagues. Alternatively, video yourself and watch the end result back dispassionately. Don't be afraid to ask others, people whose views you respect and trust, for their opinions of you. Demand honesty and don't be offended or hurt by anything they say. Assess it all frankly.

Just before you go on, ask yourself, 'What is the worst thing that can happen here?' You're not going to die. You're not going to be shot. You have an audience of people waiting to hear from you. They want you to do well because they would rather be interested and entertained by what you say than be bored or irritated. Challenge the things that are making you anxious. Tell yourself there is nothing wrong with feeling nervous.

And when it comes to the big moment, if there are friendly faces in the audience, speak directly to them. Looking people in the eye shows confidence, respect and empathy all in one, as well as signalling thought, feeling and intent. Some people do it naturally, others find it strange. But it can be practised, improved.

You can do it with a large, unfamiliar audience too. If your eyes are scanning the room, but you stop and look different people in the eye as you do so, everyone gets a sense that you're talking to them. I've felt it on both sides, as the speechmaker and the speech-listener. Don't tell Tony Blair I said so, but Bill Clinton is the master of that little tactic, and Emmanuel Macron runner-up.

People have a tendency to pepper their speeches with facts and statistics. Both are important, of course, but what brings a speech alive are big-picture arguments and, above all, stories about people – including yourself – which illustrate them. You should never be afraid to share your own experience to make a point. You'll find it will help your self-confidence, too. People relate to stories more than they do to stats, and nothing helps raise your morale more when speaking than sensing that your audience is really engaging with what you're saying. If it is a prepared speech you're making, as opposed to something off the cuff, have a written script, but don't feel bound by it if you feel a point is landing well and you want to develop it. Learn the points and the lines you want to emphasise (and when you deliver them, make sure you're looking at the audience, not down at your notes). Pace yourself, too. There is no need to speak faster than you normally would (when nervous, a lot of people speed up without realising it). Avoid ums, ahs, errs and clichés.

Afterwards, enjoy the relief. Congratulate yourself. But, also, assess honestly where and how you could have done better. Learn for the next time. There is no such thing as perfection. Everything we do is work in progress. I have always relished a good argument, and I enjoy the feeling of knowing that, as I am making a speech, the vast majority of the audience are listening intently. I can always tell. I love seeing people nod along, and if I see them afterwards I make a point of telling them how much I enjoyed their reaction. I like to pick up on the quizzical looks too, to guess what it is that is drawing the doubt on their faces, and address it. But I also know when I am not on form, and I try to assess, frankly, why that happened. It will usually relate to lack of preparation, or a lack of oomph because my mindset was wrong.

Not only is perfection impossible, I would argue, but an obsession with it is very unhealthy. Mete Coban, founder of My Life, My Say, has an interesting take on this, pointing out three recurring trends he sees in the young people he is supporting on the first steps of a new venture. First, whether starting a business or trying to get into politics, 'they want things to be perfect before they take the first step. But that never happens.' Second, because they're growing up in a faster-moving world, one in which instant gratification plays such a role, they expect results too quickly. 'Consistency over time is very underrated,' he says. Third, 'they place unrealistic expectations on themselves by thinking that they can only succeed by coming up with the next big idea.' 'Of course,' he says, 'we want to tackle all the issues in the world, but those who are most successful are those who understand where their strengths are and execute a clear plan very well over a period of time. Sometimes young people want to take on every single issue and don't know where to start, or don't end up becoming the best at anything because they try to do ten things rather than two or three that they are determined to be very good at.'

An obsession with universal acclamation is equally unhealthy. Some people's opinions are worth listening to. Others' very definitely aren't. Why would I allow my confidence or well-being to be affected by a *Daily Mail* journalist venting to please his boss, or a social media troll sitting in his underpants on his mum's sofa using me as the object for his bile? Absolutely pointless, and a total waste of the energy that we've already established we need if we're to change the world. So, unless they have a point, or can do you real harm, do not fret about the people who want to stop you, and who use abuse as their only means of doing so. You will feel a little more self-confident every time you acknowledge to yourself that someone's abuse has simply bounced off you.

The big point here is that we are all uniquely placed to create the impression we want to. We cannot influence how others feel about us other than through who we are, what we say and do, and how we say and do it. So focus more on that, who you are, what you say and do, how you say and do it, and less about what you think others think of you, or are likely to. You'll certainly feel better about yourself if you do. And you'll be more confident.

None of what I've just said means that it's possible to eliminate anxiety altogether. I would argue that that's not a desirable state to achieve in any case. *Match of the Day* presenter and former England striker Gary Lineker once told me: 'I hate it when there is a penalty shoot-out and the commentator says: "It's a lottery." They are the ultimate test of a player's technique under pressure. I love penalties. I loved taking them. I love watching them.' Former cricketer Ebony Rainford-Brent said something similar about the mindset needed when a player is chasing a win in the later stages of a match. 'You have to learn to love the pressure. Using nerves to improve performance is a big part of elite sport.' It is why I resist the idea of the comfort zone. We need new challenges. If we slip into thinking that the things we are used to doing are the things we do best, we stop looking for new things to do that might test us in new ways but also provide purpose and pleasure.

There is a big difference, though, between energising pressure and debilitating stress – or as another of the Post-it notes on my wall puts it more simply: 'Pressure good, stress bad.' Panic attacks are stress. That's bad. Pressure can make you perform better. That's good. It tells you that what you are doing matters. Handled properly, it aids concentration, preparation, workrate and energy, which all combine to improve performance.

Finally, you should never underestimate how much other

people can help you. Getting yourself a good mentor can be life-changing or certainly career-enhancing. A coach/mentor I know who runs 'confidence workshops' swears by a group exercise that involves everyone having large pieces of paper stuck to their backs. The participants all walk around the room, stopping to write other people's qualities down on the paper attached to their backs. The one rule is that only positive traits can be listed. Each member of the group is then encouraged to keep their piece of paper and refer to it whenever they question themselves. A variation on this theme is to ask one member of the group to leave the room and then ask everyone else to write down that person's positive qualities on a whiteboard. Once the whiteboard is full, flip it over and invite the person back in the room. Ask them to write down their own positive traits. Watch them dry up after a few lines. Flip the chart over. Watch them burst into tears of pride.

Some people employ more esoteric techniques. Take Tony Blair, for example. Even his harshest critics would acknowledge that my old boss commanded the House of Commons, and generally exuded confidence, flair and mastery of detail in a decade of answering Prime Minister's Questions. Yet, as I saw Wednesday after Wednesday, he never stopped feeling anxious ahead of the weekly grilling by MPs. To help him, he had a ritual of touching the red ribbon he kept in his pocket, which had been given to him by Communist miners' leader Mick McGahey at a colleague's funeral when Tony was a young MP. A somewhat fearful flyer, Tony also touched the red ribbon whenever he was on a plane, just as it was about to take off. I can recall the near panic on the occasion when he realised he had left it in his flat above 11 Downing Street, in the suit he had worn the day before. Heaven knows what the people in the seats behind us on the flight thought as they watched their prime minister having to be assured by his press secretary that the pilot's skills, and the technical capacity of the plane, were unlikely to be affected by the fact he had forgotten Mick's red ribbon.

P.S. He still has it, and still touches it when planes take off. It's of a piece with another of his superstitions, which was to wear the same pair of shoes for every single one of his PMQs sessions, and to polish them every Wednesday morning. Bizarre. But, then, just as there is often no apparent logic to anxiety, sometimes the illogical is what helps us through it.

Rules for confidence-building

- Write down a list of your positive qualities, and things you've done well.

- Then ask people you trust for their feedback, especially with regard to how you might do even better.

- Try to do something – today – that you have never done before.

- Learn to love preparation, planning and practice.

- If people are asking for something to be done, put your hand up. Volunteer.

- Join groups related to anything you're interested in.

- Look at people in both your own life, and in public life, who you see as confident, analyse what they do, and assess whether they possess traits you can emulate. I think some of our best communicators these days are football and other sports managers, and I learn lots from studying them. If I think of my favourite teachers at school, all of them were effective communicators.

- Identify good role models with a view to becoming one.

- Seek out a good mentor.

- Test your plans and opinions with people you trust.

- Enjoy congratulating yourself, and enjoy compliments from others.

- Compliment others. Don't allow your ego and personal aspirations to get in the way of building up others.

- When you're being criticised, hear the criticism rather than the critic. You might learn more that way. But also don't let it get out of perspective. It's just someone's opinion. Whether or not you agree with it, it doesn't cancel out all your positive qualities.

- Enjoy pressure, resist stress.

13.

Acquire Persevilience

If Timothy Snyder can invent a word – sado-populism – then so can I, and here it is. Persevilience. I can't believe Shakespeare, my favourite word- and phrase-maker of all time (search 'words and phrases invented by Shakespeare' to see why) didn't go for that one. It would have taken up half a line of drama written in his usual iambic pentameter style. Made for *Hamlet*.

> To be, or not to be; that is the question;
> Whether 'tis nobler in the mind to suffer
> The slings and arrows of outrageous fortune,
> Or to summon all persevilience!

Persevilience, as I hope one day to see it recorded in the *Oxford English Dictionary*, is the marriage of perseverance and resilience. They are not exactly the same thing, but they are closely related, and both are key to making meaningful change.

Back to our old friend GGOOB, Getting Good Out of Bad. Why do we want to change the world in the first place? Because there is so much that is bad – that needs improvement. We therefore take the bad and seek to transform it into good. It's an age-old human reaction, and it's the key to progress. And it's because what is bad can become a spur for action that it's possible to say that sometimes the very things that seem terrible when we're experiencing them can turn out to be turning points leading to something much better, something transformative.

Put the book down for a few minutes, and try to think of something that went wrong in your life, but that you now look back on as a good thing. Some of the best, most loving, most committed parents are those who had bad relationships with their own fathers and mothers. They got good out of bad by being determined to be better parents than the ones they had. Great sportsmen and women often talk of their defeats as being more important to their ambition and development than their victories. When he was inducted into the Basketball Hall of Fame, Michael Jordan made a point of thanking the coaches who didn't pick him, the journalists who didn't rate him, the fans who wrote him off.

Much of the emotional power in the films my son Calum makes about the Paralympic Games comes from stories of what made the athletes Paralympians in the first place. It might be an account of a disability they were born with, or an injury they sustained as a child or young adult – a setback that could have destroyed them, but instead drove them to become winners in one of the toughest sporting environments on earth. In some cases, they also used their setback to help others. Paralympic athlete Noelle Lambert, who had her left leg amputated below the knee following a moped accident in her late teens, is a case in point. When she had recovered from the operation, she took up sprinting and competed at the Paralympic Games in Tokyo 2020. She also founded the Born to Run Foundation which helps provide specialised prosthetics to younger adults and children, and she helps others by sharing her own experience. GGOOB.

I often describe my nervous breakdown, back in 1986, as being the worst thing that ever happened to me. But I would also say it turned out to be the best.

At the time, it was terrifying. I started to hear voices. I thought I was being tested by a higher power. And I believed that if I failed the test, I would die. The experience was humiliating, too. I hated being a young high-flyer suddenly crashing to earth. I hated the huge taste of failure my breakdown induced in me – after all, I hate failing at anything.

Looking back, I shudder at some of the things I was doing at the time, and the different course my life could have taken had I not had a lot of luck in getting out of the situations I landed myself in during the months and weeks that led up to my breakdown. There are one or two I cannot even bring myself to recall in print – things I did when out of control through drink that could have caused enormous damage to life and limb. I still shudder when I recall the time I hurled a chair into a crowd, and thank my lucky stars that it somehow landed in one of the few tiny gaps between people.

But then, post-breakdown, came the good. My partner Fiona stood by me. I learned the value of real friends. I got my old job back. I discovered that you really can learn from mistakes. I acquired an inner strength that I still draw on today, not least if I am ever feeling anxious and/or depressed, and I measure that anxiety or depression against the fear I felt back in 1986 as my mind literally exploded in a terrifying cacophony of music, rows, and smashing glass that seemed so real I couldn't understand why I didn't have blood on my face.

Back at the *Mirror*, and no longer boozing, I saw my career take off again. And then, in 1994, Tony Blair became Labour leader following the death of John Smith from a heart attack and asked me to work for him. I initially said no, persuaded by Fiona, friends and family that the role would put us under intolerable strain (our third child, Grace, had just been born). But deep in my gut, I knew I had to do it, so I changed my mind. Fiona, friends and family were right: it did put the family under strain, and if Fiona were not as strong as she is, I am not sure we would have survived it. But if you really think you can make a difference, you have to try to make it, particularly if you feel, as I did, that you have been given a second chance.

So maybe you should put this book down for a moment, and reflect, in the spirit of getting good out of bad, on things that have happened in your life, or may be happening right now, which have forced you to call on your powers of perseverance and resilience. Think of the setbacks and difficult moments and episodes you managed to get through or get over. Have you had periods of ill health but feel stronger for having got through them? Did you lose your job but then get another one which paid you more and gave you more satisfaction? Can you gain strength and inspiration from knowing that though you have lost friends and family, for example, you managed to keep going, and though you miss them, you are still able to function and lead a full life?

In which case you have shown powers of persevilience. The resilience element is the ability to recover from setback, particularly if you don't merely recover, but end up better and stronger than you were before the setback occurred. Perseverance is more about keeping on keeping on, whatever the setbacks and difficulties, and however long it takes to meet the challenge or solve the problem you're facing.

They are both great GGOOB words. Resilience requires the setback, the injury, the shock that calls upon your resilience in the first place. Perseverance carries with it an assumption that what you're grappling with is difficult. After all, you don't hear people say, 'I must persevere with this fabulous holiday that I am having.' Or 'I honestly don't know how I can persevere to the end of this wonderful piece of music I am listening to.'

The two qualities work together. If you have the resilience to recover from a setback, and learn lessons from it, your perseverance will strengthen. If you persevere with something even when it is not going fully according to plan, or you are not enjoying it, then that will add currency to your resilience bank. The more currency you have in your resilience bank, the more you can draw on to fuel your perseverance. The more you persevere, the greater your resilience becomes. Persevilience is born.

Once, if I had had to rank the two words I would have said that ultimately resilience is more important than perseverance. Now I believe that perseverance is the crowning strength. It's why I have made the word Persevilience. And this is not merely because Resiliverance sounds a bit weird, and less Shakespearean.

'The winner is the loser who evaluates defeat properly,' said Colm O'Connell, an Irish missionary who became a great coach to the athletics team in Kenya. I love that sentiment. It makes me think of the list of persevilient heroes I contemplate if I am starting to lose my mind in a queue or a traffic jam. I calm myself by saying: 'If Nelson Mandela could stand twenty-seven years in jail, I can get through this . . .' Or I think of Malala Yousafzai – Malala, as she is known pretty much all over the world. At the age of fifteen she was shot in the head because of her activism for girls' and women's education in Pakistan. Since then she has devoted herself to promoting the cause that led to the shooting in the first place, becoming the youngest-ever Nobel Prize laureate. And she's still only in her mid-twenties! Or I think of the families who have never given up fighting for justice for the ninety-seven Liverpool fans who lost their lives in the Hillsborough Stadium disaster of 1989. Check out *Anne*, a TV programme from 2022 about Anne Williams, whose son Kevin was one of the ninety-seven, and who devoted the rest of her life to pursuing justice for him and the others who died. She herself died, aged just sixty-two, in 2013, several years before Maxine Peake's brilliant portrayal of her struggle. The fact her story is still being told means she is still fighting now. It's the same thing with *Till*, one of the great films of last year, which told the story of Emmett Till, a posthumous icon of the civil rights movement, who at the age of fourteen was tortured, lynched and dumped in a river as punishment for flirting – allegedly – with a white woman. The star of the film is his mother, Mamie Till-Mobley, who fought for just-ice, not just for her son, but for all African Americans. She died in 2003. But neither she nor her son were forgotten, and in March 2022 the Emmett Till Antilynching Act, which made lynching a federal crime, was signed into law by President Biden.

What unites those different examples – the political activist lan-guishing in jail, the young women's rights campaigner so feared by opponents they wanted to kill her, the mothers determined to get to the truth about what happened to their sons, and then get good out of bad for others – is their absolute belief in the right-ness of their cause, and their determination to keep believing, and keep acting to give meaning and purpose to those beliefs, whatever the obstacles in their way. I guarantee all of them will have had moments of doubt. Mandela had times when he felt he would die in jail and that all of the efforts being made on his behalf would come to nothing. Malala inevitably worries that someone might try again to kill her, a fate she would be better placed to avoid if she kept her head down, stopped campaigning, stayed safe. I guarantee Anne Williams will have had moments when she felt the bureaucratic forces ranged against her were too strong, insurmountable, and wondered whether she should not just put it all behind her and try to rebuild her life. Mamie Till left the trial of her son's killers before the verdict came in, disgusted at what she had seen and – rightly – convinced the all-white jury would let them go free, whatever the evidence (the killers later admitted to the murder, and got paid for the interview in which they did so). But, somehow, every one of these heroic figures found a way to dig ever deeper into their emotional reserves and find the faith and the fight to keep on keeping on.

Such extraordinary persevilience may seem out of reach to many. And I'm not saying persevilience, even in its less extraor-dinary forms, is easy. It requires belief, guts and determination.

It requires us to believe wholeheartedly in what we are doing, and to carry the conviction that it matters. It can be exhausting, burning its way through our physical and mental energy reserves.

But there are ways in which we can try to build up those reserves to make it that bit more attainable. Essentially, we have to look after our physical health. We have to look after our mental health. And we need to understand that physical and mental health are two sides of the same coin.

I honestly cannot believe how unhealthy my lifestyle used to be; and I honestly don't know how Fiona, my partner of forty-two years, put up with my chain-smoking and my heavy drinking. She's always been a health freak, very conscious of diet, became a vegetarian before it was trendy, and has swum a mile virtually every day since we met. I haven't smoked now for thirty-five years, and not been drunk since 1986, but it took me to my early forties to get with the programme and to understand that three things I had never taken seriously – sleep, diet and exercise – really were just about the most important components of a physically and mentally healthy lifestyle.

I accept, of course, that there are supremely fit people who have psychological problems, just as there are non-exercisers who are very happy. But, as a rule, if you're physically fit, your mental health will be better; and if you're mentally in good shape, you're more likely to keep yourself physically in good shape too. How does this help sort the world out? Well, if you're not in decent shape physically and mentally, you are less likely to be persevilient.

It's all about energy. Wake up well rested, and you can feel that extra energy the moment you come round. Wake up groggy and grumpy, wishing you were still sleeping, and the cylinders of mind and body take longer to fire. It sets the tone for the entire day.

I used to see sleep as a waste of time. I was so jealous of people who said they could get by on three or four hours. That was my goal. The less sleep, the better. Madness. I am sure it is one of the reasons for my breakdown. I was never fully rested. And if the quality of your sleep is poor, and in addition you're waking up with a hangover, you are never going to get into top gear. Even to get near it, you have to dig deeper to find energy, push yourself harder – so the tiredness kicks in, but if you don't rest, it simply makes you ever more wired.

So now, I treasure my sleep. I love going to bed early. I love the feeling of waking up, feeling rested, ready to go, energetic. It doesn't happen every day, because I do get insomnia from time to time, and bouts of depression that make me either sleep too much or too little, which causes me to wake up demotivated and empty. But in general, I sleep so much better because I consciously embrace sleep as a virtue rather than considering it my time-destroying enemy.

Another warning: the risk of burnout is real, and pacing yourself is vital. It is all too easy to be completely consumed by campaigning and that is great . . . *unless* it becomes so consuming that everything else – health, livelihood, relationships, other interests – falls by the wayside. If every youngster burns out within five years of starting out in politics, we're not going to get anywhere very quickly. I am the worst person to be giving advice on this, because I have always had mild – and sometimes not so mild – workaholic tendencies. So don't listen to me; listen to my nephew Jamie.

For me, pacing myself means trying not to attend more than three councillor or Labour Party things per week. Some weeks, that is unavoidable (e.g. the first and last weeks of every month when a lot of the meetings take place), so I will attend no meetings the week after. Diary management is important and it's OK to miss a meeting. It's also OK to delegate to others. And it's OK to say no. Activists shouldn't be yes-men and -women who just do whatever they are asked – they need to be discerning about what is a good use of their time (high- vs low-impact tasks), what aligns with their skillsets, and what will help them to build their own political reputation. I have been a branch secretary in the past . . . what, in reality, did I get through doing this, other than the pain of having to organise, call and minute meetings? Not a huge amount, so I don't do it any more. Someone who wants that to be their activism does. I can focus on the things I think I am better suited to.

In the context of persevilience, you might enjoy the tips I used to give to staff ahead of election campaigns – the only form of activity, as Bill Clinton put it, 'designed to make everyone look like their passport photo'. As you'll see it's all about keeping energy supplies topped up.

Rules for campaign persevilience

- If you see water, drink it. (Yellow piss is loser's piss.)

- If you're offered alcohol, ask for water.

- If you're offered drugs, call the cops.

- If you see fruit, eat it. (Banana is the King of Fruit.)

- Beware of the caffeine overdose.

- If you see chocolate, leave it. (Full disclosure, I failed at this one almost every day.)

- If you see a bed, sleep in it, preferably not with a stranger.

- Nobody is so busy they can't do some exercise every day.

- If you can't go for a run, go for a walk, and use it as thinking time.

- See stairs as your friend, lifts as your enemy.

- If you have a problem, share it.

- If you have an idea, test it.

- One thank you is worth more than ten bollockings.

- Read books, not newspapers.

- Listen to music, not the news.

14.

A Tale of Two Campaigns

On a recent random day, outside the Parliament Hill Lido on Hampstead Heath where I swim most mornings, I had two random encounters, the first with someone I know, the second with someone I had never met before, and have never seen again since. Our conversations form the spine of this chapter, for they provided me with good examples of two campaigns – one which ended in victory, the other which ended in defeat – in which all the elements of campaigning I have just explored – the trinity of leadership, teamship and strategy and the personal qualities of confidence and persevilience – were tested to the full.

On my way to the lido that day I bumped into Lara Spirit, one of the young people whose views I have sought at various stages of writing. She lives near me, and near the lido, so I see her fairly regularly. On the day in question, there had been more bad news about the impact of Brexit, with enormous delays at Dover border controls dominating the news.

'It's so depressing,' she said, 'when you think how close we got.' By 'we' she meant the People's Vote campaign, on which she and I had worked together, trying to secure a referendum on the final Brexit deal. It did, as she rightly said, feel at times as though we had the momentum needed to win. Ultimately, though, we were unsuccessful – partly, we both felt, because we failed on questions of leadership, teamship and strategy, and partly because we didn't have the winning mindset instilled from top to bottom.

As I came out after my swim, a woman who was arriving for hers, who I had not seen before, was walking towards me.

'Oh hello,' she said, cheerily. 'How's your son Calum?'

I said he was fine, we chatted a little, and I asked how she knew him.

'I'm a friend of Bill,' she said, with a little wink and a smile as she headed to the changing rooms. 'Give Calum my best,' she added over her shoulder. 'Tell him I'll see him soon.'

Some of you will know what 'friend of Bill' means. For others, I will have to explain, but before I do, I would like you to remember these five thoughts from previous chapters . . .

No one person can make a difference. (Nonsense.)

Get Good Out of Bad. (Always, if you can.)

We achieve more together than we do alone. (For sure.)

Persevilience comes from turning setback into progress. (New word, great mindset.)

Campaigns need leaders. Leaders need teams. Teams need strategies. (Holy Trinity.)

To know about Bill, you have to know about Bob. Theirs is an almost fairy-tale story of the fusion of teamship and leadership, in which the local, very personal actions of a leader who never saw himself as such led to a global organisation that has helped and saved countless lives. Bill is all the proof you need that one person can change the world, and that the change he inspired can keep doing good in the world long after that person has left us.

There are many famous Bills in the world. Clinton. Gates. Shankly. But if you tell a stranger you're a 'friend of Bill', you almost certainly don't mean any of the above. There are many famous Bobs in the world. Marley. Hope. Dole. Geldof. Paisley.

But if your life or anyone you know has been touched by alcoholism, there is only one Bob, just as there is only one Bill. They were the co-founders, in 1935, of Alcoholics Anonymous. A 'friend of Bill' is someone who attends AA meetings. Like the woman at the lido. Like my son, Calum.

AA is a global organisation that came about when Bill, a broker and an alcoholic, who was on a business trip in Ohio, asked whether there was another alcoholic around whom he could talk to, and who could help him stick to his new resolve not to drink. He was put in touch with Bob, a surgeon who had struggled most of his adult life with alcoholism.

Despite the occasional relapse, that meeting ultimately yielded lasting sobriety for the two men. They therefore decided to apply the same principle – recovering alcoholics supporting other recovering alcoholics – to help others. First a handful, then dozens, then hundreds, before, in 1939, they produced a book, *Alcoholics Anonymous: The Story of How More Than One Hundred Men Have Recovered from Alcoholism*. Known to devotees as 'The Big Book', it sets out a programme, called the Twelve Steps and the Twelve Traditions, that flowed from Bill and Bob's discussions about alcoholism. It's a very spiritual work in many ways, and there's an element of a religious 'seeing the light' to Bill's initial encounter with Bob. But, ultimately, though God figures large in the Steps and Traditions as designed by Bill and Bob, many non-believers have benefited from the programme, by making it about belief rather than any kind of specific religious faith.

As word spread, AA groups began to spring up all over North America, then beyond. Today, there are more than 120,000 AA groups, with over two million people active participants. Achieving more together than they do alone. Getting good out of bad. And all because one man – Bill – had the insight that he needed another alcoholic – Bob – to guide him through tricky moments. Friends of Bill. Brilliant. Bill changed the world.

I don't imagine Bill had OST in mind as he cast around for someone to help him through his tricky moment in Ohio, but retrospectively his experience can be fitted within that frame.

O: Stay sober tonight.

S: Mutual support.

T: Find someone to give it.

Then, as that first meeting developed into an organisation:

O: Help others stay sober.

S: Mutual support through AA meetings.

T: Anonymity, sharing of stories, 'sponsor' system, Twelve Steps.

Bill's full name was William Griffith Wilson. He came from Vermont in the US, and he lived from 1895 to 1971. Bob was Robert Smith, born in Vermont in 1879, died in 1950, seven years before I was even born. Yet I think I can make the case that their philosophy, and the organisation to which their own alcoholism gave birth, has helped to get Calum's life back on track, after a time when we honestly feared his alcoholism would kill him. He is now ten years sober, and an AA regular. He has developed persevilience, and AA has helped. Because AA is group persevilience in action. Bill and Bob, like many addicts, continued to struggle with the issues that led to their addiction in the first place. But, as their sobriety extended and strengthened, they developed an inner confidence, strengthened further as they saw the effect that the organisation they founded was having on others.

A part of me is hesitant about writing the full names of 'Bill and Bob', given that anonymity lies at the heart of AA's founding principles. Indeed, when Bob was named among *Time* magazine's

100 most important people of the twentieth century, he refused to let them use a photo of him. But theirs is a story that deserves to be told far and wide. It is a perfect example of how so-called 'ordinary people' can do extraordinary things that change the world. Change is not just about politics. Such a simple idea, started in such a simple way, and yet today there is barely a town or city that doesn't host regular AA meetings. The creation of similar groups for gambling, drugs, sex and other addictions can also be seen as part of the Bill and Bob legacy. That is an incredible achievement.

Bill never saw himself as a leader. In fact, AA is often referred to as 'a benign anarchy'. His biographer, Susan Cheever, in her book, *My Name Is Bill*, wrote: 'Bill Wilson never held himself up as a model: he only hoped to help other people by sharing his own experience, strength and hope. He insisted again and again that he was just an ordinary man.' Maybe. But he did something truly remarkable by taking his own addiction, his recovery, and applying the lessons he learned from both to devise a philosophy, a programme and an organisation that helped others, and will do so for the rest of time. That is a legacy. And when your own son is one of those helped by it, it's hard not to see the guy who started the ball rolling not just as a real leader, but a real hero too. Bill and Bob really do strike me as a wonderful example of both my Holy Trinity, and *the* Holy Trinity, at work.

And now, less happily, the People's Vote campaign. Because, as ABBA remind us, the winner takes it all, it has already been airbrushed into history as a footnote. But it was quite a thing while it lasted. From a standing start, PV, as it became known, organised three of the four biggest marches London has ever seen and, having started with the support of about as many MPs as you could squeeze into a black cab, had won round close to 300 towards the end.

O: A second referendum on the actual Brexit deal.

S: Persuading the public to pressure MPs that a second referendum was the way to resolve the mess.

T: Many and varied, see below for the main ones.

Interestingly, although the campaign reached across the generations, it was to a large extent driven by young people working for two particular groups, 'For our Future's Sake' and 'Our Future, Our Choice', FFS and OFOC (variations on the same joke, but united in a single-minded pursuit of their goal). PV's argument was that while the 2016 referendum had yielded a narrow win for those seeking to leave the EU, now that it was becoming clearer what Brexit meant in practice, and apparent that major constitutional change was involved, there should be a referendum to confirm that the country was happy with the eventual deal. It was not an easy message to communicate, in the face of Leave's success, and the relentless accusations that we were seeking to defy 'the will of the people'. But we were confident we could win the argument.

FFS and OFOC came to all the important meetings of the campaign and exerted real influence on decisions, strategically and tactically. They worked unbelievably hard for a fraction of the wages they could have commanded elsewhere. Lots worked for nothing, not least the thousands of volunteers that were engaged around the country. Though the media was always keener to take older, better-known faces, we were pushing these young people on screen too, and they did a great job. They also toured schools and university campuses to spread the message in a way that put the main political parties to shame. And they organised a mass lobby of Parliament that was so large and so effective that the serjeant-at-arms complained about them. Their sense of teamship was at times remarkable. It was a pleasure to be around them.

Overall, the PV campaign was one of the most energetic and energising campaigns I have ever worked on, including the May 1997 election (when some among the PV team were not even born).

But the fact is we lost.

I hate losing, and have spent a lot of time thinking about why we lost. In my opinion, our objective was a clear one. Our strategy – generating public pressure on MPs – was pretty good. However, I think it also contained two flaws. Firstly, as I'll explain in a moment, I suspect we became part of the polarisation problem we were trying to address. Secondly, our conviction that our cause was a just one led us to underestimate our opponents. That's never a good mindset to have, and it's one reason why the initial referendum was lost. I have to hold up my hand here. So convinced was I back in 2016 that, when push came to shove, Remain would win, I largely kept out of the campaign. By the time David Cameron's right-hand-man Craig Oliver asked me to help the pro-Remain politicians prepare for the big TV debates, it was too late: our chances were already slipping away. Chancellor George Osborne's economic message was being overwhelmed by the emotional appeal of the Leave message and its characterisation of the Remain argument as 'Project Fear'. Underestimating the opposition remained a strategic weakness three years later, though a lesser one than in 2016.

PV's tactics, by contrast, were generally pretty strong: email and letter-writing campaigns to put pressure on MPs; marches and rallies; polling of public/political party members/unions/business sectors/regions and constituencies to show the changing mood; a diversity of voices; the mobilisation of young people to show that their generation was being betrayed; targeted ads; regional campaign groups. Looked at purely through the OST frame, we were in good shape.

Ultimately, where I think the whole thing fell down was in

the formal leadership within the campaign, and in the erratic leadership provided by the politicians outside it. The latter problem became particularly apparent just at the time when we had achieved momentum, and it proved catastrophic. The Liberal Democrats, at the time arguably the most anti-Brexit party, became seized by an absurd conviction they were on the verge of electoral triumph, so fell into the trap the Tories were laying to get the opposition parties to back an early election in December 2019, which they would make all about Brexit. The Scottish Nationalists, who had more realistic prospects of doing well in a general election, and using their success to step up their fight for another independence referendum, fell even more willingly into the trap. Labour had no option but to go along with it, and a Parliament in which momentum towards a second referendum on Brexit was growing, voted to end itself and give Johnson the gift he had been longing for.

In any case, by then, the campaign had largely imploded, thanks to a collapse in trust and respect between members of the board and the people running the campaign on a day-to-day basis, a situation made worse by personality clashes and factionalism. Chairman Roland Rudd, with the support of a board largely divorced from the nuts and bolts of the campaign, sacked the people actually running the operation, who were not just highly effective in what they were doing, but also a major reason for the phenomenal motivation of the young people in the team. Rudd denied everyone access to the all-important data we had built up, locked the office doors, destroyed morale and drained all the energy that had been achieving so much. If anything is going to make young people cynical about political engagement, it's when things like that happen. And, of course, when leadership implodes in that way, teamship goes out of the window.

In pure campaigning terms, the PV campaign did some pretty

remarkable work. But, ultimately, the lack of clear leadership structures did for us. People left meetings with their own idea of what had been agreed. Personal agendas took over from collective goals. And when the pressures really piled on, the seeds of distrust, and the lack of strategic clarity, grew into something more damaging and, eventually, amid the factional fallouts and the clashing egos, utterly destructive. It is hard for a young campaign team to feel confident when their supposed betters and elders have locked them out of the office. And it is hard to adopt a persevilient mindset when you can see, hear and feel that the entire campaign is collapsing from within.

Added to that was the fact that, as I have already hinted, we became part of the problem we were trying to solve. The referendum had been a deeply polarising event, in horribly polarising, Trumpian, modern media times. These days, you will hear people saying it would have been better had we backed a softer Brexit rather than held out for a second referendum. It's a valid criticism – in that such a deal would have been far better than the disastrous one we ended up with. But it's valid only up to a point. If a soft Brexit was possible in 2016 or even 2017, by the time we launched People's Vote, such a compromise was the least popular of all the options. Theresa May's proposed deal would almost certainly have disintegrated before the ink of her signature had dried on it. Britain was a divided country, its politics was shrill and we were in a knife fight where waving a teaspoon around would have done no one much good.

The problem was that while such polarisation may have yielded us a support base of millions, it also hardened the opposition of the Leavers and Tories whose support we needed but which it became ever more vanishingly unlikely that we would secure. I endlessly debated on TV, radio and in public meetings, with prominent Leavers like Nigel Farage and Jacob Rees-Mogg. They could fire up their true believers. We could fire up ours. But reasonable debate that might change lots of minds one way or the other? Not so much.

The story of the People's Vote campaign offers deep lessons for the way politics is conducted and explained. It also demonstrates that when polarisers polarise, the many people who do not live inside a political bubble and just want to get on with their lives, are likely to turn away from the whole political process. I discovered after the event that our social media team was putting filters on PV's Facebook ads which excluded anyone who watched *Top Gear*, played bingo, didn't have a degree, or liked Piers Morgan. FFS! (And I am not talking about For Our Future's Sake.) It was a good way to get clicks, likes and shares from your own side – but the opposite of how you reach out to your opponents and persuade. Indeed, the many people who followed and listened to Piers Morgan – a Remain voter who felt Brexit nonetheless had to 'happen' (whatever that meant) because of the referendum result in 2016 – were exactly the kinds of people we should have been trying to win over.

Former journalist and Labour adviser Tom Baldwin, who I had persuaded to take on the formal role of strategy and communications director, put it like this: 'We had to get noticed, to get on the pitch. But to get noticed, raise the funds, get people marching, writing to MPs and all the other things you need to shift opinion, we ended up not just preaching to the converted, but really pissing off the people we were trying to convert.' It was a criticism often levelled at us by Jeremy Corbyn and his team. Ironically, it was a mistake he made as well in his time as Labour leader. When you believe so much in the rightness of your cause that you lose sight of the people you need to win over, and the different methods and arguments that might be needed, you're on a journey to nowhere.

Barack Obama put it very well. 'This idea of purity, that you're never compromised, always politically "woke" and all that stuff.

You should get over that – the world is messy, there are ambiguities. People who do good stuff have flaws. People you are fighting may love their kids. The danger I see in young people, especially on college campuses, accelerated by social media, is this sense that the way of "me making change" is to be as judgemental as possible about other people and that's enough. If I tweet or hashtag that you didn't do something right, or you used the wrong verb I can sit back and feel good about myself: "See how woke I was, I called you out." That's not activism. That is not bringing about change. If all you are doing is casting stones, you are not going to get very far in changing things.'

Telling someone they have no right to a view is not a great opening gambit if you're hoping to win them over. It's why I don't support the increasing tendency towards a cancel culture and the non-platforming of people with whose views a vocal group happens to disagree. Social media has done much to harm thoughtful public debate, and culture warriors continue to exploit grievances rather than engage with them, and yet I still believe that if you have the better argument, ultimately you give yourself the better chance of winning. But, if you're fighting a political campaign, you also need more than that. You need to be able to persuade above the noise. And it is in all of our interests, not least in order to defeat the 3Ps from Part I – polarisation, populism and post-truth – that we actively seek to carve out space for persuasion and genuine argument, not just shouting and mobilisation. That is partly what *The Rest Is Politics* podcast tries to do. Obviously, mobilisation is important, but as a result of the assault on truth that damages so many important debates today, it is going to be hard to generate an honest conversation about the future without engaging in some kind of truth and reconciliation about the past. Whether it's Brexit here, or guns and abortion in the US, the shouting drowns out the debates that we need to have.

I still think we were right to try to get that second referendum, and the way Brexit is playing out has only strengthened my view. I still look back on the People's Vote campaign as having embodied some of the best principles of teamship within the team actually doing the work. But teamship alone is never enough. We failed on leadership. Because we failed on leadership, our teamship suffered. And because of both those failures, we failed on strategy. You cannot win, and you certainly can't win well, unless all three – leadership, teamship and strategy – are working in harmony.

PART THREE
Taking the Next Step

15.

Get Your Message Across

So you've decided to get involved. Good. You're determined to make a difference. Great. And you're confident that you can. Even better. Remember this, though. However brilliant your idea, however clever your strategy, however committed you may be, if you can't get your message across, you're finished before you start.

This may seem so blindingly obvious a statement to make that it doesn't need stating. And yet it's extraordinary how often dedicated and talented campaigners treat communicating their message almost as an afterthought – as though, provided you have right on your side, everything else will fall into place. Sadly, the world is not like that.

If you look at the most effective communicators, they tend to have three things in common. They know what their story is and how to frame it. They know how to keep it simple. And they come across as themselves, not merely as a mouthpiece for a cause or movement. Much as I dislike Donald Trump for his malign role in US politics and world affairs, I recognise that he is a past master here. His speeches at rallies may be long, meandering and often delusional, but the central messages he delivers are straightforward and clear. And whether he was transmitting them via social media or to a stadium audience of thousands, they have always come across as authentically 'his'.

More positively, an ability to communicate and connect is also one of Ukrainian president Volodymyr Zelensky's core strengths. Thanks no doubt in part to his experience as an actor, he is confident and fluent in front of the camera, whether that's in more formal settings, or filming one of the selfie videos that have been viewed by millions around the world. The messages he has been communicating in recent times into homes and phones everywhere are simple. *The Russian invasion of Ukraine was wrong. This is an existential fight. Our people are fighting courageously. We can win. But we need support.* He knows that if he's to make those messages land, he has to say the same things again and again, as though he's saying them for the first time. And he comes across as genuine, his trademark green T-shirt giving him both a touch of ordinary guy and military leader.

Another of Zelensky's great skills is to appreciate the many ways in which a message can now be transmitted. He understands how to tweak the delivery of that message to suit the medium through which it is being broadcast. In the course of a single day he may address an international body like the UN; visit a child in hospital, who says she knows him from TikTok; make a selfie video; and conduct an interview with a foreign broadcaster. The same basic messages are broadcast each time, but communicated in different forms. Those pieces he does to camera that involve conversations with 'ordinary' members of the public, or 'ordinary' soldiers, are rough at the edges, as though to emphasise a sense of real-life reportage. The ones he does to, say, a foreign parliament, are earnest and direct. US president Joe Biden's announcement of $800 million in new military aid might have happened without Zelensky's stirring speech by videolink to Congress the day before, in which he played moving films of what was happening to the people in Ukraine. But I am sure the speech, and the manner in which Zelensky made it, helped ensure that Biden experienced next to no political pushback in the US for committing to such enormous political and financial support. It was the same approach, resulting in even greater financial backing from the US, when Zelensky visited the White

House and Congress just before Christmas last year, one of the stand-out political and diplomatic moments of 2022. His New Year message, delivered shortly after his return to Kyiv, was a communications masterclass. At seventeen minutes, it is long for a straight address to camera (though there is occasional film over-lay telling the story of the war so far), but it is beautifully crafted and beautifully filmed, and certainly worth viewing if you are interested in how to communicate well in moments of crisis and challenge. Zelensky talks rarely, if at all, about himself, focusing instead on the people. The story is an awful one, yet somehow, as the final shot comes to an end, you feel much more hopeful than when you started.

Zelensky and his team also 'get' social media, endlessly putting out short films and other materials to promote across all the main channels. These, in turn, generate coverage across mainstream media, too, in a never-ending loop. One of their great weapons is humour, usually at Putin's and the Russian army's expense, in the form of memes, cartoons, or anything else which allows them both to poke fun and to highlight the cultural differences between the two sides. Putin's formal addresses, staged photos and carefully controlled media interactions come over as hope-lessly old-fashioned and unconvincing by comparison.

On occasion, Zelensky and his team target specific people via social media to great effect. It was on Twitter that the Ukrain-ian minister of technology, Mykhailo Fedorov, published an open letter to the CEO of Apple, Tim Cook, asking the tech giant to block the Apple Store in Russia. They did. Fedorov used a similar tactic with Tesla CEO Elon Musk when asking for Starlink Inter-net satellites. Musk obliged.

Zelensky's other great insight is that in an era where the mes-sages coming at us are constant and relentless, you can never afford to let your voice fall silent. When I was starting out with Tony Blair, we could more or less claim to be 'setting the agenda' if we were leading a few TV and radio news bulletins and a couple of broadsheets, and at least getting noticed in the tabloids. These days, thanks to the explosion in TV and radio channels, 24/7 news on TV and radio, websites, streaming, podcasts and, of course, social media, we have a media landscape in which 'the agenda', as it was understood back then, barely exists. Or, if it does, the pace of change, the proliferation of outlets, and the media's constant need to move on to the next big thing, means that it rarely remains 'the agenda' for long. It takes a US presidential election result, a Russian invasion of Ukraine, the death of the Queen or a global pandemic for there to be the sense of a single established 'agenda', and even with events as huge as those, the world moves on a lot faster than it used to. Coverage of the Queen's death in September 2022 dominated the media and public debate in most parts of the world. The coverage in the UK was on a gargantuan scale and overseas the attention given to her funeral was enormous. My favourite picture of that day was sent to me by a friend, Alastair Morrison, who runs Pinsent Masons law firm: taken from the back of the sizeable business-class cabin on an Emirates plane heading from Dubai to Sydney, it shows every single passenger watching live coverage of the funeral on the individual screens in front of them. 'This', he messaged me 'is what you call soft power!' And yet, including in the UK, once her funeral had taken place, things – 'the agenda' – moved on quickly, shortly thereafter to be filled by a somewhat well-publicised book by one of her grandsons!

So, while Vladimir Putin's invasion of Ukraine inevitably dominated the agenda in most countries of the world for some time, President Zelensky was all too aware that coverage of his country's plight would not be sustained unless he could keep communicating in new and innovative ways. He was conscious that our attention spans have shortened. He knew that our capacity to be shocked has been weakened by the relentless reporting of bad news, which means, tragically, that the fact of war, and of its horrors, is all too quickly normalised for those not directly affected. He realised that part of his role as a leader, both as commander-in-chief and communicator-in-chief, was therefore to pump out the same messages, again and again and again, to keep the world's focus where the Ukrainians wanted it to be.

Thanks to the Internet, anyone today can seek to employ the tactics of a Trump or a Zelensky to get their message across. Obviously, there are some huge downsides to this. As former foreign secretary David Miliband pointed out to me recently, people's obsession with gaining as many likes and shares as possible on Twitter and elsewhere means that what we often end up with is 'the opposite of argument': relentless shallow opinion. Campaigning via social media can be vicious, too. In certain hands – Trump again comes to mind – it can be downright dangerous. Consider, for example, whether Jair Bolsonaro would ever have become president of Brazil, Latin America's biggest country, in 2019 without social media to exploit and manipulate. A campaign narrated by traditional media, with a mix of supportive and antagonistic newspapers, and broadcast media seeking to challenge as well as merely cover what he said and did, would have given Bolsonaro a much harder ride than he got by overwhelming the media space via his own social channels. Rather than engage the mainstream media, Bolsonaro made a virtue of bypassing it, presenting it as part of 'the enemy, the elite' that he was heroically combatting on behalf of 'the people'.

His online campaign was everything one would expect from a right-wing populist: a blend of lies, vicious personal attacks, and the wholesale vilification of certain groups, such as the LGBTQ+ community. But, of course, making controversial but compelling content galvanised his base. It also demonstrated that it is possible to mount an enormous, motivating network campaign across a

major country without recourse to a huge budget, a huge professional team, or the support of conventional media.

That very fact, though, should give encouragement to those
seeking to get a hearing for their infinitely more honourable
causes. Cambridge Analytica insider-cum-whistleblower Christopher Wylie has provided chapter and verse on how that company
harvested data on an industrial scale to target potential Leave
voters with individually crafted, often untrue messages. But in
his book *Mindf*ck* he also describes how when he first encoun-
tered the Cambridge Analytica company, he could see that the
technology that it was developing could be used for good. He still
believed this even after he'd met alt-right self-styled guru Steve
Bannon. He accepts he was naïve. But that doesn't make him
wholly wrong. Either way, I find it hard to conceive how any campaign for radical change for the better, on pretty much anything,
is going to be won without understanding social media, embracing it, and seeking to use it for good.

Miriam González Durántez comes to mind in this context. The
daughter of a Spanish politician, the much-commented-upon
wife of former UK deputy prime minister turned Meta executive Nick Clegg (not surprisingly, she has developed a loathing of
the *Daily Mail* to match my own), a lawyer and activist, she is also
the founder of Inspiring Girls, an organisation dedicated to raising the aspirations of young girls around the world by connecting
them with female role models. She is fully alive to the dangers of
social media for the girls and young women she seeks to inspire,
yet also appreciates the essential role it plays in the work that she
and others like her are doing every day.

'Social media', she told me, 'has already changed the world
on a scale that our generation can hardly comprehend. #MeToo
would not have been possible without social media. The Arab
Spring revolution would not have been possible without social
media, even if it then failed. You personally are in a really good

position to reflect as to whether the invasion of Iraq could have happened if social media had existed – my view is that it would not.' As for her own organisation: 'We have gone in five years from a standing start to being established in thirty countries. We could not have done that without social media.'

She said that in half of the countries where Inspiring Girls operates, the movement got going because people there, mainly but not exclusively women, read about it on social media and got in touch, often with Durántez herself via direct messages, using Instagram and LinkedIn. 'An organisation like ours needs constant exposure to attract role models, and especially diversified role models, because if you look at role models in traditional media, the same women keep coming up again and again,' she said. 'For a charity like us, making noise through traditional media is really difficult. They tend to want bad stories, not good. Or they just want to interview me and ask personal questions which don't help the organisation. Being able to give volume to the charity via social media gives us incredible freedom. Without it we would not manage to make sufficient noise to catch the attention of both role models and schools.'

She points out the 'horses for courses' aspect of the online world. Inspiring Girls makes huge use of Instagram, since this best spans the generations. When it comes to recruiting role models, LinkedIn is the place they tend to turn to. They know that in the UK, a lot of teachers use Twitter, and most of the schools they enlist come via Twitter DMs. TikTok, by contrast, represents a challenge: the sorts of role models sought by Inspiring Girls often feel uncomfortable with that particular route to their intended audience, as it is felt to be very much a place for the young.

Just how pervasive and powerful a push across social media can be was demonstrated by the #ThisLittleGirlIsMe campaign Inspiring Girls ran for the International Day of the Girl in 2021.

Run from Durántez's laptop in California, it created more buzz, LinkedIn reported, than any other campaign across its network. More than twenty million people got involved on Instagram, leading to an upsurge both in role models and girls to whom they were matched. Traditional media in many countries, seeing the reach of the campaign across social media, then covered it too, further driving the kinds of people Inspiring Girls wanted to get involved to do so. As Durántez says (in reference, this time, not only to her own campaign but to Zelensky): 'Simple things, like just expressing a view, can change world trends and even political events – so there are no excuses not to try to make a difference.'

Utilising social media inevitably involves learning to cope with the abuse and toxicity that is such a depressingly inevitable element of it. I've developed a pretty robust approach, adopting the simple mantra: 'Don't let the bastards get you down.' And, I reckon, having been on the receiving end of a fair bit of abuse and toxicity, that I've reached the point where it just doesn't get to me. With apologies to those who post them, I very rarely look at all the comments on my articles and social media postings. There are too many, and there are only so many times you can be called a war criminal before it ceases to have any impact at all. If I felt I was, it might. But I don't, because I'm not, so it doesn't.

True, every now and then, a complete stranger on social media, or sometimes face to face when I am out and about, will say something that makes me sit up and think. That's all to the good: it's important to have your ideas and views challenged – after all, it's why in a democratic system we have an opposition. But being held to account and prompted to evaluate your views is not the same thing as being abused. I welcome criticism as a means to test what I think and either to get me to shift my ground or strengthen the view I already hold. Sadly, though, that's not what a lot of social media is about.

I completely understand why the whole business of quantifying likes and friends is an anxiety minefield; why cruel, anonymous comments and cyberbullying can at a stroke shatter someone's confidence. All I can say is: don't let them. Easier said than done perhaps, but essential, because in the modern world nobody who tries to make a difference, no matter how personable and well-intentioned, will be spared abuse and toxicity. It is vital not to allow abuse from others to frame your own reality. Instead, focus on your own views of yourself, and those of the people you trust and respect. I care what those close to me think. I don't care what a coward in the shadows chooses to type on their keyboard. When social media abuse escalates to death threats, I simply pass those on to the police, though in general I think if someone is going to kill you, they are unlikely to advertise it in advance on Twitter.

I also have a rule of never blocking anyone. It simply makes them feel important! And I constantly bear in mind something that former Australian prime minister Julia Gillard – a feminist icon for her speech in the Canberra Parliament in 2012 taking on the misogyny she had endured as a woman politician for most of her career – said to me. After Gillard had described social media as a 'vile sewer', I commented that surely she could understand why many young women could not face a life in the public arena because of it. To this she replied: 'Yes, but if you let that be the deciding factor, you let the bad people win. You have to do what you believe in.' It's up there with another of my Post-its: Bobby Kennedy's pre-social media aphorism: 'If there is nobody in your way, you're not going anywhere.'

Gillard said that women are abused more than men, and women of colour abused more than white women. However, if she is ever asked by a young woman if she would 'do it all again', the answer is 'yes, in a heartbeat, because you can do things that change your country, change the world. That is so much more satisfying and important than anything bad the abusers say about you.'

Gillard also told me about Ngozi Okonjo-Iweala, currently director general of the World Trade Organisation, the first woman and the first African to hold that position (prior to that, she had been both finance minister and foreign minister in her native Nigeria). Co-author, with Gillard, of a book called *Women and Leadership*, she would invariably say to any young woman who talked of the barriers and the fears holding her back from going into politics: 'When I was finance minister of Nigeria, I lifted two million women, subsistence farmers, out of poverty. Why wouldn't you want to do that?' Gillard laughed as she told me this, and added: 'You can't do that just by tweeting about it.'

That leads me to the other piece of advice I would give from my analogue generation to today's digital generation: don't treat social media as the real world. True, its growth rate and reach have been, and continue to be, extraordinary (interesting factoid: it took the telephone seventy-five years to reach fifty million users, the radio thirty-eight years, television thirteen years, the web four years, and the Angry Birds Space app thirty-five days. Oh, and there are only nine countries in the world with more people living in them than Elon Musk has followers on Twitter, 150 million). When it comes to political activism and protest, though, it is important to recognise the limitations of the digital environment. It's very easy to start an online petition and for it to get a few hundred signatures organically. Then what? Once you're at that point, you have to be prepared to act physically – as Greta did.

The web generation can do pretty much everything they want to online: date, shop, game, bank, learn, gamble, chat with mates, promote their views. But there will always be a place for physical campaigning. As Alex Smith put it to me in relation to his work, both on the Obama campaign, and then running his charity: 'The Internet is just a tool – it can't be allowed to become a lifestyle or a place to conduct all business. Using your OST framework, for me the Internet is not the objective, or the strategy, it's just a tactic – one amongst hundreds or thousands available. The strategy is to get people in a room together, talking, listening, engaging, learning and then acting (whether in overcoming difference, building movements, in business or in politics). So don't just rely on your online activities.'

He is right. The Internet is so all-pervasive in our lives that there is a risk we see it as O, S and T all in one. It is most definitely a T – in my case, for example, it's a means to educate myself, make arguments, rebut lies, call out opponents, hold the powerful to account, raise awareness and campaign on issues I care about like mental health, try to keep issues fading from the media and the public mind, sell books and tickets for events, promote my podcast, articles and interviews, and post my daily Tree of the Day. But digital activism alone is never enough. You have to get out and do, not just sit there and say.

This is where traditional media comes in. First, because many decision makers, policy makers, opinion formers and generally influential types still look there first, so if you want them to hear your message, that is where to land it; and second, in part because of that, it still has influence. TV, radio and print journalism all continue to pack a punch, and can sometimes help you cut through in a way that might be difficult to achieve in the virtual world.

That's not to say that I'm unaware of the many drawbacks that exist with much of the current 'old' media landscape. 'Media' may sound a lovely neutral word. In practice it's frequently partisan, often shockingly so. Biased media outlets exist in democracies everywhere, from Spain to the US, from Latin America to the Balkans. Among totalitarian regimes, of course, the media are essentially an extension of state power.

In the UK, while freely admitting my own centre-left leanings, I would argue that the national press is today more overtly right-wing than it has ever been, and that the advent of new, more openly politically motivated TV and radio stations suggests that a similar bias is making its way into broadcast media, too. On many days the *Express*, the *Mail*, the *Telegraph* and the *Sun* are more extensions of the Downing Street press office or right-wing think tanks than they are objective seekers after truth. Rupert Murdoch, the most influential media owner of my lifetime; Viscount Rothermere at the *Mail*; the Barclay brothers, who jointly owned the *Telegraph* until the death of David Barclay in 2021; these are all men of the ideological right using their papers less to reflect the world as it is than as political weapons that promote their outlooks and commercial interests. The *Mail* under Paul Dacre's editorship offered arguably the most extreme form of weaponised bias. The paper would adopt a political position on a given story or debate and then shape its reporting both to support that position and to destroy those who disagreed with it. It capitalised on and exploited our rightly held belief in the concept of a 'free press', successfully resisting demands for any degree of accountability. And it conflated opinion and fact, misleading its readers accordingly.

It's not just that papers like the *Mail* exist. It's that in our sado-populist world they exert a baleful influence on so much of the rest of the media. By claiming to speak for the national mood or the national interest, by insinuating that those who disagree with them are traitorous left-wing woke pinkoes, they intimidate other news organisations into a position where they feel obliged to treat the hard-right newsmongers as some kind of neutral arbiter on current events. The BBC has all too often proved depressingly supine in this respect. Fearful of right-wing media attack, worried that its political foes are looking to change its funding model, it struggles to keep its nerve and tends to allow its agenda to be set for it by the bullies. The result is coverage that too often comes across as an echo of the government's line, and a willingness to self-censor that smacks of cowardice. It's not the only culprit. I learned more about the real story of life inside care homes during the Covid pandemic from the Channel 4 drama *Help*, starring Jodie Comer and Stephen Graham, than from millions of words in the papers or hours of broadcast across TV and radio. The news media didn't get to the truth. They provided a reflection of what the authorities said. One particular scene in *Help*, where a care worker fought and failed to get an ambulance to a dying man while, in the background, health secretary Matt Hancock's disembodied voice could be heard promising that he would put his arms around care homes, made me want to scream at the failure, not just of our politics but of our media.

I think contemporary journalism suffers from another problem, too. In its desire to grab attention, to get eyes and clicks on its stories, it prioritises sensation and scandal over stories that have a genuine public interest. I am reminded here of something I heard US journalist Carl Bernstein say when we were sharing a platform at a conference in Italy. He declared that he was proud of his role in uncovering the Watergate scandal, and President Richard Nixon's part in it, but felt that, overall, while Watergate may have been one of the greatest stories of all time, it was 'a disaster for journalism'. His reason? It gave rise, he argued, to a new generation of journalists who felt that the only real story is one that brings people down, the mightier the better. Given there aren't that many of those, there is a desire to attach a -gate suffix to stories which are frankly not remotely in the same league as Watergate.

A few years ago, UK newspaper proprietors and editors climbed over each other in their eagerness to defend press freedom from the modest reforms proposed by Lord Leveson, following a series of media scandals (most notoriously the revelation of phone hacking by some tabloids). Given the sorts of stories they choose to run, and their unwillingness to invest in great investigative journalism, it's a moot point what they thought they were defending.

Woodward and Bernstein were given months to uncover Watergate. *Sunday Times* editor Harry Evans had a team of reporters working for eight months before exposing the Establishment cover-up of Kim Philby's spy ring. Few editors today would allow anyone eight days on a story, or even eight hours, let alone eight months. They prefer quick, easy results that serve their agendas.

Rant over. Let's try to get good out of bad here. Because, though there is a lot wrong with our media, there is a lot right about it too. And, in any event, it has an influence on the public debate. So if you're in the business of making change, you have to know how to engage with it and get your message heard, on terms that assist you. You might choose to establish a red line or two (I happen to draw one at the *Mail*, which is not allowed in the house, and with which I never do interviews). But as a rule, you should not elect to be so purist as only to go after the news outlets whose editorial line you agree with. You need to keep the doors, and your options, open. And it's probably as well to have the following T.R.U.T.H. Post-it somewhere near at hand:

1. TENACITY. You will send a well-crafted news release and receive nothing back. You will leave a voice message with a news desk and hear nothing back. You will fire off a message, see that it's been read, and still get nothing back. This is par for the course. Expect it, especially at the beginning. Tweak your release, refocus, refine and go again. There are limits (your story may not be good enough), but stick with it.

2. RELIABILITY. It is possible that a response to emails and calls may come very late or very early in the day, or on weekends. Be ready. Respond to emails quickly. Keep your phone on and your volume up. The more you get to know journalists, the more you will discover that being reliable helps you climb their list of go-to people.

3. UNDERSTAND. Journalists, particularly junior reporters, are often low paid and are all extremely busy. Silence on their part is likely to be down to one of two reasons: your story is not of sufficient interest (amongst competing stories) or they have not had a chance to look at it (and may never get that chance). It will not be personal. Whilst this can be frustrating, you have to understand that silence is the inevitable consequence of the pressures journalists face.

4. TEAM. Try to build and maintain a team, even if it's informal. Share your work with a friend who is good at writing or who is at arm's length to your cause. Get a second opinion, listen and act on it. Try to step back from what you've written and distance yourself from the emotions your cause inspires in you. Remember, it is not how worthy your story is, but how news-worthy it is. Only the latter will achieve the exposure necessary for the change you seek.

5. HONESTY. When you want a particular job, it can be tempting to exaggerate on the application form or to hyperbolise during an interview. Avoid this temptation when dealing with the media, no matter how much you want to see your story in print or on screen, or how passionate you are about your cause. Yes, if it's unique, make your case, and yes, be enthusiastic, but stick to the facts. Always. It builds trust.

So what makes a good story – the sort of story that the media are likely to pick up on? And how to make sure it gets a public airing?

First and foremost, you must have something new to say. A new point of view, a new piece of research, a new event, a new take on an old story, a new perspective, a new campaign, a new graphic, a new face backing your cause. There's a reason why 'leaked' documents appeal, rather than ones that have already been 'published'. They're novel and fresh. People in politics some-times joke about MTBLs – 'memos to be leaked' – but the fact is, they exert a strong appeal. Often the best way to ensure some-thing gets read is to mark it confidential.

You need a genuine talking point. The media will be more inter-ested if what you have to say is something that can be attacked as well as defended, that invites debate – not least because it will increase online engagement. Journalists are taught news values and should be able to sense a story's potential almost immedi-ately. There are many important causes, so why yours and why now? Does it pass the 'so what' test? In other words, will people actually care about your story? Will it get people talking in the pub, the boardroom, at the kitchen table? Is there a theme with a rich vein attached to it? One-off stories come and go. For a mes-sage to get out there, people need to hear it many times; and that sometimes means the same issue and theme being illustrated by a number of different stories, stories that people can relate to. Narratives about, say, climate change or poverty in Africa or the long-term impact of Brexit require constant refreshing via stories that have an immediate impact. It takes pieces about a heat wave, forest fires, storms and floods to stimulate general interest in cli-mate change. It takes the story of queues of traffic at Dover, or a big employer relocating, or a new and dramatic piece of eco-nomic data, to get Brexit back on the news agenda.

All that said, there's a difference between offering the media something new and offering them something wholly contrary to the way they currently think. Sometimes it's necessary to go with the flow a little before seeking to switch its direction. If someone is judged to be 'up', the press will love a story about how he or she rescued a child from drowning at the local swimming pool. If that same person is judged to be 'down', such a story may be written up as a strange assault on a child in front of shocked and outraged families. Changing either of those narratives can be tough. More positively, if a newspaper is running a campaign for something you support, and you have a story which helps that campaign, you know where to place it.

Once you know what you want to say, you need to remember the Marilyn Monroe poem, and 'think in ink'. News, or press, releases matter. They force you to run your story through a filter so that only the most important aspects remain. They force you to write in a journalistic style, prioritising the crux of what it is you are trying to say (there are plenty of courses available to help you learn how). They bring key messages to life through their use of quotes. They get you to think in terms of soundbites – the colourful, memorable, catch-all phrases that journalists need to sell a story internally. They serve as the basis for briefing notes, interview notes, social media posts and blogs. If you are working on your own, and have to write the news release solo, you will probably find that after a while you can repeat it almost verbatim. This is helpful when pitching to journalists down the phone. If journalists do take your story, then it is also useful for them too as there is ready-made content they can cut-and-paste. Spoon-feed as much of your content as you can to journalists. They tend to be busy.

Not only do you need to think in ink, you need to think in headlines – it's the way, after all, that newspapers and broadcasters tend to think. Write the headline for them, and make that your main point. And keep it to fewer than ten words. This will serve not just as the heading of your news release, but the subject heading of any email you send, and probably the hook on social media when you look to share it with a wider audience. Obviously, if the news release is a complex one, it's OK to use subheadings, or toplines, as well. These will serve to summarise your argument further, almost into a mini-script, and so prove helpful when you're pitching the story in thirty seconds, or when you're converting it into a Twitter thread. Journalists often have concentration spans shorter than easily distracted goldfish. You have to accept that, and work with it.

In terms of getting the story into the right hands, it obviously helps if you already have contacts. Otherwise, it's a question of choosing an outlet that suits your target audience, and identifying journalists or producers who have written or broadcast stories that relate to your theme. A lot of people get nervous when speaking to journalists. This may possibly be because of worries about what's 'on the record', 'off the record', 'background' or 'deep background', or because of their general reputation for untrustworthiness. But it's generally the case that if you have a good story, you will find a journalist who will help you.

That said, don't expect a media outlet that has never shown any interest in your cause suddenly to develop a fascination with it because you've chosen to get in touch. The *Guardian* and the *Mail* differ from each other not simply because they treat the same story in different ways, but because they have different agendas.

Once you've selected your target publication, you should avoid going too high, too soon. Ambitious reporters, rather than section editors, are more likely to give you time. It's also worth remembering that there's an art to knowing when to reach out. Not many professions are as governed by time as journalism. Deadlines are both the friend that motivates and the foe that limits possibilities. So be aware of the rhythm of the day and of the week, as it impacts upon journalists you are seeking to influence. There is no point contacting a Sunday newspaper with an idea for an investigation for that week's paper on Saturday afternoon. If your story relates to a future event, contact diary managers at newspapers and broadcasters via a diary note, providing details, and call up to see if it has made the diary. There are plenty of easily available directories on this kind of thing. Look for time-related hooks. People are more interested in health or diets after Christmas, when they have eaten too much, and before they go on holiday, when they realise they're going to have to take their shirts off.

Finally, while your focus should be on the written word, you should never ignore the power of pictures. I hate clichés, and it is definitely a cliché to say that a picture is worth a thousand words, but that really is the case. Think of any major news story from the last year. The Queen's funeral. Liz Truss resigning. Bombs hitting Kyiv. Argentina winning the World Cup. What enters your head? I am guessing it is not newsprint or a webpage, but something visual: an image or a piece of film. So what image is associated with your news story? What appears in your head when you read your release? Could you recreate it in a new and interesting way (particularly valuable for social media posts)? Could you describe it and offer it to media outlets so they send photographers or camera teams? Could your spokespeople be available to comment in front of a scene that tells your story? Could journalists engage with your cause by interviewing service users, for example?

Janet and John guide to news management over.

Before I leave the area of journalism altogether, I would add a plea. As much as I criticise it, as much as I bemoan its faults and excesses, I would urge you not to rule it out as way of helping to change the world for the better. It's true that in all too many places, good journalism tends to get drowned out by the bad, the loud, the short-termist, the self-serving, the political agenda of the media oligarchs, and the blah-blah-blah of the 24/7 channels. But despite that, the role of a journalist remains vital to getting the truth out there and holding the powerful to account.

And the fact is, whatever the current faults of the trade, there are plenty of good journalists, including among the main broadcasters and on most of the national and regional newspapers. The BBC has some tremendous foreign and domestic correspondents, while Ros Atkins' explanatory films, which came into their own during the pandemic, have continued to represent the best of

BBC journalism: informative, interesting, analytical, fact-based, clear. Much of Sky News' coverage of the war in Ukraine has been outstanding. Likewise Lindsey Hilsum's reports on Channel 4 News. ITN has done a huge amount to expose the reality of poverty and poor housing in Britain in general and its impact on children's health in particular. Pippa Crerar, now political editor of the *Guardian*, did much to uncover the truth about misconduct in Downing Street during the pandemic when she was doing the same job for my old paper, the *Daily Mirror*. She has rightly been showered with awards for her work. It was the *Daily Telegraph* which led the way in exposing the MPs' expenses scandal. Local and regional broadcasters showed Boris Johnson up for the blowhard blusterer that he is when he made himself available for a round of interviews with them. And, OK, putting a lettuce into a race with Liz Truss to see which would last longer might not win a Pulitzer Prize, but the *Daily Star* has been responsible for some of the funniest front pages of recent years, which have also made serious points.

Further afield, I think also of the two *New York Times* investigative reporters, Megan Twohey and Jodi Kantor, and the painstaking processes they went through to expose the scale of the sexual abuse perpetrated by Hollywood producer Harvey Weinstein. The film made about the scandal, *She Said*, rightly portrays them and their bosses in a heroic light. Miriam González Durántez is right when she says that the #MeToo campaign would not have been set ablaze without social media. But I would argue that it was brilliant old-fashioned journalism that lit the flame. I would also argue that among some terrible publications in Britain, there are good ones, too, both print and online, including relatively new ventures such as *Byline Times* and the *New European* (full disclosure, I am editor-at-large of the latter). New voices can emerge quickly if they have something genuinely interesting to say.

And then, alongside full-time journalists, there are the people who serve the cause of good journalism in other ways. I think, for example, of the lawyer Peter Stefanovic, who – literally every day – provides an online rebuttal to the lies told by ministers. I think of the former tax lawyer Dan Neidle, who led the way on Nadhim Zahawi's tax affairs. I think of the sometimes brilliant social media takedowns of traditional media lies and bias. I think of the podcasts that dissect what is going on and expose stories and facts that might otherwise get buried. I think of the 23,000 'reporters', readers who in 2009 helped the *Guardian* dissect the expenses claims of MPs and crunch their way through 460,000 documents the paper posted on its website. All such people make a difference.

So, though this book is aimed at persuading people to get stuck into politics, I would urge that journalism has an important role in the political debate. The Murdoch–Dacre generation is fading out, and new media and a new generation are eroding their power and influence, hopefully democratising our media.

Even if you don't decide to take a direct role, do educate yourself in the arts of proper journalism, and learn how to distinguish fake news from the genuine article. As we currently have a government that is not that keen on fact as the basis of its communications, or the teaching of a true reflection of the country's past in history lessons in school, it may be too much to expect that genuine media literacy and understanding be added to the school curriculum. But it is needed.

This analysis by BuzzFeed News is just one of many illustrating the scale of the challenge we all face in sifting what we read and hear: in the final three months of the 2016 US presidential campaign, the top-performing fake election news stories on Facebook generated more engagement than the top stories from major news outlets such as the *New York Times, Washington*

Post, Huffington Post, NBC News, and others. During what many would regard as the most important months of the campaign, the twenty top-performing false election stories from hoax sites and hyperpartisan blogs generated 8,711,000 shares, reactions, and comments on Facebook. Within the same time period, the twenty best-performing election stories from nineteen major news websites generated a total of 7,367,000 shares, reactions, and comments on Facebook. Then, as the election drew closer, into the period when undecided voters were making their minds up, and people who tend to zone out of politics were zoning in, engagement for fake content on Facebook skyrocketed and surpassed that of the content from major news outlets.

One day, perhaps, we will take a leaf out of Finland's book, and teach children how to spot fake news. In the meantime, here are a few pointers for young and old alike.

- Source. Find out what/who the main source is. Are they legitimate? Reliable?

- Date. Check when the piece was written/broadcast. (There's stuff on the Internet and social media that is years old, yet looks new.)

- Context. Have the facts been wrenched out of context to fit an obvious particular narrative?

- Cross-reference. Before you rely on something/base your argument on it/repeat facts from it, CHECK IT against other accounts that deal with the same topic. Just because one person states something as accurate or true, it does not automatically mean that it is.

- Omission. Try to be aware of what might have been left out. You want 'the truth, the whole truth and nothing but the truth'.

Missing out salient information can be as powerful as lying, so look out for it. Cross-referencing helps to expose omissions.

- Pause. Think before you react to things you read and hear. If you don't, you risk promulgating misinformation and losing credibility. (Don't retweet anything without taking time to check it – a lesson I learned very expensively when retweeting a tweet about a Tory MP which turned out to be untrue and defamatory!)

- Fact-check. The Internet makes establishing basic facts (as opposed to opinions) quick and pretty easy. Obviously, there are information sites out there that have particular agendas to push, but it's not difficult to spot which ones do so. When in doubt, go for sites that are generally reckoned to be pretty accurate. Again, for all its faults, the BBC should be included. Likewise, some of the major international news agencies. Added to which, there are new sites entirely devoted to fact-checking. FullFact is one such: a good example of people recognising a damaging trend – increasing disinformation from politicians, public institutions and journalists – and deciding to do something about it. It is a bad sign of the times that we need fact-checkers; a good sign that people and organisations are meeting that need.

16.

How to Become a Campaigner

All politicians have to be campaigners, but not all campaigners have to be politicians. For many people, the idea of being a campaigner is more attractive, maybe easier too, than seeking a political role, not least because it doesn't have to be a full-time preoccupation. These days I think I fall into that camp: I regard myself as active in various political causes, but I also allow myself time for many other things.

Given that I am urging everyone to get stuck into politics, it's perhaps only right to address two questions I am often asked in this context: 'Why don't you start a new party?' (this happened especially during the Corbyn era); and 'Why have you never become an MP?' The former is easily answered. My answer to the latter will show, I hope, that while I fervently believe we need more good people in politics, I accept that it's not for everyone, and that it's not the only way to make a difference in the world.

The 'new party' question first. The reason why I have never seriously contemplated the launching of a new political party is that, even though I was expelled from the Labour Party for voting Lib Dem in the European elections of 2019 as a protest against Labour's Brexit policy, I have always felt tribally Labour. I am not sure I could do something which might harm the Labour cause, and so ultimately help the Tories. That being said, if Labour fails to oust the Tories at the next election, given how much improved they are under Keir Starmer, and how awful the Tory government has been in recent years, then something pretty major has to happen.

As to why I have never become an MP, there is a practical, factual answer: for various complicated reasons, personal, professional and political, the time was never right. But there is also a more psychological, emotional one. Since leaving full-time politics in 2003, I have worried that if I went back full-on into the political arena, I would be putting at risk things I have only relatively recently learned to value: my own health and key relationships chief among them. I suspect that at some level I will always regret not having become a politician in my own right. However, I am as close to certain as I can be that, even if I had proved to be a good one, the downsides would have been considerable, possibly even overwhelming. I still recall the words of a man who was once my sporting hero, then became a political opponent, and over time a good friend, when I was closest to going for it, back in 2015: Seb Coe.

'Al' – he is one of a small number of people who does the Paul Simon thing and calls me Al without my getting annoyed – 'I am on my knees. I know you, and I know Parliament, and I am telling you now . . . you will go insane. You will hate it. You will lose everything you've got going for you, like your freedom. You can do tons more outside. Please, I am begging you, just say No, and if you are ever tempted to say Yes, you call me!'

We will never know if it would have driven me insane, because I heard, and I heeded, and I felt he might have had a point. While I determined to stay close to the pitch, I therefore decided not to step on to it. As it happens, my partner Fiona came even closer to becoming a player, going for selection as Labour's parliamentary candidate in Hampstead and Highgate, and looking likely to get it, before waking in the middle of the night and asking: 'Why am I doing this when we have just got our life back?'

I'm acutely aware, then, that in this area I haven't fully walked the walk. However, what I hope both Fiona and I have demon-strated, and still do, is that Parliament is not the only place to 'do politics', and to make a difference. The campaigning arena is also absolutely crucial to making our world a better place. Athlete-turned-broadcaster-and-businessman, Brendan Foster – another great friend, and one of the soundest citizens you could wish to meet – messaged me on the day Boris Johnson was finally evicted from office to say, 'I reckon if you hadn't led the charge about his dishonesty and his disregard for the Nolan Principles from way out, when everyone else was treating him like a cuddly toy, he might still be there.' He pointed to the fact that shortly before Johnson's fall, his Cabinet colleague Nadhim Zahawi was sent on a tour of the studios, and in a succession of interviews warned his Tory colleagues that it was 'people like Alastair Campbell' who were urging them to dump their leader. It struck me at the time as a pretty desperate tactic, comic even, but Brendan said it showed how I had managed to get inside their heads. He was flatteringly exaggerating my role, of course, because I have no doubt that Johnson was always going to come a cropper. In some-thing as complicated as the rise and fall of a prime minister, there are so many factors at play, and they are impossible to quantify. But I'd like to feel that the campaign I had very deliberately cre-ated around those Nolan Principles, along with the thousands of tweets I'd put out, the flood of articles I wrote and the dozens of interviews I gave, was at least in the mix somewhere, making a difference.

For her part, Fiona has devoted decades to campaigning for better state schools, during which time she's done stints as a very active governor and chair of the schools our own children went to (and continuing to do so long after they left). She also chairs and volunteers for several charities, regularly dragging me off to be her driver when she is collecting supplies for our local food bank. A cynic – or the *Daily Mail* – would doubtless say that makes her a 'do-gooder'. I would counter that only in a country where the *Daily Mail* is the most read paper could 'do-gooder' be a term of abuse. In Rothermere-Dacreland, far better to be a do-badder, I assume. It's the same with their evident distaste for 'virtue-signalling'. Presumably they would prefer us all to signal vice and evil instead? 'Doing good' is a great objective for anyone. Add it to woke, and those Nolan Principles, and you have the makings of a good moral compass. A reminder: Honesty. Openness. Objectivity. Integrity. Selflessness. Accountability. Leadership.

My point, then, is that I fully appreciate that we do all have limits, some imposed by ourselves, some by others, some by the norms of the world we grow up in. But limits are not an excuse to be a mere bystander. So, though I said in the introduction that I would love it if this book inspired someone to become an MP who then went on to become prime minister, I would be equally delighted if it motivated someone to become a campaigner, to volunteer, to join a party or a cause, to visit prisons, to start up groups aimed at helping elderly people who are lonely, to decide to go for a low-paid job with a charity rather than a high-paid job with a bank or a hedge fund.

Let me take you back to the TV series I mentioned at the beginning of the book, *Make Me Prime Minister*, and to the three young women who made it through to the final. As they stood at their lecterns in front of Union flags and giant banners spelling out their names, *Channel 4 News* presenter Krishnan Guru-Murthy moderated their debate in front of several hundred people at London's Bloomsbury Theatre. Then he asked me if I had a last question for the three contestants.

I had spent several weeks with them, had got to know and like them, seen them deal with highs and lows, progress and setback, above all seen them improve, as communicators and critical thinkers, and in their understanding of politics in all its often maddening complexity. But the question I asked was what, if they won, they would do with the platform and the profile that victory in the TV show would provide. They gave very different answers. Kelly Given, who had focused on housing as her main issue, and who has autism, said she wanted to use her voice to fight for better understanding of, and greater compassion for, the marginalised and often ill-treated autistic community. Holly Morgan returned to the theme of her main presentation, institutional racism, stating she would use all her energy and passion to fight to eradicate it, and to educate those – we had seen a few in the audience Q & A – who failed to see that racism was a problem not just for ethnic minorities, but for all of us, because it holds people back as individuals, and therefore holds us all back as a country.

Natalie Balmain, on the other hand, raised an issue upon which I had not heard her previously express an opinion at any point in the two months we had known each other. Her main policy proposal had involved dealing with tax avoidance by big multinationals, and the fact that that she was about to go on to win suggested that she, and her policy, had gone down well. But when it came to what she would do with the platform and profile were she to be crowned Channel 4's Alternative Prime Minister, she said this: 'I think our politics is broken, the party system is broken, people don't feel their democracy is working, they feel their votes don't count, and so don't trust the whole process. So, I would get engaged in fighting to change the electoral system so we have a fairer voting system and people feel that their involvement actually means something.' Her words went down well with the audience, and perhaps tipped things even more in her favour, helping to cement the victory I would announce a little later.

As she spoke, I remember thinking: 'Wow! That's smart!' Not the fact that she had that view, but that she had not made a big deal of it during the previous weeks, as Sayeeda Warsi and

I eliminated people en route to the final. She won the series by focusing on what she needed to do to survive week to week. In the final she presented a policy that she believed in and promoted well, coming over as warm and empathetic, with a lot of emotional intelligence. But then, in front of an audience that was getting their first sight of her, who had seen none of the ups and downs of the previous weeks, she read the room, and when asked what she would really love to achieve if she could, she indicated she intended to focus on the thing she really believes needs to change, and got a very powerful response. OST operating on various levels perhaps.

The Scottish National Party would be mad not to snap up Kelly, and I hope that Labour likewise see in Natalie what Sayeeda and I did, given she hopes to become a parliamentary candidate. But some of the things they learned through the series, and some of the ideas I lay out here, will hopefully be of use to them and the other contestants, no matter what path they take. Whatever they now turn their minds to, they are all 'in politics', because to greater and lesser degrees, everything has politics in it somewhere. And, indeed, everyone is political in some way. Who doesn't have an opinion about tax levels, about crime in their communities, about the state of the roads, about the quality of our leaders, about racism, about the education of their children, about Putin, about China and America, about the impact of social media? We may think we do not do politics; but politics does us. We might as well all make it a two-way thing.

I totally get why so many people turn away from it. It's complicated. It's difficult. It's hard to follow, full of jargon and processes that look bewildering. The party I have historically supported, for example, has rules of Byzantine complexity governing who can become a candidate or even an activist in the first place. I can well understand why someone might complain that just getting by in life is hard enough, without making it harder by feeling you have to keep tabs on all the big issues. And when the scale of challenges is so monumental, it is all too easy as an individual to think we are all too small, too weak to make a difference.

How does any one individual, having reflected on, say, sado-populism and the decades-long development of the political, intellectual, financial and organisational forces behind it, persuade him- or herself that they can take it on alone? They can't. The forces are too strong. But anyone can build an argument alone. You can read and research alone. You can educate yourself alone. You can then join with others. You can win an argument with others. You can literally spread the word, build networks, as the sado-populists did, and continue to do. You can start local, and build out. You can start small, and go big. Once you feel yourself making a difference, you can develop the confidence to go wider, further, deeper in making the case for the change you believe in. You can develop a mindset that says: 'I may not be able to change everything, but I can change something, and that is what I am going to do.' Change-makers come in many forms. There is no template. No right or wrong way of doing it. You don't need to ask permission. It's up to you to decide if that is what you want to be. And if you do . . . then go for it! It's as simple as that.

Of course the scale of the campaign you choose will determine what you need by way of practicalities; whether that's in terms of money and other resources, premises, staff, volunteers, outside advisers, materials, access to information, data, or support from politicians. But I'd make two points here: every campaign in the world started as one person's idea; and one person can do a lot to start a campaign. Of course, they can achieve even more with others, but the first step is vital. Building the team can follow.

Fourteen years ago, when I wrote a novel about the relationship between a psychiatrist and his patients, I vowed to myself: 'I am going to use my novel to change the way this country talks and thinks about mental health, because, with any luck, that will help to change the way governments and healthcare systems deal with the issue.' Have I achieved everything I set out to do in the mental health arena since then? Has all my writing, broadcasting, campaigning and lobbying done what I wanted it to? No – not least because I wasn't initially clear what it was exactly I wanted to achieve. But have I helped move the dial? Definitely. Have I, and those I campaign with, achieved everything that could be achieved to get parity between physical and mental healthcare? No. Far from it, and in recent years I feel we have made huge progress but are now going backwards again. But the progress made inspires me to keep going, as does the progress still to be made. And I remain confident that, long after I am gone, we will eventually get to a place where people look back on today's attitudes to mental health and mental illness and wonder how on earth it took so long to demolish the walls of taboo, stigma and ignorance, and the acceptance of inadequate services.

I'm pleased I followed my instincts. Fiona was concerned about me putting my mental health challenges 'out there'. She feared it would worsen my own mental health and draw more attention to our family. My mother was worried my campaigning would place my brother Donald, who had schizophrenia, in the public eye. But I *felt* strongly that I had to do it, and am glad I did; for the cause, and also for myself. And when the then chancellor George Osborne stood up in Parliament, and announced an extra £600 million for mental health, naming me, Lib Dem MP Norman Lamb and Tory MP Andrew Mitchell as the drivers of the all-party campaign which argued for it, that was a day when being 'in politics' felt good, and meaningful. That same feeling will have been shared by Motor Neurone Disease campaigners Doddie Weir and Rob Burrow, both former rugby players who became MND patients and then campaigners, when Boris Johnson's government announced they were investing £50 million into research for a cure. When Weir died last November the money, two prime ministers later, was still to be allocated, prompting Burrow to protest: 'How many more warriors die before this stupid government give the £50 million they said they would give?' Even when you win, sometimes you need to keep on fighting. But everyone who fights, makes a contribution.

And the fact is that major campaigns need different types of people. They need the leaders and the big names who will make the big interventions, organise stunts, conduct public debates, and get media attention. But they also need the volunteers who will knock on people's doors or stop them in the street to find out what they think; who will organise meetings, street stalls and petitions; who will produce campaign materials, run social media campaigns, make phone calls, stuff envelopes and raise money. And, among those volunteers, they need a younger contingent who aren't there just to carry out menial tasks (which is what often tends to happen), but to show how the skills that are second nature to them, but may be unfamiliar to their older peers – particularly social media and modern communications skills – can be deployed to create a great campaign.

Those skills, like the skills you develop in your own day-to-day life and work, are transferable. What you learn in one campaign you can take to another: whether you are trying to save a local amenity under threat, seeking to persuade a council to fund a new service you think your community needs, or doing your bit to save the planet, feed the hungry, or give hope and opportunity to the poor. Whether big global goals or small local projects, so many of the principles of campaigning are the same, and the best way to learn is to do, and the best place to start is often in your own local community. The skills that are needed – whether that is good writing, public speaking, face-to-face communication, the ability to negotiate and compromise – are skills worth having and developing anyway, which will also help you in anything else you set out to do. Having a multi-generational campaign team also enables you to speak to more people more effectively. A communication that gains support from a sixty-year-old might not resonate in the same way with a twenty-year-old, and vice versa. Having the ability to target different age groups with the same overall message, but perhaps with different styles and tactics, will increase the reach of the campaign.

If you do decide to get involved with political campaigning, I hope it is with a view not just to changing the world, but also to changing how politics itself is done. The two must go together. Our current system feels as though it is breaking, but until it does, it is the only one we have, and we need new blood to come in and change it.

If you choose to campaign for political change, I'd ask you to consider Natalie's plea for a fairer voting system, and also my desire for two other pieces of electoral reform: compulsory voting and lowering the voting age. The former I believe would give us more democracy, not less, and better democracy at that. Again, I call on Julia Gillard as an expert voice, as Australia is one of the twenty-two countries in the world where compulsory voting already exists. People are, of course, allowed to deface their ballot, scrawl abuse or 'none of the above'. But they do have to take part, or risk a fine. Gillard believes compulsory voting, and the consequent high turnout, gives greater legitimacy to those who are elected. More importantly, she argues that it makes those seeking election focus much more sharply on the interests of all sections of the electorate, not just those who are 'likelier to vote'. 'It means your politics ultimately has to be in the mainstream where most people live, and want to live. If Mr, Mrs and Ms Average are not voting for you, you can't win. It means that a lot of the so-called culture wars which prevail in the US for example do not translate to Australian politics. We are less liable to get carried away to extremes.'

When I first suggested lowering the voting age to my daughter Grace, then in her mid-teens, she said: 'Dad, you've met my friends. Some of them literally know nothing about politics.' My response was: 'I can introduce you to people of my age who know even less.' Having observed teenagers during the Scottish independence referendum campaign walking to school arguing about housing and nuclear weapons, instead of celebs or social media likes, I think I was right. Seven out of ten sixteen- and seventeen-year-olds in Scotland then went on to vote, which is surely a good thing, even if they did mostly vote contrary to the way I would have done. And, when you consider that the EU referendum was about major constitutional change, with consequences that would go well beyond a single parliamentary term, and so have a far greater impact on the very young than the very old, it is surely absurd that there was almost no mention of extending the vote to that younger age group. David Cameron never even thought about it. He didn't think he would need their support. He also probably thought that lowering the voting age would favour Labour in future parliamentary elections. Cameron's decision to hold the referendum as a way of keeping his Eurosceptics quiet was an example of doing the wrong thing for the wrong reasons. And he did the wrong thing for the wrong reasons in failing to extend the franchise to older teenagers. That's politics.

And that's the sort of politics we need to campaign to change. It means getting the new blood flowing, and the old blood welcoming it, for the extra vibrancy and vitality that new blood can bring. It means knowing what you can do, but also knowing what you can't. So, perhaps, as I close this section, I should add 'be realistic' to the things we need to be as we set out on the road to doing the things we need to do to change the world. Be confident. Be energetic. Be healthy, physically and mentally. Be resilient. Be media savvy. Be engaged, and clear about how. Be ambitious, but realistic.

Here are a few more suggestions to bear in mind as you decide what specific steps to take on your political journey.

- Remember: campaigning is a mindset. You have to set your mind to it and make it come fully alive.

- Get properly involved in campaigns for the causes you really believe in. Don't just tweet about them.

- If you can afford to, set up regular donations to the causes you believe in. If you can't, think about raising money for them another way.

- Become a school governor, NHS trust board member, trustee of a charity you support, Student Union officer, committee member of a sports or social club. Useful, worthwhile and all good experience.

- Whatever your age, find younger people who would benefit from your support, and offer it to them.

- Consciously try to be a role model and/or a mentor.

- Have role models and mentors, too.

- Speak to strangers with curiosity and without judgement. Learn about people's lived experience of the world.

- Read the views of people you disagree with and try to understand why they hold the beliefs they do. This isn't just a question of respect. It's a question of understanding the arguments you are up against and working out how to counter them.

- Challenge a friend to change their mind on something (and be open to changing your own mind on something too).

- As Michelle Obama says, 'start at your own kitchen table' – with your family and friends.

- If you have one, join your work diversity group or staff engage-ment network to engage in change where you work. If your workplace doesn't have one, start one.

- Never stop informing yourself about the issues you care about; but keep learning about the ones you're not so engaged by too. All knowledge is useful and you should try to keep it current.

- Bear in mind another of my presidential Post-its, this one by Theodore Roosevelt: 'Nobody cares how much you know, until they know how much you care.'

17.

How to Get into Politics

I have dwelt at length on *why* people should embrace the idea of being involved in politics. In this final chapter I want to turn to *how. How*, after all, ultimately answers the two key questions: 'But what can I *do*?' and 'But what can *I* do?'

Wanting to do something, even if you don't necessarily know what that something might be or are not sure how to bring it about, is an essential first step. But if you're thinking about a fully-fledged political career, you need much more than that: you need a burning inner desire to bring about change, or to protect and preserve the things you believe in. Or both!

Take this from Emily Paterson, twenty-two, just out of university: 'I want to go into politics but I don't know how to start.' I get lots in that vein. I get lots, too, from young people, including schoolchildren, who want advice on how to get their friends interested in politics. In my reply to Emily, I told her that to some extent she had already started, by asking me the question. But, I added, she had to want that career for the right reasons. Passion is so important. If you don't have real passion inside you, then I recommend you do something else. Seeking to become a politician solely because you want status, power or fame, or because you want to be at or close to the centre of national decision-making (or one day a contestant in the *I'm A Celebrity* jungle) are terrible reasons. I accept that plenty think that way. I believe they deserve to fail.

I also said to Emily, that if she did feel that passion, and she sensed politics was right for her, then she should 'just go for it'. It sounds easy, and I accept it is not. But it is absolutely the attitude required. Go for it though you might stumble en route. Go for it though you might fail. Go for it with your eyes wide open, knowing that whatever happens, whatever setbacks you endure, you'll learn lessons and gain experiences which will be useful next time round. Go for it even though you might not see the change you believe in come in your lifetime (but tell yourself, as I do on mental health, that you're part of change that might well come after you're gone: the work you do now is worth it on that basis alone).

If, having read that, you're still on for it, the *bad news* is that there is no simple, single straightforward route into politics. Most people who try for a political career fail either to get onto the first step of the ladder, or, more commonly, to climb as high as they think their talents should take them. The *good news* is that there is no simple, single straightforward route into politics. Anyone can do it! No formal qualifications are required, and there are many different ways of getting where you want to end up.

Ultimately, if you want to bring about major change for the whole country, you need to think in terms of securing a place in Parliament. It may have many flaws, but, to be blunt, if you're not in the system, you can't change it. Natalie won't win her fight to change the voting system unless the country elects a Parliament and a government committed to that change. Outside pressure only takes you so far. 'We need Proportional Representation . . . we need to get rid of the Lords . . . we need a written Constitution . . .' I hear these cries all the time. They are all ideas whose time may seem to have come. But without parliamentary support, they're simply not going to happen. There is a lack of the formal organisation and lobbying to change the minds of opinion-formers and policy-makers that is so essential to get a campaign over the line – the kind of set-up that, for example, brought the Brexiteers success in 2016 (and bear in mind that it took the diehard anti-Europeans forty years to achieve their goal).

As to how to become an MP, or an elected representative in the parliament/assemblies of the devolved administrations, at the moment – in the UK at least – you generally have to join a party. Independent candidates who win seats in parliamentary elections are rare indeed, and are usually single-issue campaigners. Great, but their reach is limited. This isn't true in every democracy. In France, for example, where first the president is elected, then the parliament, it's possible for a new party with a new approach to win almost from a standing start. This, after all, is what Emmanuel Macron managed to do. But such success is rare, even within a presidential form of government. In a parliamentary system, such as the UK possesses, and with our current electoral system, it's virtually impossible.

Interestingly, former French president François Hollande believes the UK system has significant strengths in this regard. 'Of course you have problems,' he told me, 'but you still have two strong parties as the heart of your political environment. If people don't like the Tories, they can vote Labour. If there is a Labour government and they don't like it, they can see an opposition ready to follow them. In France, in Italy, the parties have been hollowed and weakened, young people are less sure where to turn. That helps the extremes: a far-right government in Italy, the risk of a far-right government in France.'

For most politically motivated people, it's usually fairly straightforward to work out which party you want to belong to. But, obviously, that's not true for all. If it were, why would anyone ever change the way they vote? People's views and beliefs do and can shift. I, for example, am instinctively anti-nationalism, and I fought hard to help keep Scotland in the UK in the 2014 independence referendum. But post-Brexit, and after twelve years of broadly incompetent and unresponsive English nationalist government from London, I am far more understanding of the Scottish Nationalists' arguments, even if I can also see their weaknesses and failings in other areas. Of course, there are many reasons people change who they vote for. Tactical voting, protest voting, or loss of confidence in a party. Labour's surge in the polls last year was at least in part driven by public loss of confidence in the Tories.

I'm also aware that many people's understanding of politics comes from their parents, and that their inherited loyalties may change if they decide to take a mental step back and compare the parties objectively for themselves, drawing on current, nonparental sources of information. Even looking at a party website can be helpful, at least in terms of giving a sense of a party's direction of travel. So can checking out party leaders' conference speeches. I know from experience that those are the ones that leaders – the good, hard-working leaders anyway, not the ones who think they can bluff and bluster through anything – put the most work into, in terms of crafting the overall message and shaping their overall priorities. They are pretty easy to find online.

It's a fact, too, that political parties change over time, sometimes dramatically, as happened to both Labour under Jeremy Corbyn, and the Conservative Party as it morphed into a Brexit Party and then further into its current right-wing manifestation. You might therefore find that the party you were thinking of joining is moving away from you. That's certainly how former Conservative leader William Hague feels. Regarded as a Eurosceptic when he was in charge and campaigning to be 'in Europe but not run by Europe', he accepts that he is now seen by many in his party as a 'soggy centrist, not a true believer'. 'I haven't changed,' he says; 'the party has passed me by.'

For a politician such as Johnny Mercer, choosing a party was something of a late journey of discovery. The ex-soldier had never even voted in an election until he became an MP. When he decided to try for elected office, it was with the sole aim of winning a better deal for Britain's 2.2 million military veterans. It was only after talking to people already in Parliament that he decided that, on balance, he was a Tory. (It's to his credit that he did ultimately manage to move the dial on veterans, despite being 'stiffed' by both Johnson and Truss. Under Sunak, he became veterans' minister for a second time.)

Once you've chosen and joined your party, which is usually as simple as filling in an online form and paying a membership fee, you may well find that a very good way of deciding if you definitely want to be an MP is to work for one. Volunteering is often an excellent route into a job, and, in my experience, the best MPs and the people around them know how to put someone's skills to good use. MPs tend to split their teams between the constituency, where case work, correspondence and organising visits will be a big part of the job, and Parliament, where you might be more engaged in managing the diary, making sure the MP is where he or she is meant to be, drafting speeches, answering phones, talking to journalists. There is an apprenticeship scheme in Parliament, whilst the Parliamentary Academy Scheme has as its stated goal encouraging young people, aged sixteen to twenty-four, who do not have a university degree, to get into a political career. These apprenticeships, which involve working for an MP for a year, are paid, and have a recognised qualification at the end of them. Politics is like the media: all too often internships and the like depend largely on who you know, which risks merely serving to perpetuate the barriers that stop many young people from thinking they can get into Parliament. You can. It's just that you might have to fight harder than the person with the right connections. You will also find lots of jobs advertised at the 'working for your MP' site, www.w4mp.org – these are often with MPs, but also with bodies that have a role in parliamentary affairs.

Taking the next step – seeking to become an MP – requires

you to be at your most persevilient. Set your OST. I know all parties will have their own selection systems, but as a minimum you will need to be known within the local party, be broadly liked and respected by its members, and be broadly in tune with their views and attitudes. My experience of Labour shows me that the successful candidates have a number of things in common. They know who their local members are; know who the movers and shakers are and how to persuade them to back their cause; know how to reach out to other key players in meetings as well as on a one-to-one basis, and understand the importance of developing a profile across the local media and with local groups active in the community. It's not easy. It's hard work. It takes time, effort, energy, commitment, and even with all that, many more lose than win in the race to be selected.

Further persevilience is required to stay the course as an MP. You have to learn to cope with its many downsides and challenges. As François Hollande says, 'Politics is harder than ever. Social media is harsh, brutal. There is hatred and abuse. Most people in politics could earn more money in business. You have no weekends, no holidays, your private life is not your own.' Unquestionably, it's even worse for women politicians, who often have to endure a level of hostility and hatred that would drive most of their male colleagues to quit, and worse still for women of colour. Labour MP Diane Abbott endures levels of social media abuse which are frankly sickening. And while there will have been many factors, personal and political, weighed up by Jacinda Ardern before she announced, in January 2023, that after six years as prime minister of New Zealand she finally had had enough and that she would be stepping down from the role, the viciousness of social and mainstream media attacks would have been in that mix. I know from people in the security world that she was one of the three democratic leaders most targeted by the Russian bots and troll farms. (Only President Macron and Justin Trudeau came in for more of their treatment.) Not only that, but she faced endless attacks from conspiracy theorists, anti-vaxxers and anti-globalists, who are convinced the world is controlled by the UN (as if!) or the Davos crowd or billionaire George Soros. She struck most reasonable people as one of the best and brightest, certainly one of the most empathetic, leaders of modern times. She developed a profile globally that went way beyond that of most leaders of New Zealand, a relatively small country better known for its rugby than its politics. It was precisely because of that empathy, and what came across to most as a genuine compassion, that people in many parts of the world saw her as a breath of fresh air. It saddened me hugely that she should have chosen to quit, though I respect her reasons for doing so (among which was a desire to have more time for her family). I just hope the sustained abuse she received doesn't dissuade other equally talented women from thinking about politics as a possible career choice.

If you have to endure abuse as a politician, you also need to understand that you will not necessarily agree with everything your party requires of you, and that a degree of flexibility is essential. As Johnny Mercer put it to me: 'I knew next to nothing about politics until I became an MP, and you learn you have to swallow an awful lot of shit. I swallowed so much shit, voting for this policy, that policy, all to try to keep the veterans agenda going down the path. However determined and resilient you are, there is a residual build-up that does stuff to your character.' Sometimes you have to compromise more than you would like. However, provided you know what you believe and believe it deeply, it is possible to compromise on ideas and policies without compromising on values.

Finally, you have to accept that most people do not get to the top, that the best are often weeded out, and that, sadly, the charlatans sometimes win. My podcast partner Rory Stewart was one of the contenders in the leadership contest that resulted in Boris

Johnson becoming prime minister. Johnson later expelled Stewart and other anti-Brexit MPs from the party when they refused to support the madness of a no-deal Brexit. He says that he was desperate to win, desperate to stop Johnson, who he feared would be dreadful for the country, and was devastated no longer to have his Cumbrian seat in Parliament. Looking back on his time in Westminster he reflects how 'brutalising, dehumanising and remote from people' politics had become. Fortunately, in his new role as the head of a major development charity, he is still seeking to make a difference, albeit from outside Parliament.

So far, I have focused on making a difference through becoming an MP. But it's not the only way to exercise influence and bring about change within politics. Policy advisers, strategists, civil servants, writers, think tanks, designers, researchers, organisers, NGOs and volunteer campaigners: they all have a role to play. Politics cannot function without them.

And then, of course, you have local and regional politics. 'All politics is local' is one of the most famous phrases ever uttered about politics. It seems to date from the early 1930s, but was made famous by the former speaker of the US House of Representatives, Tip O'Neill, half a century later. Its central point is that to win and keep a seat at the top table you have to know how to win support in your local patch, and then keep addressing local concerns. That may suggest a degree of cynicism or opportunism on the part of national politicians who feel they have to throw a few scraps to their supporters to safeguard their position. But that's not really what it's about. It's a recognition that local politics is vitally important to people's day-to-day welfare, not to mention a significant power counterbalance to national politics. For politicians at every level of government it also provides a valuable reality check on what really matters to people.

Tony Blair tells a very funny story about campaigning on a

London council estate in the 1983 election, when Labour had a policy of abandoning nuclear weapons unilaterally. Standing on the doorstep of one particular flat, he tried to persuade the woman who lived there of its merits. She told him her main concern was rats running around the estate. Tony persisted in arguing the moral imperative of ridding the world of nuclear weapons (as I've just said, you sometimes have to toe the party line on things you don't fully believe). She responded by saying: 'How is that gonna help me get rid of the rats?' He didn't really have an answer. He did, however, understand the power of local politics in national politics. He was hugely fortunate to be selected for Sedgefield, his constituency in County Durham, because his local party was run on the basis of real grassroots work, along with the determination of a small group of party workers that Labour should be more in tune with the actual concerns of voters than with the obsessions of political activists. This was crucial both to the crafting of New Labour and to the strategies that it went on to devise.

So go local, and be informed. Being informed doesn't just mean spending a bit of time online to make sure you're on top of the main news. Being informed means going deeper than that. Read widely. Question everything, being sceptical without being cynical. Go to events. Sit in on council meetings. Join groups. Explore. If you went to a local political party meeting, and decided it was too dull, too process-focused, too dominated by people who seem a bit weird and fanatical, you would not be the first. You might decide there and then that you can't face another one. Or you might reflect that the average age needs lowering, the quality of debate needs raising, and you can help on both fronts. So you go again.

Before you know it, you will find yourself wanting to, or being asked to, stand for election as a local government councillor. Go for it. Or maybe you're a student considering one of the positions up for grabs on one committee or another. Lots of students' unions will tell you it is hard to fill all the positions. So go for them. (And, by the way, though studying politics is obviously a good way to learn about politics, so is history, so is economics, so are languages, and so is . . . life. Don't think you have to get a degree in politics, or indeed anything else, to have a successful career in politics.)

I love the story of Josie Potts, a school cleaner who had never thought about politics, but who one day confronted her Labour MP John Mann in their Bassetlaw constituency, and gave him an absolute monstering about the damage drugs were doing to her community. Such was the impression she made on him that a few days later he went back to find her. He told her she was exactly the sort of person he needed in the community to help him try to deal with the problem. She has now been a councillor for over a decade. And all because someone encouraged her to get involved and showed her how.

Then there is Nina Parker, one of my daughter Grace's best friends at school, who used to come on holiday with us. Even then I could tell that she was fascinated by politics – she often joined in the discussions she heard the adults having. She is, as her friends sometimes groan, utterly obsessed about climate change, and about the need for younger people – for whom it is the greatest concern, whatever the populists may claim – to get more involved, and feel more empowered to make change. 'When the system feels so broken, why leave it to the people who broke it?' she asks, not unreasonably. She has made her first foray into elected politics as a Camden councillor. 'The climate crisis was one of the main reasons I put my name forward as a councillor,' says Nina. 'Because local politics is one of the most effective ways to orchestrate positive change.' It's a wonderful attitude to take with regard to such an overwhelming challenge. Do what you can, where you can.

She adds for good measure: 'Can you please use my favourite stat somewhere in your book . . . 80 per cent of women aged eighteen to twenty-four voted Remain in the referendum. Imagine if young women ran the country . . . I think we would be a lot healthier than we are now.' I had a similar thought watching the final of *Make Me Prime Minister*.

I appreciate that I have said plenty of bad things about politics and politicians in the preceding pages. I genuinely despise Boris Johnson for what he has done to the country and its politics, just as I despise Trump for what he has done in the US, and I worry that, unless we counter it, their malign influence may outlive them both. I have very little time for those who enabled and supported them, defending their indefensible conduct, turning a blind eye to their moral corruption and character flaws, and that includes the two Tory leaders who followed Johnson into Downing Street, having spent several years supporting him.

But there remain plenty of good politicians amid the bad. They are the ones to support, to work for, to build up. They are the ones, who, like former New Zealand premier Helen Clark, can say, 'There is no better feeling than feeling someone has come to you with a problem, and you helped them resolve it in a way that made their life better.' We need to drive bad politicians out and replace them with good ones. That means we need fresh talent, and we need to treat that talent – and indeed all good politicians – with the same respect we do a doctor or a teacher. That, I admit, includes me. The policy Rory Stewart and I have adopted on our podcast of 'disagreeing agreeably' has prompted me to think that I may have contributed in some ways to the lack of respect for politicians currently so prevalent, because, not least on Twitter, but in the mainstream media too, I really like to tear the Tories apart. In general, I accept, we would all be better off if we could show more respect for people whose politics we don't share. To go hard on policy differences, but avoid personal attacks unless essential to the argument. To look for compromise, because in most situations the possibility of finding one will be there.

François Hollande follows his plea for 'the brightest and the best people' in politics with an impassioned case for their vital necessity. 'Being a politician used to be a great ambition for so many people,' he says, 'but that has changed. But what is the alternative? Democracy is the system we have always known, and it is now threatened by outside forces; by the bellicose nature of authoritarian regimes like Russia, China, Iran, plenty of others; by the anarcho-capitalists like Elon Musk and the giant companies who want a world without borders and restrictions on them; but also by our own divisions and doubts and disengagement. I don't think enough young people understand the seriousness of what we face. We are too complacent. Our whole systems are under threat to authoritarianism. The challenge for the next generation is this: do you want to fight for our values, do you want to fight for democracy? If you do, then get involved in that fight, not by joining the army, but by joining political parties and campaigns.'

I share his concern. And I share his worry that too many people feel disconnected from mainstream politics and the political process. It's something I am often struck by when I talk in schools. I almost always sense in a great many of the students the passion and the drive, the huge interest in themes and issues that I would define as political. Education. The environment. Inequality. Child poverty. LGBTQ+ issues. Racism. Misogyny. Online abuse. Animal cruelty. Employment opportunities. Policing. I did an online event with a sixth form politics class two days after the heavy-handed policing of a vigil for Sarah Everard in protest at her murder by a police officer, and the anger was off the scale.

Unfortunately, I also sense too little understanding of the means by which politics is capable of addressing their concerns. (Although, in the case of the mismanaged policing of the vigil, it was hard to push back on their argument that the system, either of politics or of policing, was incapable of delivering for them. It is at times like these that you realise why trust levels in our Parliament and government have fallen below 20 per cent, a third of what they are for several parliaments in Europe.)

If, as I often do, I ask for a show of hands on the question, 'Would any of you think about going into politics to fix things?', very few hands are raised. I try to convince those present that by caring about the issues they care about, they are already 'in politics' and then try to persuade them that some of them at least should think about trying elected politics when they're older. But all too few see becoming a politician as the route to effecting change – or, if they do, are willing to admit it. Sometimes I detect an active distaste for the political process. On one school visit, I watched a session of Prime Minister's Questions with a class of fourteen-year-olds. At the beginning, some were amused. As it went on, they were repelled. It was really quite stark to see their reactions.

I suspect that part of the reason for this disconnect is that they have grown up in a world so saturated by the Internet and social media that their natural instinct when confronted by something they disapprove of is not to turn to conventional politics and political processes but to leverage technology via a tweet or a post. Fair enough. But it's not enough. For all the noise that can be made using online tools, and the speed with which it can be made, on its own it rarely moves the dial in a sustained way. That, in turn, I suspect, then fuels the sense of politics being remote and irrelevant. It is not that many young people are not engaging politically with the world. It is that their form of politics does not mesh with current political systems. As a result, at election time, turnout among younger voters is often worryingly low. Sixty-four per cent of young people voted in the Brexit referendum. Forty-three per cent voted in the general election a year earlier.

To my mind, one of the key challenges that lies ahead is marrying modern forms of engagement with the existing political process. It's a challenge that opens some big questions, such as: who's responsible for harmonising politics and social media, the politicians or the big tech companies? How can we build incentives for both in order to harmonise the two fields? Given the way their algorithms are designed to work, are social media companies ever going to be fit for purpose to exist in the traditional political framework? Is the traditional political system too outdated to be able to meet the challenge? Whenever I see the older generation, as represented by members of parliaments around the world, in discussion with the younger generation, as often represented by young tech leaders, it feels like two groups of people speaking the same language, technically, but who are nonetheless in need of interpreters. I know that I don't fully understand the modern world, especially the role of technology, as well as I understood the political and campaign landscape in which I was directly involved while I was in full-time politics. Reading Christopher Wylie's book, for example, I could see how far behind a technophobe like me had fallen, and I could see too how the opponents of Trump and Brexit were far too cavalier about the dangers of the other side understanding these changes better, exploiting them better, and exploiting the decency and ignorance of their opponents. But I think I still have a good enough understanding of human beings, and of how to build strategies and campaigns.

Fortunately, whatever older cynics say, the intellectual engagement is certainly there among the young, even if it doesn't currently translate into political activism of the sort I grew up with, or into a universal belief that it is worth getting involved, or even worth voting when given the chance. Indeed, I think it is possible to make the case that there have never been so many young people involved in movements for change worldwide. Whether on the streets or online, they are expressing themselves, fighting for improvements in their lives and the lives of others. Look at the courage shown by those protesting against authoritarian regimes, or the sheer volumes of young people mobilised in the fight for sustainable development. What they need to be persuaded of is the essential link between voting and the preservation of democracy, of voting and bringing about change. They also need to understand that their staying away from the voting booths plays into the hands of the cynics who want to regard younger people as self-obsessed and detached from 'reality'. It also works in favour of those who currently control the levers of power. It leaves them in place.

As a country, we are not prone to revolution. But we need a youth revolution – a peaceful one, in which younger people serve as the gatekeepers to enhanced political engagement, rather than merely as also-rans within existing political frameworks. Older people have a role to play in this revolution, too. Unfortunately, I have to say, I don't yet detect in my generation the willingness, or the capacity, to bring about the transformations necessary. They tend to defend the status quo. They also tend to equate their age and experience with unshakable wisdom. One complaint I hear again and again from young Labour activists is that even after Jeremy Corbyn managed to attract so many younger people into the party, meetings are so often dominated by small numbers of people in their sixties and seventies. Such a dynamic puts younger people off speaking and, after a while, turning up.

As I draw to a close, I want to encourage my generation and experienced older activists to do one thing: open your eyes to the talent, energy and passion around you. Don't knock it. Don't block it. Don't envy it. Instead, recognise that it may operate at different times of the day, week and month to you. That's OK. Recognise that it may come with other commitments and limitations. Those can be worked through. Recognise that the most significant thing you can do is accommodate, encourage, nurture and promote that talent if, like me, you want to change the way we do politics. If you don't, the campaign or party will quickly become out-of-date and easy for opponents to attack, undermine or render irrelevant. 'But what can I do?' Contribute by sharing your experience and knowledge with the next generation, inspiring them wherever you go.

Though I am very proud of New Labour's achievements, and proud of that era, especially by comparison with the Tory era we are living through, the extent to which the key figures of that time remain so central to the current debate sometimes alarms me. My old boss's think tank, the Tony Blair Institute for Global Change, produces policy ideas every bit as interesting as those coming from elsewhere in the policy development world; both he and Gordon Brown made valuable contributions during the pandemic, and Gordon's interventions in the cost-of-living crisis, as prime minister Johnson and the chancellor, Nadhim Zahawi, holidayed while inflation soared, reminded everyone of his intellect, and his economic and political clout. It reminded me in particular of the time G7 leaders were meeting during the global financial crisis of 2008–9, and one of them said: 'We don't have a plan,' and Barack Obama said: 'I think Gordon has a plan.' Which he did.

But what the continuing presence of the key New Labour figures also reveals is that we did not regenerate sufficiently in power. There was perhaps an assumption that one day Tony would go, Gordon would take over, and then a new generation would come on, probably with David Miliband at its head. But, truth be told, we didn't really plan beyond Tony and Gordon. Talent was not developed in the generation below them. When David lost to his brother Ed, and then especially when Jeremy Corbyn succeeded the younger Miliband, that point was firmly underlined. A reminder of the last eleven general elections from a Labour perspective: LOST, LOST, LOST, LOST, BLAIR, BLAIR, BLAIR,

LOST, LOST, LOST, LOST. That helps explain why Keir Starmer is right to stamp out complacency.

There are new initiatives, such as the Jo Cox Women in Leadership Programme, the Labour Women's Network, or the non-partisan 50:50 campaign, and I believe the Labour front bench is getting stronger. But it has taken a long time, and we have to take some responsibility for that. It is too easy for us to sit there and say, 'Well, we won three in a row, why has it gone tits up since then?' In part because we were so busy dealing with the present, we overlooked how quickly the future arrives. Succession planning, and bringing on the next generation, is crucial to longevity.

Today, I believe our generation has to see itself as the runners in the third leg of a 4 x 100 metre relay race. We have run 90 metres flat out, we are shouting at the next runner, the next generation, to get them moving; we are preparing to pass on the baton, knowing we have to let it go, though we know the spotlight, the power, then moves on with them; then we are shouting our encouragement and support as they run to the line, and hopefully to glory.

To younger and newer activists, I say this. I can sense your passion and your frustrations, and admire and share them. But don't be naïve. Unless you are one of a very privileged few, the system can often feel like it is stacked against you. But take heart from the many people who were not born into privilege, and yet have managed to make the system work for them, and have thus been able to work for the benefit of others. You can do that too.

When I was young, I thought sixty-five – my age – was ancient, borderline dead. So I guess I am technically old, even if most days I don't feel it. But I am definitely up for letting the young take over.

And as I close, I hope you can heed the words of two people even older than I am, both recent guests on the podcast: ex-New Zealand prime minister Helen Clark, aged seventy-three, and former UK deputy prime minister Michael Heseltine, now ninety (he was born on the same day that Hitler took power in Germany: 21 March 1933).

'If you are thinking about a political career, and have doubts,' says Lord Heseltine, 'don't do it, because it is a grinding, gruelling profession with some upsides but plenty of downsides. You have to have energy and will and commitment and vision. If you have that, it is the centre of the stage, it is where you can make a difference, and the difference you make is up to you. It is the most exhilarating, satisfying, bewildering commitment you will ever make. And if I was twenty-one again, and you asked me whether I would make the same decision, that politics was the place to be? Absolutely. My only resentment is that the one thing I no longer have is time.'

'If a young woman asks me if I think she should go into politics,' says Clark, 'I say "yes" without hesitation. But I warn them: "Don't expect anyone to roll out a red carpet for you. You have to roll it yourself, and then kick the door in."' Wise words.

Change will only happen if you put your phone down and find like-minded people with whom to develop and implement campaigns. Read plenty. Think deeply. Engage regularly. Be like Greta, who did something about her unease about climate change. Fundamentally, don't be a bystander and don't be blown off track by the fads and commentary of the here and now. If you want our political, charitable, legal or other systems to improve, you can and must be active – and I hope there are sections of this book which you can put into practice.

Above all, you need to speak out. Share your ideas with your parents, your mates, your teachers. And then go a little wider into your local community until, eventually, you're talking on platforms to hundreds if not thousands of fellow activists, bringing our country back from the political brink to a place where, once again, practical politics is delivering for 'ordinary people'.

Heed the Emeli Sandé song:

> *You've got the words to change a nation*
> *But you're biting your tongue*
> *You've spent a lifetime stuck in silence*
> *Afraid you'll say something wrong*
> *If no one ever hears it, how we gonna learn your song?*
> *So come on, come on*
> *Come on, come on.*

It's over to you, youth. Your country needs you. Your world needs you. Your time is now. And the old must let you sing.

My top ten reasons to think about going into politics

1. It needs shaking up. A lot. Now.

2. It really matters. Politics, good and bad, touches all parts of our lives.

3. It is really interesting.

4. Sometimes, it is even good fun.

5. It doesn't matter how old you are, what qualifications you have or haven't got, or where you come from. There's no fixed route into politics. You do it your way.

6. Politics doesn't have to mean just government or Parliament.

7. It gives you the platform to turn your ideas into action.

8. It offers you the chance of really changing the world. I am not saying there aren't other ways to do that, but that political context will always be there.

9. It is in constant flux, always changing. No two days are the same.

10. If you make it to the top, and do it well, you're talked about and written about for ever, and your ideas and legacy outlive you.

Acknowledgements

As I said many pages ago, this book was largely inspired by people who have contacted me to share their frustrations and concerns, their ideas and ambitions, or just to ask for a bit of encouragement or advice. So I owe them thanks for that inspiration, and I really hope that within the book is something that helps some of them to make a difference. The more the merrier; the bigger the better!

I was aware when I started out that this would be the work of an older man aimed in part at younger people, urging them to get more engaged and more involved, and even more aware that their world is a very different one to the one I grew up in and in which I worked in politics. So at various stages I have sent either sections or full drafts to a number of people, mainly, though not exclusively, much younger than me. They have been enormously generous with their time, insights, experiences and, above all, ideas for improvement. Every single one of them said something which made me see an issue afresh or prompted me to dig out a new piece of research or simply take their comments and thoughts into the main narrative. So widely was I disseminating different chapters at different times that I am sure I may have forgotten one or two whose help I nonetheless appreciate. If so, and they get in touch, I can add them in time for the paperback! But I would like very much to thank the following for their many and varied contributions: Jamie Naish, Alex Smith, Moisés Naím, Sarah Hunt, David Miliband, Miriam González Durántez, Peter Kyle, Mete Coban, Georgia Gould, Kevin Keith, Nina Parker, Tom Baldwin, Tarik Salih, Ryan Wain, Richard Brooks,

Acknowledgements

Rory Stewart, Sayeeda Warsi, Peter Hyman, Lara Spirit, Andrew O'Neill, Nathan Lloyd, Nadia Whittome.

At Penguin Random House it was a pleasure to be back working with editor Nigel Wilcockson. He and I worked on *Winners* together and he brought the same commitment and professionalism to this one. His obsession is structure and the book is so much better structured than when I sent him the first version. Thanks, too, to Josh Ireland who did a great job on the copy-edit, to Joanna Taylor who kept us all on deadline, to Isabelle Ralphs who masterminded the publicity campaign, and also to my agent Jonny Geller, as ever a great support and guide to the wonderful(ish!) world of publishing. Thanks also to Fiona for allowing me to be a passenger-seat audiobook, as I read the first draft to her on our drive back from France last summer, and took in her many and varied comments then and since. As she constantly reminds me, I would be absolutely lost without her. She, and our three children, Rory, Calum and Grace, mean more and more to me the older I get, and contribute so much to all that I do.

Thanks above all to you for reading this book. 'But what can I do?' The answer is simple: whatever you set your mind to. So get out there and change the world. It needs you. Us. Them. Everyone. We achieve more together than we do alone, remember.

Index

Index

Index

Alastair Campbell was born in Keighley, Yorkshire in 1957, the son of a Scottish vet. Having graduated from Cambridge University with a degree in modern languages, he went into journalism, principally with the Mirror Group, before joining Tony Blair as his spokesman and strategist from 1994 to 2003. He continued to act as an advisor to the Labour Party during subsequent election campaigns. A consultant strategist, writer and broadcaster, he is still engaged in politics in Britain and overseas, a leading advocate in the field of mental health, and co-presenter of the UK's most popular podcast of 2022, *The Rest Is Politics*.

He lives in North London with his partner of forty-three years, Fiona Millar. They have three grown-up children. His interests include open water swimming, cycling, bagpipes and Burnley Football Club. His first book, *The Blair Years*, was a number one *Sunday Times* bestseller. He has since published eight volumes of diaries, a book on the Northern Ireland peace process, four novels, two memoirs on living with depression, including the bestseller *Living Better*, and *Winners*, which also went straight to number one in the *Sunday Times* charts. Now aged sixty-five, he says he will never retire.